T0341223

Artificial Intelligence and Machine Learning in Business Management

Artificial Intelligence and Machine Learning in Business Management

Concepts, Challenges, and Case Studies

Edited by

Sandeep Kumar Panda

Vaibhav Mishra

R. Balamurali

Ahmed A. Elngar

CRC Press is an imprint of the
Taylor & Francis Group, an **Informa** business

First edition published 2022
by CRC Press
6000 Broken Sound Parkway NW, Suite 300, Boca Raton, FL 33487-2742

and by CRC Press
2 Park Square, Milton Park, Abingdon, Oxon, OX14 4RN

Library of Congress Cataloging-in-Publication Data
Names: Panda, Sandeep Kumar, 1985- editor.
Title: Artificial intelligence and machine learning in business management
: concepts, challenges, and case studies / edited by Sandeep Kumar
Panda, Vaibhav Mishra, R. Balamurali, Ahmed A. Elngar.
Description: First edition. | Boca Raton : CRC Press, 2021. | Includes
bibliographical references and index. | Summary: "The focus of this book
is to introduce Artificial Intelligence (AI) and Machine Learning (ML)
technologies into the context of Business Management. With the maturing
use of AI or ML in the field of business intelligence, this book
examines several projects with innovative uses of AI beyond data
organization and access. It follows the Predictive Modeling Toolkit for
providing new insight on how to use improved AI tools in the field of
business. Taking a multidisciplinary approach for using AI, this book
provides a single comprehensive reference resource for undergraduate,
graduate, business professionals, and related disciplines"-- Provided by
publisher.
Identifiers: LCCN 2021031675 (print) | LCCN 2021031676 (ebook) | ISBN
9780367645557 (hardback) | ISBN 9780367645564 (paperback) | ISBN
9781003125129 (ebook)
Subjects: LCSH: Management--Technological innovations. | Artificial
intelligence--Industrial applications,
Classification: LCC HD30.2 .A775 2021 (print) | LCC HD30.2 (ebook) | DDC
658--dc23
LC record available at https://lccn.loc.gov/2021031675
LC ebook record available at https://lccn.loc.gov/2021031676

ISBN: 978-0-367-64555-7 (hbk)
ISBN: 978-0-367-64556-4 (pbk)
ISBN: 978-1-003-12512-9 (ebk)

DOI: 10.1201/9781003125129

Typeset in Times
by SPi Technologies India Pvt Ltd (Straive)

Dedicated to my sisters, Sushri Susmita, Sujata, Bhaina Sukanta, nephew Surya Datta, wife Itishree (Leena), son, Jay Jagdish, and late father, Jaya Gopal Panda, and late mother, Pranati Panda.

Sandeep Kumar Panda

Dedicated to my father, Ravindra Kumar Mishra, my mother, Shakuntala Mishra, and other members of my family and friends.

Vaibhav Mishra

Dedicated to the Almighty Lord (God Father Shiva) and all Divine Brothers and Sisters of Brahma Kumaris World Spiritual University, Mt. Abu, Raj.

R. Balamurali

Dedicated to my parents, to my love, Eman - your smile brings happiness to my life, and also to my kids, Farida, Seif, and Malek.

Ahmed A. Elngar

Contents

Preface

The focus of this book is to introduce Artificial Intelligence (AI) and Machine Learning (ML) technologies in the context of Business Management. The advent of AI & ML technologies has the potential to deeply impact the traditional ways of managing businesses. The book consists of the introduction of Artificial Intelligence and its relationship with other technologies. The reader will also get to know the impact and challenges associated with this. The remaining few chapters will cover the impacts of AI and ML in various fields of business and management like operations management, marketing management, human resource management, finance and strategy. The chapters of the book will give insights into the implementation and impact of AI & ML to business leaders, managers and technology developers and implementers.

With the maturing use of Artificial Intelligence or Machine Learning in the field of business intelligence, this book examines a number of projects with innovative uses of AI beyond data organization and access. It follows the Predictive Modelling Toolkit for providing new insight on how to use improved AI tools in the field of business. It explores cultural heritage values and risk assessments for mitigation and conservation and discusses on-shore and off-shore technological capabilities and spatial tools for addressing marketing strategy change and change in retail, insurance and healthcare system etc. Taking a multidisciplinary approach for using AI, this book provides a single comprehensive resource for undergraduate, graduate, business professionals and related disciplines.

Nowadays, AI improves a lot in the area of supply chain to track the product, to provide intelligence in insurance field, to finance field etc. In this regard, the traditional approach of teaching and learning is not meeting the requirement in the policies of Industry 4.0 revolution. Hence, we edited this book to minimize the gap between academia and Industry.

The book is organized into 15 chapters:

Chapter 1, *Artificial Intelligence in Marketing*, discusses how AI help to the marketing people to better understand the speech (recognition) by applying techniques like text mining, with latest advancement in programming it has made modelling of direct marketing responses and predicting churn using classification trees and training machines to better understand customer needs etc.

Chapter 2, *Consumer Insights through Retail Analytics*, describes an in depth understanding on how Indian retail companies such as 'Shoppers Stop' and 'Future Group' are exclusively using customers' purchases and other transaction data to predict their future purchase behaviour and design product placement strategies.

Chapter 3, *Multi-Agent Paradigm for B2C E-Commerce*, discusses the business applications of KBS, CBR, ANN, GA and MAS along with negotiation, customer relationship management and customer orientation. From computational point of view, agent characteristics, multi-agent system paradigm and its communication protocol also been discussed. Lastly, the chapter describes the Belief-Desire-Intention (BDI) architecture for mental state and other cognitive parameters such as preference, commitment, and capability required for computation of trust in any AI based e-business system to formalize the internal architecture of complex agents.

Chapter 4, *Artificial Intelligence and Machine Learning: Discovering New Way of Doing Banking Business*, illustrates the impact of AI and ML application on finance with the principal focus on Banking sector, how AI affects customers, maintains the customer relationship, influences business performance and finally how AI will change future of Banking sector. Artificial Intelligence (AI) is one of the front digital transformation strategies that can spread in the area of finance today.

Chapter 5, *Analysis and Comparison of Credit Card Fraud Detection Using Machine Learning*, discusses fraud detection technique to protect or prevent the cardholder from huge losses. To determine the fraud transaction various deep learning architecture like Long Short-Term Memory (LSTM), Gated Recurrent Units (GRU), Convolutional Neural Network (CNN), and Multilayer Perceptron (MLP) have been used.

Chapter 6, *Artificial Intelligence for All: Machine Learning and Healthcare: Challenges and Perspectives in India*, deliberates on the healthcare sector as its main thrust area to study the application of Machine Learning. The role of ML is to help the common people to access healthcare facilities without any constraints.

Chapter 7, *Demystifying the Capabilities of Machine Learning and Artificial Intelligence for Personalized Care*, discusses Machine Learning enabled Artificial Intelligence, which detects the abnormality at an early stage, where physician, as well as patient, can be alarmed earlier about a future disease or health conditions, enabling early intervention to provide early treatment along with personalized recommendation and how physicians, as well as patients, look at these technologies along with small case studies.

Chapter 8, *Artificial Intelligence and the 4ᵗʰ Industrial Revolution*, focuses on briefly understanding the threats of governance over data privacy, net ethics and cybersecurity issues and underscores the need for broader cyber laws and policymaking in the future. The transformative impact of Artificial Intelligence, Machine Learning and embedded technology will shape the new economy and market space. How will the economies, markets, ecosystems and organizations react and respond in this ever-expanding yet interconnected world remains to be seen.

Chapter 9, *AI-Based Evaluation to Assist Students Studying through Online Systems*, focuses on the AI techniques used to grade the performance of students in an Online Learning Environment and provides a feedback to improve the Learning Process. A simple implementation based on Markov Decision Process is present to understand this approach.

Chapter 10, *Investigating Artificial Intelligence Usage for Revolution in E-Learning during COVID-19*, examines the portrayal of AI in E-learning during COVID-19 and apart from discovering the role of AI during this pandemic. The study has also investigated the future of AI in E-learning post COVID-19.

Chapter 11, *Employee Churn Management Using AI*, describes an AI model which can help the Human Resource Management to anticipate which representative can leave the association in not-so-distant future by investigating the past informational index of the association in a significant manner.

Chapter 12, *Machine Learning: Beginning of New Era in the Dominance of Statistical Methods of Forecasting*, briefly covers the popular empirical studies covering statistical and ML (AI) methods used for the purpose of forecasting and their outcomes and suggestions for the future scope of study.

Chapter 13, *Recurrent Neural Network-Based Long Short-Term Memory Deep Neural Network Model for Forex Prediction*, provides the historical data of different countries on a daily basis that are compared separately using Back-propagation Neural Network (BPNN), Functional Link Artificial Neural Network (FLANN) and LSTMs. Comparing daily exchange rate prediction of these three models, LSTMs model outperformed with maximum accuracy with faster convergence.

Chapter 14, *Ethical Issues Surrounding AI Applications*, highlights ethical issues and approaches that are currently being undertaken to address in the different domain.

Chapter 15, *Semantic Data Extraction Using Video Analysis: An AI Analytical Perspective*, deliberates on extracting vehicle numbers off of vehicles from a CCTV captured video through four steps, including conversion of video to a continuous image sequence, image segmentation, character segmentation and character recognition, with preprocessing at every stage to improve the quality of input data available for the next step. In the era of the growing complexity of problems along with the increasing functionalities offered by video analytics, this can be the most basic and generic solution supporting many applications.

Acknowledgements

First and foremost, we would like to thank the Almighty Lord. In the process of putting this book together we realized how gifted we are. You have given us the power to believe in our passion and pursue our dreams. We could never have done this without the faith we have in you, the Almighty.

We would like to express our thanks to many people who have helped during the preparation of this first edition.

We thank all the authors who spent their valuable time, knowledge, insights and ideas by contributing various chapters in the book. We also thank all authors for their kind co-operation extended during the various stages of processing the document.

We thank Mr Kanugonda Lokesh Reddy, M.Tech, for formatting the book chapters by placing the figures at appropriate places.

We thank the IFHE (The ICFAI Foundation for Higher Education) Management and Advisor, Director, Dean, and Faculty Colleagues of IcfaiTech (Faculty of Science and Technology) and IBS (Icfai Business School) for providing the necessary infrastructure, platform, ambience, encouragement, suggestions and moral support which helped us in shaping the book nicely and completing the task in an effective way.

We are very much grateful and thankful to CRC Press, Taylor & Francis for providing the opportunity to edit the book *Artificial Intelligence and Machine Learning in Business Management: Concepts, Challenges, and Case Studies*. In this regard special thanks go to Keith Povey Editorial Services Ltd for much improvement of the English language and syntax. We strongly believe that the book will have a positive impact on the readers.

Last, but not least, we would like to thank all the prospective readers of the book. It has been written with you in the mind. We welcome suggestions, tips for improvements, criticisms and appreciation. Your invaluable inputs are very much required for our future endeavours.

Contributors

Rachna Agrawal
Associate Professor
Department of Management Studies
J. C. Bose University of Science and
Technology
YMCA, Faridabad, Haryana

Vaidik Bhatt
Department of Operations & IT, ICFAI
Business School (IBS), Hyderabad,
The ICFAI Foundation for Higher
Education (IFHE) (Deemed to be
university u/s 3 of the UGC act
1956)

Aditi Bansal
Department of Computer Science and
Engineering
College of Engineering and Technology
Bhubaneswar, Odisha, India

Dhiraj Bhattarai
School of Computer Engineering
Kalinga Institute of Industrial
Technology (Deemed to be
University)
Bhubaneswar, Odisha, India

Sujata Priyambada Dash
Department of Management
Birla Institute of Technology
Mesra, Ranchi, India

Rishi Dwesar
Marketing and Strategy Department,
IBS
IFHE University
Hyderabad, India

Pradosh Kumar Gantayat
Department of CSE
DRIEMS Autonomous Engineering
College
Tangi Cuttack Odisha, India

Ajay Kumar Jena
School of Computer Engineering
Kalinga Institute of Industrial
Technology (Deemed to be
University)
Bhubaneswar, Odisha

Rachita Kashyap
Marketing and Strategy Department,
IBS
IFHE University
Hyderabad, India

Dr Puspalata Mahapatra
School of Computer Engineering
Kalinga Institute of Industrial
Technology (Deemed to be
University)
Bhubaneswar, Odisha, India

Bireshwar Dass Mazumdar
Department of CSE
IERT Allahabad
Allahabad, India

Sambit Mohanty
Software Developer CTSC
Hydrabad, India

Subhadarshini Mohanty
Department of Computer Science and
Engineering
College of Engineering and Technology,
Bhubaneswar, Odisha, India

Subasish Mohapatra
Department of Computer Science and
    Engineering
College of Engineering and
    Technology, Bhubaneswar,
    Odisha, India

Vidushi Pandey
Department of Information Systems
Indian Institute of Management
    Kozhikode, Kerala, India

Vijay Shankar Pandey
Assistant professor
Institute of Management Sciences
University of Lucknow
Lucknow, India

Sanghmitra Patnaik
KIIT Deemed to be University
Odisha, India

Parthasarathi Pattnayak
School of Computer Applications
KIIT Deemed to be University
Odisha, India

K. S. Perianayagam
Chief Technology Officer
Sahara Net Corp Ltd.
Lucknow, India

Pooja Rani
Research Scholar
Department of Management
    Studies
J.C. Bose University of Science and
    Technology
YMCA, Faridabad, Haryana

Namita Rath
Faculty of Management Studies
Sri Sri University
Cuttack, India

Minakhi Rout
School of Computer Engineering
Kalinga Institute of Industrial Technology
    (Deemed to be University)
Bhubaneswar, Odisha, India

Shubhagata Roy
Department of Operations & IT
IBS Hyderabad
IFHE, Hyderabad, India

P. Sashikala
Department of Operations & IT, ICFAI
    Business School (IBS), Hyderabad,
    The ICFAI Foundation for Higher
    Education (IFHE) (Deemed to be
    university u/s 3 of the UGC act 1956)

Alok Kumar Sahai
Faculty of Management Studies
Sri Sri University
Cuttack, India

Saloni
School of Computer Engineering
Kalinga Institute of Industrial Technology
    (Deemed to be University)
Bhubaneswar, Odisha, India

Musarrat Shaheen
Assistant Professor, Dept. of Human
    Resource, ICFAI Business
    School (IBS) Hyderabad, IFHE
    (Deemed to be University)

Nidhi Shukla
Institute of Management
    Commerce and Economics
Department of Shri Ramswaroop
    Memorial University
Lucknow, India

Anand Sinha
Sahara Net Corp Ltd.
Lucknow, India

Sarita Kumari Singh
School of Computer Engineering
Kalinga Institute of Industrial
  Technology (Deemed to be
  University)
Bhubaneswar, Odisha, India

Farrah Zeba
Assistant Professor
Department of Marketing and Strategy
ICFAI Business School (IBS)
  Hyderabad
IFHE (Deemed to be University)

Editors

Dr Sandeep Kumar Panda is currently working as an Associate Professor in the Department of Data Science and Artificial Intelligence, IcfaiTech (Faculty of Science and Technology) at ICFAI Foundation for Higher Education (deemed to be University), Hyderabad, Telangana, India. His research interests include Cryptography & Security, Blockchain Technology, Internet of Things, Artificial Intelligence and Cloud Computing. He has published many papers in international journals and in international conferences of repute. He received "Research and Innovation of the Year Award" hosted by WIEF and EduSkills under the Banner of MSME, Govt. of India and DST, Govt. of India at New Delhi on January 2020. He has seventeen Indian patents in his credit. His professional affiliations are MIEEE, MACM and LMIAENG.

Dr Vaibhav Mishra is currently working as an Assistant Professor at the IBS Hyderabad, IFHE University, India. He has completed his engineering in computer science from Uttar Pradesh Technical University, India. Subsequently, he completed a MBA and PhD from the Indian Institute of Information Technology (IIIT), Allahabad, India. During his PhD, Dr Mishra got the MHRD scholarship. He has a few certificates in his account like Six Sigma (Quality Management) – 'Green Belt' from KPMG, ISO 20000-1:2005 (IT Service Management, lead auditor) from BSI, R-Programming-Practical Approach from IIT Kanpur. He has published research articles in international journals of repute (indexed in SCOPUS and ABDC), such as International Journal of Bank Marketing (A), International Journal of Electronic Business (C), etc. He has also reviewed the journal articles for various journals like Information & Management Elsevier (ABDC-A*), International Journal of Indian Culture and Business Management–Inderscienece, International Journal of Sustainability in Higher Education, etc. His areas of interest are Management Information System, Database Management System, cryptocurrency, cloud computing, E-commerce, ERP Systems, Quality Management and Data Mining.

Dr R. Balamurali is currently working as an Assistant Professor & Coordinator in the Department of Computer Science and Engineering, Faculty of Science and Technology at The ICFAI Foundation for Higher Education, Hyderabad, India. His research interests include Energy Efficiency in Wireless Sensor Networks, Wireless Body Area Networks, IoT, AI and Deep Learning. Dr Balamurali is a life member of Indian Society for Technical Education (ISTE). He received his B.E. Degree in Computer Science and Engineering from PET College of Engineering, India in 2002. He completed M.Tech. in Information Technology from Satyabhama University, Chennai, India in 2008 and the Ph.D. in Computer Science and Engineering with specialization in Wireless Sensor Networks form SRM

University, Chennai, India in 2017. From June, 2017 to June, 2018, he worked as a Post-Doctoral Fellow at Bennett University, Greater Noida, India. He has published research articles in international journals and Conferences of repute.

Dr Ahmed A. Elngar, He is Assistant Professor of Computer Science, Chair of Scientific Innovation Research Group (SIRG) Director of Technological and Informatics Studies Center Managing Editor of Journal of Cybersecurity and Information Management (JCIM), Beni-Suef University, Faculty of Computers & Artificial Intelligence, Egypt. Dr Elngar is the Founder and Head of Scientific Innovation Research Group (SIRG) and Assistant Professor of Computer Science at the Faculty of Computers and Information, Beni-Suef University. Dr Elngar is a Director of the Technological and Informatics Studies Center (TISC), Faculty of Computers and Information, Beni-Suef University. He is a Managing Editor: Journal of Cybersecurity and Information Management (JCIM) Dr Elngar has more than 25 scientific research papers published in prestigious international journals and over 5 books covering such diverse topics as data mining, intelligent systems, social networks and smart environment. Research works and publications. Dr Elngar is a collaborative researcher He is a member in Egyptian Mathematical Society (EMS) and International Rough Set Society (IRSS). His other research areas include Internet of Things (IoT), Network Security, Intrusion Detection, Machine Learning, Data Mining, Artificial Intelligence. Big Data, Authentication, Cryptology, Healthcare Systems, Automation Systems. He is an Editor and Reviewer of many international journal around the world. Dr Elngar won several awards including the "Young Researcher in Computer Science Engineering", from Global Outreach Education Summit and Awards 2019, on 31 January 2019 (Thursday) at Delhi, India. Also, he awards "Best Young Researcher Award (Male) (Below 40 years)", Global Education and Corporate Leadership Awards (GECL-2018), Plot No-8, Shivaji Park, Alwar, Rajasthan-301001, India. Also, He have an Intellectual Property Rights called "ElDahshan Authentication Protocol", Information Technology Industry Development Agency (ITIDA), Technical Report, 2016. Dr Elngar's great many activities in community and environmental service include organizing 12 workshops hosted by a large number of universities in almost all governorates of Egypt. He is involved in a workshop on smartphones' technologies and their role in the development of visually impaired skills in various walks of life.

1 Artificial Intelligence in Marketing

Rachita Kashyap and Rishi Dwesar

Marketing and Strategy Department, IBS, IFHE University, Hyderabad

CONTENTS

1.1 INTRODUCTION

During the early days of AI in the 1950s, scientists were asking questions like "Can machines think?" and were looking into deep, complex issues of mechanizing emotional intelligence. However, in today's world of Amazon's Alexa, Apple's Siri, Google Assistant etc. machines have become far more capable, yet AI still has a long way to go. In simple terms, AI can be explained as human intelligence exhibited by machines and can be broadly classified into Artificial Narrow Intelligence (e.g., smart speaker, self-driving car, AI in farming and factories) and Artificial General Intelligence (machines can do anything a human can do). The benchmark for AI is to be as good as human intelligence, and to possess ability to reason, see and communicate like humans do. Though capability of AI has improved by leaps and bounds over the years, it is still far off from that benchmark in comparison to human intelligence. Nevertheless, recent advancements in the field of AI reflect a very promising future.

AI is Machine Learning (ML) driven. ML deals with training a computer to perform specific tasks and functions automatically. Usually, these tasks are exhaustive, repetitive and often too complex for humans to do efficiently. Machines can learn

DOI: 10.1201/9781003125129-1

1

through supervised, unsupervised and reinforced learning. In supervised learning, several input and output sets are provided to the machine. Through this approach, data is fed to an algorithm and the machine tries to recognize the relationship between the input and the output. When the machine has stopped learning – in other words, has learned optimally – the learned model can predict the value or the class of new data points. For example, a system can be trained to differentiate between a kangaroo and a koala. By feeding the system with dozens of images of both animals, the system will learn about the features which distinguish each and so improve its prediction. In unsupervised learning, data is analyzed without trying to make any predictions. It is focused on learning and understanding the underlying structural properties and associations in between the observed data. This kind of learning can be used in detecting outliers, classifying and segmenting customers and the market. In reinforcement ML, the system does not have historical data to draw conclusions upon; instead, the algorithm learns by taking different actions and evaluating their successes and failures. Reinforcement learning is used by Facebook in advertising on its platform. The system tests the advertisements on full spectrum when it is flighted for the first time. With time, and when sales rise, Facebook's algorithms analyze the data available, and it then shows the advertisements to certain sets of customers, in certain geographical locations, at certain times of the day and using certain on-screen placements.

1.2   AI, ML AND DATA SCIENCE

We often see AI, ML and data science in use together, and they are considered to be lucrative career options today. Data science can be defined as a broad field of study which pertains to data systems and processes which are aimed at maintaining datasets and deriving meaning from them. With the advent of technology and the Internet, today almost all organizations generate a large volume of data through their daily transactions, and it becomes problematic for these organizations to monitor, store, organize and extract important information from this data. Data scientists use a combination of tools, algorithms, applications and principles to extract useful information from various random data clusters, and then use this information to guide business processes to reach organization goals. The information extracted can be used to study ongoing data trends in any field of business and is helpful in presenting business forecasts and setting courses of action based on insights found and inferences made. The best example of ML is Netflix suggesting movies to the customers based on their movie-viewing behaviour and Amazon recommending books based on the past purchases of customers on the website. With the help of ML, marketers can provide customers with customized content as well as suggest other products that they may wish to purchase.

ML is a field of study that gives computers an ability to learn without being explicitly programmed, whereas data science deals with extracting knowledge from data. Deep learning is a big artificial neural network which mimics the network of neurons in a human brain. It is a subset of ML and is called "deep learning" because it uses deep neural networks for learning. The machine uses different layers to learn from the data and the depth of the model is represented by the number of layers in the

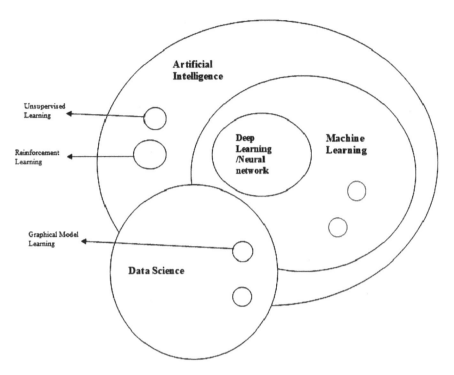

FIGURE 1.1   Relationship between AI, ML and data science.

model. Deep learning is a new term used within the world of AI. Refer to Figure 1.1 Relationship between AI, ML and Deep Learning.

The relationship between AI, ML and data science is given in Figure 1.1.

1.3   AI AND MARKETING

In one century, human civilization has developed by leaps and bounds in terms of technology, healthcare, economy and in every possible materialistic dimension. In the years to come we are likely to witness replacement of human-driven cars to self-driving cars, doctors operating remotely through robotic surgical devices, nanotech self-cleaning clothing, 3D printers facilitating instant delivery of goods, meaning manufacturing time can be brought down, implantable communication devices replacing mobile phones, and many other technical advancements. It would come as little surprise if all advertising and marketing tasks were to be managed wholly by computational systems. Currently, marketers use a lot of technology, but in the coming decades, AI and ML methods will take the marketing game to a new level.

Practitioners and academicians have anticipated that AI will change marketing strategies and customer behaviours. According to a survey conducted by Salesforce, AI will be the technology most adopted by marketers in the coming years. With the help of AI, business processes are being automated and so machines are then able to perform preset tasks with higher accuracy and far less human intervention, such as transferring data, sending promotional mail to existing as well as potential customers, updating customer files, replacing lost ATM cards, reading documents to extract key points using natural language processing etc. With the help of AI, companies can gain insights from the vast amount of transaction and customer data which will include not only numeric data type, but also text, images, audio recordings of customers conversing with the customer care service provider, facial expressions, and even voice tones. By employing AI in daily functioning, companies can better predict customer choices, deploy appropriate digital marketing strategies or anticipate potential credit fraud.

Marketing bots are one of the most popular forms of automation right now. A bot is basically a piece of software which can be programmed to carry out a specific set of actions on its own. Bots are usually cheap to setup, and easy to program and run. Bot-powered commerce is our modern-day manifested destiny and is the future of marketing. For example, in order to purchase a bulb for your newly bought reading lamp, you need to visit different websites, scroll through a number of pages, fill out forms regarding your shipping address, give payment information and so on. But if there is a bot, you just need to tell it to find a bulb for your reading lamp, and it will guide you through different bulb hues, voltages, etc. and then place the order for you. Behind the screen, the bot leads you through a concatenation of questions in order to better understand your intent, and deliver the right information to you. AI bots can provide both customer as well as sales support services, are available 24/7, have very low error rates, and their deployment can be scaled up or down according to demands.

Here are a few functions that a bot can perform which can be beneficial to any business:

1. Assist website visitors looking for answers about products.
2. Help in conducting marketing research.
3. Qualify leads.
4. Help in tracking individual team members' work and keep the whole team updated with each other's work.
5. Personalizing advertisements for customers.

With all the descriptions suggested above, AI offers the potential to reduce the costs incurred and increase revenues. Revenues can be increased by making informed and improved marketing decisions (e.g., product recommendations, competitive pricing, personalized promotion, enhancing customer engagement). The costs may decline due to automation of simple marketing tasks and free up human agents to handle more complex marketing tasks.

There is a misconception that AI is replacing humans in their jobs, but firms can use AI to amplify their employees' capabilities. For example, Stitch Fix, a leading clothing and service provider, use AI bots in assisting their employees to provide a better service to their customers. With the help of AI, stylists identify the best clothing styles for their customers by integrating all the data provided by the customers while expressing their preferences, general style trends, handwritten notes, Pinterest boards and preferences of other customers in the same segment. Ginni Rometty (CEO of IBM), in his media interactions has often indicated that AI would not lead to a world of man "versus" machine but rather a world of man "plus" machines [1].

1.4   BENEFITS AND DETRIMENTS OF USING AI IN MARKETING

1.4.1   BENEFITS

A) **Personalization and relevant messages**

AI fuelled predictive analytics can help companies by tapping the right customer base and analyzing their browsing history, and then showing appropriate advertisements to the right set of people. This can help companies understand their customer preferences better and then make appropriate recommendations. This is being used widely by Amazon and Netflix, saving billions by keeping customers hooked to their services and avoiding cancellation of services. As a marketer, AI gives you much power in terms of developing certain data points which lets you guide your customers to the right product.

B) **Streamlining the marketing efforts**

Through deep learning AI can study consumer behaviour patterns and predict which segment of customers are likely to make a certain kind of purchase. This can help businesses in targeting the customer base more accurately without wasting time and money on less probable leads.

C) **Cost saving**

According to various research surveys conducted worldwide, around 85% of the interactions between brands and customers are going to happen online. As compared to other advertising mediums like prime time tele advertisements, print advertisements, billboards etc. online advertising is cheaper as well as more precise in targeting the right set of customers with the aid of AI.

1.4.2   DETRIMENTS

A) **Human control is still required**

AI cannot function without human intervention, as it lacks the creativity, flexibility and imagination which makes humans the epicentre of the marketing world. Humans have various tastes, preferences, experiences etc. which enable them to make better decisions than machines, which are run on algorithms comprising from formulas, statistics, commands etc.

B) **Algorithms can be wrong**

Due to bad data AI can develop biases. For example, automatically preferring and shortlisting CVs of white males over people belonging to other ethnicities, genders, colours etc. because previously most of the successful people in those positions were white males. And this makes AI infer that white males are better suited for those positions over other people.

C) **Automated chat boxes and machine answering calls is not always the solution**

Many people, especially those of older generations, are not comfortable talking with machines instead of human customer care agents. And moreover, we all know how exasperating it can be when we have an urgent matter at hand, and are looking for solutions from a robot. Therefore, chatbots should be installed by businesses only after careful research on their customer segment and product offerings.

1.4.2.1   Amazon Go (Caselet)

Amazon.com, Inc was founded by Jeff Bezos in 1994 under the name Cadabara (1994–95). It started as an online marketplace for books but later ventured into selling furniture, electronics, apparel, food, toys, jewellery, software etc. It is considered one of the Big Four technology companies (alongside Google, Apple and Facebook) and presently focuses on e-commerce, AI, digital streaming and cloud computing. In 2018 Amazon announced its two-day delivery service, Amazon Prime, which today has 10 million subscribers worldwide. Prime Video, Amazon Music, Audible and Twitch are subsidiaries of Amazon through which downloads are distributed, and audiobooks, videos and music are streamed. Amazon distributes various products and services through Amazon Fresh, Amazon Studios, Amazon Wireless, Kindle Store etc. Amazon has acquired around 40 subsidiaries including Zappos, Goodreads, Amazon Robotics, IMDb, Amazon Maritime, Ring, Whole Food Markets etc.

Amazon Go opened its first store in 2018 in Seattle. It is a chain of convenience stores, with 26 sites across the US, and a further ten planned to open across the United Kingdom as of 2020. Amazon Go is not just any other grocery store: it is a store enabled with 'Just Walk Out' technology, where the customers can simply enter the store, grab whatever they need and leave, eliminating checkout lines. In order to get started with the shopping, shoppers need to have an Amazon account, a smartphone and the free Amazon Go app. As the shoppers enter the store, they need to scan a barcode within the app on their smartphone at the entrance turnstiles, keep their phones with them, and then grab whatever they need before leaving the store. Amazon has applied the technology used by self-driving cars (AI, ML, Image recognition, array of fusion sensors, deep learning, computer vision, bigdata on how humans shop etc.) to create the shopping experience in Amazon Go stores. From the moment shoppers enter the store, they are recognized and tracked with the help of sensors and cameras installed all over the store. The technology automatically detects the products taken from or returned to the shelves. It keeps a track of the products in the virtual cart, and once the shopping is complete and the shopper exits the store, Amazon charges them from their Amazon account and emails a receipt to the customer.

1.4.2.2   Technical Working of Amazon Go

Firstly, the data is acquired through several sensors in order to enable awareness of which products have been picked up from the aisle or the shelves. Some examples of the type of sensors are weight measurement, pressure detectors, dimensional measurements of the products. Secondly, several deep learning algorithms are used to understand what product the customer picked up or put back; which products to keep in the virtual cart; which products the customer picked up while making a purchase decision; how much time did the customer take to make a decision; which products are getting sold faster and where to place these products for easy access. And finally, when the customer passes a transition point on exiting the store, a bill is generated for the items present in the virtual cart, which is the result of the automated analysis done by intelligent machines working behind the curtain.

After the success of Amazon Go stores, many retailers had shown interest in this technology which is an amalgam of complex system of sensors, cameras and software that tracks each and every activity and movement of the shoppers inside the store. The Amazon Go tech bundle has been put on sale in the market. 'Just Walk

Out' technology can be installed in the pre-existing retail stores undergoing renovation as well as new stores under construction and requires only few weeks for the entire setup procedure. The brand has gone a step further by creating a new website dedicated to 'Just Walk Out' technology and covers all the technology related aspects like sales offers, most frequently asked questions about their new business line etc. The site does not cover the pricing info, but covers a variety of package related info like hardware required, software solutions etc. Amazon provides 24/7 customer support via phone or mail [2].

1.4.2.3 Issues Related to Amazon Go Technology

Amazon Go uses computer imagery and a sensor fusion tech bundle to record and analyze customer actions, and gives accurate results accordingly. But what if the customer wears a mask? Wearing a mask is a necessity during the prevailing pandemic conditions. Will Amazon Go be able to identify the customer correctly?

The number of products in Amazon Go might increase, and what if the customer does not return the lifted product to the shelf from where it was picked up? Will the customer be charged for the product? What if the customer consumes the product in the store itself (e.g., a juice bottle or candy in a box) and puts back the empty product packaging on the shelf. Can the sensors, cameras and image processing software identify such instances? What if a family with kids enter the store? How will the products picked up by the kids be charged? And it has been observed that if there are more than 20 customers in the store at a time, the software crashes; how will Amazon handle these issues? The technology is still growing and has a long way to go.

Amazon Go Stores: This is What Future Looks like is given in Figure 1.2. Figure 1.3 shows a cashier-less store that lets customers pick up the products and walk out of the store where as Figure 1.4 represent Amazon Go Cashier less convenience store. Figure 1.5 indicates an Employee stocking the shelves in a cashier less store.

FIGURE 1.2 Amazon Go Stores: This is What Future Looks like.

FIGURE 1.3   A cashier-less store that lets customers pick up the products and walk out of the store [1].

FIGURE 1.4   Amazon Go Cashier less convenience store [2,3].

FIGURE 1.5   An Employee stocking the shelves in a cashier less store [5].

1.5   MARKETING PLAN AND AI'S POTENTIAL

Applications of AI are very broad in nature. With the help of AI abilities to detect and extrapolate hidden patterns in data, marketers can identify opportunities as well as threats, and act on them in real time. Following are the ways in which we can leverage AI's potential across different stages of a marketing plan.

Stage 1: Analyzing the Current Situation

This stage involves the analysis of macroenvironmental factors. The organization develops an understanding of the current and future business environments by analyzing the current situation and understanding the business environment [6]. Marketers use tools like SWOT (Strengths Weaknesses Opportunities Threats) analysis for getting the in-depth understating of the targeted market. With the help of AI assisted features like social listening, getting data-driven information on purchasing patterns, product demand and customer satisfaction can assess and estimate demand, market trend and respective customer sentiment. With the help of ML, an AI backed consumer research agency investigated the online consumer discussions and suggested that a brand should not just focus on itself while analyzing the online forums but also other competitor brands [4]. This can bring an understanding on competitors' behaviour and help in gauging the respective target segments reactions.

Stage 2: Understanding Markets and Customers

This stage involves the analysis of microenvironmental factors. The organizations try to develop understanding related to consumer behaviour, including factors affecting their loyalty, attitude, purchasing patterns, product category demand and also the market share demand. AI can assist the marketers in processing the vast data available through their social media accounts, mobile activity, web searches and contact centre interactions [5]. For example, at the Consumers Electronics Show held in Las Vegas, 2019, Neurodata Labs and Promobot (a robotics manufacturer) demonstrated a multimodal emotion detection, for the purpose of customer experience management [6]. This AI-enabled system uses a combination of eye movement, heart rate, voice, body gestures and facial expressions in order to determine customers' emotional states [6]. Rosbank is using this technology in their call centre, and collects information like changes in voice volume, number of pauses in speech, conversion time etc. and then converts it into customer satisfaction metric [7].

Stage 3: Segmenting, Targeting and Positioning

This stage involves extensive consumer research on certain criteria that may enable marketers to communicate messages very precisely and develop products according to the targeted customers' requirements. AI can assist managers in predicting the customers intent as well as gain more insights for better recommendation through tailored promotions. For example, marketing firm Adgorithms have a platform named Albert, that was responsible for 40% of Harley Davidson's motorbikes sales during 2016. [8]. Despite certain advantages of AI in segmenting and targeting stage, it can also lead to discrimination as whom to offer products and services further leading to unintended illegal price discrimination [9].

Stage 4: Planning Direction, Objectives and Marketing Support

This stage involves development of short-term objectives, long term goals, formulation of future strategies and customer service (Campbell et al., 2020). AI can assist marketers by integrating chatbots on websites, apps and social media channels to encourage sales (Wood, 2011). According to Salesforce (2019) [10] 24% of businesses in the US use AI-aided customer services, and 54% are looking for ways in which their customer services teams can use AI. They have also forecasted that the use of AI applications in the customer service sector would see 143% growth between 2019 and 2021. In previous research it was found that the majority of customers prefer talking to a human over a chatbot, but AI can still provide the back-end support to the agents. AI can better match the customers with the agents according to their specialization.

Stage 5: Developing a Product Strategy

This stage involves development and selection of the products to be offered by the brand involving decisions related to the features, quality, design and customization of products. Insights on the target customer and positioning can be used by marketers for developing successful products. In this stage, AI can assist in customization of the products and assisting in product delivery and logistics [6]. For example, Samsung is taking AI assistance in understanding what their existing and potential customers are saying about them. This helps Samsung in improving their products and appropriately designing their campaigns [11]. Likewise, Nike is also using AI-enabled clustering algorithms, and data collected from various geographical locations through its apps to manage their collection, to enable a concept of which products should be displayed together to develop.

Stage 6: Developing Pricing Strategy

This stage involves understanding the target customers' price sensitivity, competitors' pricing strategies and accordingly deciding on how much to charge for their offering in order to maximize profits. In this stage AI can assist the firm in tracking the buying trends and accordingly enabling the dynamic pricing (e.g., surge pricing) and detecting price related anomalies (e.g., non-profitable customers, cases of fraud and pricing errors) [12]. For example, Airbnb employees use AI and ML algorithms to suggest to customers in settings options what pricing to set for each date by analyzing the data on seasonal changes, location, special property attributes and local events [13].

Stage 7: Developing Channels and Logistics Strategy

This stage involves developing strategies related to logistics or channels that include deciding on whole distribution channels, retail channels and direct distribution channels. AI can help managers in optimizing and predicting the distribution, inventory, store display and layout. For example, Afresh uses AI-assisted management of stock and inventory [6], as does Browzzin, a social commerce app that transforms the posted pictures into shoppable content [14]. These types of platform technologies enable consumers to take pictures anywhere and then make these items in the images shoppable.

Stage 8: Developing Marketing Communication and Influence Strategy

In this stage a firm develops a communication strategy in order to create and enhance the brand's image in the customers mind by informing them about their offerings and benefits related to it. AI can help marketers in this stage by targeting the advertisements to the right customers by analyzing their search history as well as real-time data obtained from the point of purchase. Brands with the help of AI can place interactive advertisements in the videos depending on the content of the videos [15]. For example, LEGO used interactive advertisements by training and feeding AI systems with the knowledge of wide range of LEGO product offerings [16].

Stage 9: Planning Metrics and Implementation Control

The final stage involves monitoring the performance metrics of the previous development stages, identifying the problems and taking corrective actions in order to increase the efficiency. The most important aspect of this stage is identifying the anomalies in the metrics and deciding on how to respond to them. In this stage AI can replace humans as it has the capability to collect and analyze vast amounts of data obtained from real-time environment sales as well as available historical data. AI can also be used in assessing the performance of the online features and advertisements and continuously providing customers with the relevant content [6].

1.6 FUTURE

According to a report by Statista [17], ML and AI are among the most effectual digital marketing techniques used by the businesses today. In 2016 AI saw an 43% adoption rate which increased to 88% in 2019 as marketers have realized the true potential of the AI that it helps them to create better solutions for marketing related problems. AI improves the marketing approach and helps marketers in gaining deeper insights into their customer's ideations.

Following are some ways in which AI can disrupt the coming future of marketing:

1. **Advertising Networks**
   With the advent of technology, the size of the electronic devices is getting smaller with the passing days. On average, a person owns six connected devices, yet the advertising for that one person on their various screens remains incompetent. Most of the time users are bombarded with irrelevant disjointed advertisements across all the screens they are using as accidental taps or clicks are also taken into consideration. This void in personalization of advertisements can be filled by AI. It has the capacity to anonymously analyze the user data in order to target the advertisement more accurately and thus increasing

the ROI on advertisements can be increased exponentially. Google is already using AI fuelled personalized advertisement targeting on its platform.

2. **Email Marketing**

Businesses can rely on AI for personalized email marketing as it might help them in analyzing the customer behaviour and their preferences. It can empower the businesses in making a better connection with their audiences, and in turn, up their revenues. In its nascent stage, only AI can process and analyze several thousand customer touch points and effectively predict the best time of day to send emails. This knowledge, along with personalized content, can further drive more effective clicks. Potent and effective tools like Boomtrain and Persado are currently using AI for devising better email marketing campaigns. With the help of supervised ML algorithms can also be used to train the spam filters in identifying the unwanted mails [18].

3. **Content Generation**

In the current scenario AI is not in a position to write articles and create web content without human intervention, but to a certain extent it can still generate the content for websites to draw visitors. Blank forms and templates are used for entering the keywords and data in order to generate unique and customer targeted content with the help of ML algorithms. The content generated through AI is as impeccable as the professionally generated content. Reputed polishers like Forbes and Washington Post [19] are using AI powered tools like Quill and Wordsmith to increase clicks and also generate content for their websites. It shall not be long before the way marketers generate content will change forever.

4. **Content Curation**

In addition to content generation, AI can also organize the content according to customer preferences and then present the customized personalized content to the customers visiting the website. Amazon does use this technique by giving recommendations like 'people who bought xyz also bought abc'. This helps Amazon in selling more products. AI tools such as List.ly and Curata are being used by businesses for content curation.

5. **Voice Searching**

According to Statista, 42% of the worldwide population voice searched the Internet instead of typing words related to the information they were looking for. Amazon's Alexa, Microsoft's Cortana, Apple's Siri and Google assistant has made the use of AI in voice recognition extremely popular. However, there is still a long way to go as the marketers still need to figure out how to identify keywords for personalized product recommendations within natural conversational language.

6. **User Experience**

In various research studies conducted it has been found that the use of technology helps in enhancing the customer experience; for example, AI driven technologies such as providing recommendations according to the customer's location, type of screen being used by the customer, their tastes and demographics. This can further accentuate customer's experience while interacting with the brands. Academic research indicates that if the customer enjoys their experience with the website increases their probability of staying longer on the website and also increases the conversion rate of browsing into purchases. Uizard and Mockplus are two of the tools that help business in improving customer experience [3,20–30].

7. **Web Design**

Designing a website easier than ever, and as such empowers small and/or new businesses with less capital to have their own website and make their presence felt in the market. This further enables customers to choose as there will be more players in the market.

REFERENCES

1. Carpenter, J., n.d. *IBM's Virginia Rometty tells NU grads: Technology will enhance us.* Chicagotribume.com. https://www.chicagotribune.com/bluesky/originals/ct-northwest-ern-virginia-rometty-ibm-bsi-20150619-story.html. (accessed on October 28 2020).
2. Koksar, I. n.d. *"Amazon Officially selling Cashierless Store Technology to retailers."* https://www.forbes.com/sites/ilkerkoksal/2020/03/30/amazon-officially-selling-cashierless-store-technology-to-retailers/#7b4cd8176c47 (accessed on August 19, 2020).
3. Fleishman, G. n.d. Fastcompany.com. *"Checking out Amazon Go, the First No-Checkout Convenience Store."* https://www.fastcompany.com/40518124/amazon-go-store-opening?utm_campaign=Daily%20Logistics%20Newsletter&utm_source=hs_email&utm_medium=email&_hsenc=p2ANqtz-8jiPOwl-0srd8LIB4rkUStmm46Yf-HrAHiPiiRYOTtJE-bVYBrtnpCyjMPgIhZixq5H-8UH (accessed on January 11 2020).
4. Read More at: https://www.o360.ai/blog/ai-driven-persona-development-o360-consumer-portraits.
5. Dunwoodie, B. n.d. *"How AI is impacting the voice of the customer landscape."* CMS Wire. https://www.cmswire.com/customer-experience/how-ai-is- impacting-the-voice-of-the-customer-landscape (accessed on September 29, 2020).
6. Ponce de Leon, S. n.d. *"At CES, AI robots can read your emotions."* Grit Daily. https://gritdaily. com/ai-emotion-bots/. (accessed on January 11, 2021).
7. Campbell, C., S. Sands, C. Ferraro, H.-Y. J. Tsao, and A. Mavrommatis. "From data to action: How marketers can leverage AI." *Business Horizons* 63, no. 2 (2020): 227–243.
8. Vilar, H. n.d. *"UK's Nationwide analyses customer interactions with SAS. Fintech Futures."* https://www.bankingtech.com/2019/03/uks-nationwide-analyses- customer-interactions-with-sas/. (accessed on January 8, 2021).
9. Power, B. n.d. *"How Harley-Davidson Used Artificial Intelligence to Increase New York Sales Leads by 2, 930%."* https://hbr.org/2017/05/how-harley-davidson-used-predictive-analytics-to-increase-new-york-sales-leads-by-2930. (accessed on January 8, 2021).
10. Newell, S., and M. Marabelli. "Strategic opportunities (and challenges) of algorithmic decision-making: A call for action on the long-term societal effects of 'datification'." *The Journal of Strategic Information Systems* 24, no. 1 (2015): 3–14.
11. Read more at: https://www.salesforce.com/au/blog/2019/04/state-of-service--2019-s-changing-customer-service-trends.html.
12. Sentence, R. n.d. *"How Samsung uses social listening for product marketing and sentiment analysis."* https://econsultancy.com/how-samsung-uses-social-listening-for-prod-uct-marketing-sentiment-analysis/ (accessed on October 20, 2020).
13. Arevalillo, J. M. "A machine learning approach to assess price sensitivity with application to automobile loan segmentation." *Applied Soft Computing* 76 (2019): 390–399.

14. Hill, D. "How much is your spare room worth?." *IEEE Spectrum* 52, no. 9 (2015): 32–58.

15. Dorfer, S. n.d. *"Shoppable content: AI app Browzzin."* https://www.stylus.com/kppfqb (accessed on December 20, 2020).

16. Caygill, D. n.d. *"Six trends brands should know about for 2018 and the tech they need to craft responses. Campaign."* https://www.campaignlive.co.uk/article/six-trends-brands-know-2018-tech-need-craft-responses/1450488 (accessed on January 8, 2021).

17. Sweeney, E. n.d. *"IBM's interactive AI ads reach more sites, brands. Industry Dive."* https://www.marketingdive.com/news/ibms-interactive-ai-ads-reach-more-sites-brands/538558 (accessed on January 8, 2021).

18. Read More at: https://www.google.com/url?sa=t&rct=j&q=&esrc=s&source=web&cd=&ved=2ahUKEwj6_bvW_ZLuAhUEeysKHc-PARsQFjABegQIBRAC&url=https%3A%2F%2Fspaces.statista.com%2Fstudy_id59297_artificial-intelligence-ai%2520(1).pdf&usg=AOvVaw3SA_qUIKtIBNU1HQ2qfxoJ.

19. Read more at: https://hbsp.harvard.edu/download?url=%2Fcatalog%2Fsample%2FBH1037-PDF-ENG%2Fcontent&metadata=eyJlcnJvck1lc3NhZ2UiOiJZb3UgbXVzdCBiZSByZWdpc3RlcmVkIGFzIGEgUHJlbWl1bSBFZHVjYXRvciBvbiB0aGlzIHdlYiYiBzaXRlIHRvIHVzZSBFZHVjYXRvciBDb3B5IZyZWUgVHJpYWxzLiBOb3QgQgcmVnaXN0ZXJlZD8gQXBwbHkgY2hhXN0ZXJlZD8gUmVhZHklY3MgZXhwaWQ8gZW5kIEzyZ-WUgVHJpYYxzLiBOb3QgQcmVnaXN0ZXJlZD8gQXBwbHkgbm93Hkgbm93LiBBY2l3c3MgZXhwaWQ8gUmVhdXRob3JpememUgbm93LiJ9.

20. Read more at: https://www.washingtonpost.com/pr/wp/2016/08/05/the-washington-post-experiments-with-automated-storytelling-to-help-power-2016-rio-olympics-coverage/

21. Wankhede, K., B. Wukkadada, and V. Nadar. *"Just walk-out technology and its challenges: a case of Amazon go."* In *2018 International Conference on Inventive Research in Computing Applications (ICIRCA)*, pp. 254–257. IEEE, 2018.

22. Türegün, N. "Impact of technology in financial reporting: The case of Amazon Go." *Journal of Corporate Accounting & Finance* 30, no. 3 (2019): 90–95.

23. Levy, A. n.d. *"How Netflix's AI Saves It $1 Billion Every Year."* https://www.fool.com/investing/2016/06/19/how-netflixs-ai-saves-it-1-billion-every-year.aspx (accessed on January 8 2020).

24. Statista. 2015. https://www.statista.com/statistics/678739/forecast-on-connected-devices-per-person/

25. Suleman, F. n.d. *"10 Reasons that Demonstrate the Importance of Technology in Business."* https://readwrite.com/2019/08/16/10-reasons-that-demonstrate-the-importance-of-technology-in-business/? (accessed on August 16 2020).

26. Statista. 2018. https://www.statista.com/statistics/190858/most-effective-online-marketing-channels-according-to-us-companies/

27. Chatterjee, D. n.d. *"Blogger Outreach: The Definitive Guide for the Beginners."* https://readwrite.com/2020/06/21/blogger-outreach-the-definitive-guide-for-the-beginners/ (accessed on June 21 2020).

28. Statista. 2019. https://www.statista.com/statistics/1036727/global-voice-search-region-device/ (accessed on June 21 2020).

29. Kundariya, H. n.d. *"Is AI Going to Disrupt the Marketing Industry?"* https://readwrite.com/2020/08/12/is-ai-going-to-disrupt-the-marketing-industry/ (accessed on January 11 2020).

30. Davenport, T., A. Guha, D. Grewal, and T. Bressgott. "How artificial intelligence will change the future of marketing." *Journal of the Academy of Marketing Science* 48, no. 1 (2020): 24–42.

2 Consumer Insights through Retail Analytics

Farrah Zeba
Department of Marketing and Strategy, ICFAI Business School (IBS) Hyderabad, IFHE (deemed-to-be-university), Telangana

Musarrat Shaheen
Department of Human Resource, ICFAI Business School (IBS) Hyderabad, IFHE (deemed-to-be-university), Telangana

CONTENTS

2.1　INTRODUCTION

There is an urban legend, which goes like this: Not long ago, there was a large super-market chain, which discovered something very unusual in its customers' buying patterns. To their utter surprise they found a statistically significant correlation between two unrelated items: beer and diapers. They could not come to terms with how an increase in the sales of diapers could lead to a significant increase in the sales of beer as well. Members of the thinktank at of the chain rattled their heads and after much deliberation extrapolated that the reason for this strange association was that it was quite likely that, as it being a Friday night, fathers were stopping off at the retail chain to buy diapers for their babies, and since they could no longer go down to the pub on usual Friday night like before parenthood, might be mitigate this by buying

DOI: 10.1201/9781003125129-2

beer along with the diapers. As a result of this finding, the supermarket chain had a 'eureka' moment and decided to place the diapers next to the beer shelves in the store. This allegedly resulted in the astronomical increase in both the sales of beer and diapers [1,2].

This strange beer and diaper association story, for no particular reason, is widely believed to be from the big retail chain Walmart [2]. Though there are many variations of this fable, the underlying tenet is that a supermarket discovered that customers 'who buy diapers also tend to buy beer'. This insight leads to a very important question: how did the supermarket determine that such a relationship could exist between two unrelated products? And the answer is retail analytics. The beer and diaper correlation, though a legend, arguably heralded the pervasive use of the customer transactions data of a supermarket to uncover unusual, unknown and quirky nuggets about customers [3]. Such a correlation is only possible when data-driven analytics is conducted in retail stores. Consumers' purchase behaviours are captured and used to predict future consumer purchases.

2.2   WHAT VALUE DOES ANALYTICS BRING TO RETAIL?

The science of analyzing raw data so as to draw conclusion from mass of information in the form of trends and metrics is termed as "data analytics". In practice, data analytics is an umbrella term that covers divergent aspects of data analysis.

The process of employing analytical tools for analyzing business trends, and calculating metrics to comprehend retail business decisions is termed as "Retail Analytics". Retail is the upcoming business domains for analytics because of its prolific data and numerous optimization problems such as optimal prices, discounts, recommendations and stock levels which can be solved by deploying analytical techniques. Especially when the retail industry is facing new challenges like uncertainty in economy, digital competition, and emergence of customers being well informed and increasingly demanding. This opens a new opportunity for retailers who can accurately anticipate the customers' wants and needs by offering the right product, in the right place, at the right time and for the right price.

2.3   TYPES OF CUSTOMER DATA USED IN RETAIL ANALYTICS

"Customer data can be collected in three ways: by directly asking customers, by indirectly tracking customers, and by appending other sources of customer data to your own", said Hanham. "A robust business strategy needs all three". For simplicity, the retail consumer data can be categorized in four domains ([4–9]; and [10]).

a) **Personal data:** This category includes personally identifiable information such as name, age, gender, address, IP address, browser cookies and others.
b) **Engagement data:** This type of data encompasses the way consumer interact with retailer's physical store visits, its website and mobile apps, also company's social media pages, and other digital footprints of the company.

c) **Behavioural data:** Under this category data pertaining to consumers' transactional details, such as buying history, trail and usage information, repeated purchases and some qualitative data like mouse movement information.

d) **Attitudinal data:** This data type is related to consumer metrics of customer satisfaction, criteria of purchases, product desirability and customer loyalty.

2.4 APPLICATION OF CONSUMER DATA – RETAIL ANALYTICS

There are several ways by which retail companies can use the consumer data that they collect so as to draw business relevant consumer insights:

i. **Enhancing Customer Experience:** Consumer data offers an avenue to the retail organizations to get a better understanding of their customer needs as to not only meet their customers' expectations. But also gain a competitive advantage by exceeding the customer expectations based on the consumer insight they gained from retail analytics. For example, by analyzing customer behaviour along with reviews and feedback, companies can gain agility in fine tuning their physical as well as digital presence of their goods, or services or brand to better align the current competitive landscape.

ii. **Crafting effective marketing strategy:** Data which is contextualized can aid the retail companies in extrapolating how their consumers are engaging as well as responding to their marketing campaigns, and thus in the process that will be able to personalize the marketing strategy as per the target market needs. The predictive power of retail analytics can empower the retail firms for the effectiveness of the current marketing strategies in meeting not only present needs of the consumers, but also be ready for all possible future needs of their current as well as potential consumers.

iii. **Transformation of data into cash flow:** Increasingly, companies who are using retail analytics to make their business decisions are the ones turning out to be more profitable that those who do not. Consequently, data service providers who deal in buying and selling information on customers are tremendous boost in their business operations. Thus, the businesses that capture large amounts of data, transforms it into valuable consumer insights and then sell it represent opportunities for new revenue streams.

iv. **Securing More Data:** In this case consumer data is often used as a means of securing information which are highly sensitive in nature. For instance, increasingly most of the retail banks are using cutting edge technology like voice recognition data to authorize a user to access their financial information so as to safeguard them for fraudulent attempts to steal their sensitive information. Thus, with growing sophistication in data capture and analytics technologies, the retail organizations will have to up their game by finding novel and comparatively more effective ways to collect and contextualize data on each and every interaction point with their customers (Table 2.1).

TABLE 2.1
Data Privacy and Retail Analytics

As per DW, the Supreme Court in 2017 reiterated that the Indian constitution guarantee a fundamental right to privacy for every citizen. Thus, the Indian government is to introduce Personal Data Protection (PDP) legislation. The bill is expected to materialize and become functional by early 2021. "The draft PDP law was based broadly on the same principles as the European Union's General Data Protection Regulation (GDPR)", said Anirudh Burman, associate fellow at the Carnegie Endowment for International Peace India in New Delhi. Thus, it is insistent that retail analysts adhere to these principles which comprise of protective laws for storing consumer data, asking for the user's consent before using private information, periodic audits for companies and rules for reporting breaches. Further the retail analyst should also be cognizant about the fact that, the PDP also includes setting up a Data Privacy Authority (DPA) to "maintain, monitor frameworks, firms and penalties to companies".

Source: MFD (n.d.)

2.5   ANALYTICS IN RETAIL INDUSTRY – HOW IT WORKS

It has been seen that retailers who have knowledge of customers make analytically smarter strategic decisions about their investments in the area of merchandising and inventory management (Anonymous, n.d.). Analytics also enabled them to implement these organizational-level strategies in individual-level offers. Rakesh Biyani, CEO (retail), Future Group concurred, "Retail analytics are very important to ensure the 'right product, at the right time in the right store'. We have used retail analytics to optimize our supply chain as well." [11]. The aim for 'sweet spot' where customer behaviour unites with what the retailer and its suppliers need to accomplish. Prior to opening a Shoppers Stop store at South City Mall in Kolkata, this company also identified this 'sweet spot' by studying the buying patterns of 'First Citizens' residing in South Kolkata and shopping at the Elgin Road Forum store. It indicated that these customers who have these memberships were among those who shop for accessories more frequently that other apparel. Based on this insight, Shoppers Stop dedicated a much larger space to the beauty section at the new store. Bhatia also added, "To target better, we have also classified our database into segments – value, premium and bridge-to-luxury shoppers (BTL), and groups based on cultural and occupational affinity." [11]. However, selecting the right analytics for the business problem is becoming a problem in itself. Analytics marketplace is teeming with vendors with extensive paraphernalia to confuse retailers with similar sounding solutions. Prudent retailers should be cognizant of practical and significant differences in employing analytic techniques, providing variants of insights and resulting in specific business benefits. It is a known fact that 'one-size-for-all' doesn't fit for all types of business requirements. For an analytics investment to yield substantial return it is quintessential to deploy the right technique that had been selected to accomplish the business goals (refer to Table 2.2).

In essence, it is now apparent that most of the competitive retailers are increasing response rates and revenues, by using models driven by retail analytics to figure out timely, customized and relevant offers to customers. Analytics provide a scientific

TABLE 2.2

Analytics Techniques According to the Business Objectives and Purpose

Analytics Techniques	Works For	Suitable For	Benefits
Collaborating Filtering	Infer customer behaviour on the basis of similarities, for instance people who bought A and B together.	For the purchase behaviours of the first-time customers.	Facilitates limited differentiation when no historical data on customer purchase behaviour is available.
Clustering Algorithms	Group customers on the basis of their similar historical behaviour pattern.	Creating broad customer segments for promotional programmes and strategic planning.	Facilitates data driven customer differentiation at a large scale to guide or justify business investments in store design, merchandising and others. Helps in generalizing lifts response rates over traditional query-based segmentation.
Regression Models	The future behaviours on the basis of identified customer attributes.	Prediction of customer behaviours and allow designing marketing and personalized treatment.	Allows predicting response rates (with the double effects) and enhances conversion rate.
Time-to-Event Models	The time when specific customer behaviour is likely to occur.	Predicting the time period when customers are most likely to buy.	Enhances response rate and enables strategy. development for boost in sales by predicting best time of sales.
Uplift Models	The particular behaviours or actions of retailers which is likely to bring a change in the forecasted customer behaviour.	Determining the worthiness of the investment for a particular action.	Cost-benefit analysis for the retailers. Helps in avoiding offers and discounts on products which the customer will buy anyway.
Decision Models	Mathematical mapping of the numerous predictive models' outcomes with the other decision-making elements such as a range of possible retailers' actions and customer responses.	Improves and helps in the complex decisions. Also, captures key results drivers including constraints for use with an optimization engine.	Helps in selecting the best offers, while keeping in view all retailers and suppliers' objectives, for each customer.

means of realizing the long-standing exhortation of customer-centricity. As such, it equips retailers to cater to unique preferences of each customer based on insights into their desires, preferences and future behaviours. Having said that, the next big question is whether there are rules of thumb for analytics in retail. The answer: Not exactly! Nevertheless, there exist a few critical steps, such as those outlined by experts in three retail analytics: studying customer's attitudes and behaviours, analysis of transactional data and predictive modelling [12]. In the first instance, retailers try to track several parameters of their premium customers including their locations, lifestyle, socio-economic background and age. Secondly, transactional data sheds light on areas such as layout planning and shelf placement proximities to home in on the right location of merchandise to maximize sales. The third area is probably the toughest and yet extremely critical – predictive modelling. Using this, retailers could get an idea of how customers' upgrade their purchase behaviour, categories they might be interested in the future as per changes in lifestyle. It also will help them taking up decisions to set up future stores on the bias of the future lifestyle of consumers in a catchment area.

2.6   METRICS IN RETAIL INDUSTRY

There exists several metrics to measure the sale effectiveness of the retail store which indirectly perform as indicators to consumer foot falls [13]. Some of the popular metrics are:

a) **Customer Traffic:** The number of customers visiting the store, irrespective of whether they are purchasing or not. That the increased number of potential customers allows retailers to predict that at least few will purchase some goods. Also, footfall is a sign that people are interested in the items you have in your store. The number of customers is the only metric which retailers can grow indefinitely.

b) **Retail Conversion Rate:** But not all the customer who visits the store do a purchase. One need to identify and target the customers who have purchases an item from the store. This is called customer conversion ratio. Conversion ratio largely depends on the type of retail goods one is handling. According to surveys of Retail Industry the average conversion rate for e-commerce sites is about 2%–3%. The formula to calculate customer conversion ratio is:

#Customer conversion ratio = No of transactions/Customer traffic × 100

c) **Average Sale:** Average sale is nothing but the Average purchase value. That is what amount of money in terms of rupees, dollars, pound, yen or euros on an average a customer has spent in the store. Further is there is increase or decrease in the amount spent. The formula to calculate average sales order value is:

#Average sales order value = Total sales value/Number of transactions

d) **Items per purchase:** This is the size of an average shopping cart. That is how many items (relative to price) on average customers are buying. That is if the number of items bought by customer is more, but the sale value is less than it means people are buying economically cheap items. You need to check this to have a reasonable high sales value. Retailers can aim for more items in a shopping cart with two equals three (2=3) marketing campaigns.

e) **Gross margin (GM):** This is the sales profit before costs. GM is the difference between total revenue generated and the cost incurred to source the items. GM can be calculated by deducting costs of goods from its selling price. In general, the rule of thumb is to always keep the GM high enough so that one has plenty of room to cut back when required. The formula is:

#Product price when sold = Product acquiring or making price + Gross margin

2.7 ANALYTICS IN PRACTICE IN RENOWNED RETAIL ORGANIZATIONS

Whether the correlation between purchase of diapers and beers was indeed a parable or not remains debatable. But what is of significance is that not far from Walmart and the likes, there is a growing trend of new-age Indian retailers, who are orchestrating real success stories in the world of analytics. Analytics is changing the rules of the game, playing a critical role in the retail business in India by furnishing retailers with valuable insights to decide on aspects like store location, assortment of merchandise, customer segments and loyalty programmes, communication strategies and even reducing cannibalization of own store [14]. For instance, an internal programme of Shoppers Stop called 'First Insight', which leverages its 'First Citizen' loyalty database, was driven by analytics. It reflected the actual buying behaviour of the Indian consumer based on a nine-year historical track of every stock keeping unit (SKU), that each First Citizen consumer ever bought from there retail chain. As, Vinay Bhatia, VP – marketing & loyalty, Shoppers Stop, who also manages the analytics team, explained, "To benefit from this data we work on models such as analysis of buying behaviour to support merchandise planning" [15].

The success of these endeavours of Shoppers Stop was quite evident in the delightful experience of Ms. Suchitra, a regular Shoppers Stop customer, at one of its Mumbai outlets. As reported by ET Bureau:

> Suchitra and her friends are among the regulars at the Shoppers Stop store at Inorbit Mall, Mumbai. More often than not, during her shopping jaunts, if she opted for an ethnic ensemble, she'd make the trip upstairs to the first floor, to pick out a pair of shoes to go with it. One day, as she was walking the store, she was quite surprised to find that the footwear section had been moved to the level below, right next to the Indian wear section. Though she had not decided to purchase anything on that day, but due to pleasant placement she ended up buying. Ethnic wear, shoes; this works.

[15]

The experts in their e-paper for *Times of India* revealed that by employing analytics, long before, Shoppers Stop predicted the behaviour of Suchitra and other customers like her. They illustrated this as:

> To Suchitra, it seemed just a coincidence that the footwear section happened to have been moved just where she wanted it. But coincidence, it wasn't. Rather, this move which is an example of an adjacency analysis conducted by Shoppers Stop, which after sifting through 24 months of customer data;

found a pattern wherein it was found that women who buy ethnic wear (sal-war-kameez-dupatta) tended to buy footwear as well. Based on this insight, Shoppers Stop moved its footwear section from the first floor to the ground floor where the ethnic wear section was located. Soon enough it found that this translated into a 25% growth in sales.

[15]

Analytics-backed business orientation took the centre stage once in a press conference held in Bangalore at the Ritz Carlton, where Rakesh Biyani, joint Managing Director of Future Group, India's largest retailer, along with Atul Jalan, CEO Manthan, the world's leading player in analytics for the consumer industry, joyfully shared their fruitful 10 months partnership of retail and analytics [11]. Rakesh Biyani emphasized the importance of the inevitable alliance of retail and analytics through this futuristic statement, he commented:

We knew every customer need was unique and we had opportunities to fine-tune our business planning and execution. With the hyper-localized views of customer demand that Manthan's analytics provides, we will be able to tailor assortments, inventory, replenishment, marketing promotions, store engagement to meet the unique needs of markets and stores. By making decisions faster and more precise, and our execution more efficient, we believe it has the potential to realize a 7%–9% reduction in out of stocks, recover an average 5%–7% in lost sales, and achieve 10%–12% reduction in churn. All of this would not be possible without the ability to spot and act on analytics-driven opportunities.

[11]

Future Group tie-up with Manthan's analytics enabled the retailer, the real-time and actionable information in over 370 stores across 166 cities nationwide by tracking more than 10 million customer transactions in a month of 13,000 product brands in a network 3,000 suppliers. Further, activities of over 25 million loyal customers and their transactions were tracked in data warehouse of Manthan's analytics [11]. Future Group had rolled out analytics to all decision makers across its business divisions. Atul Jalan, CEO at Manthan said:

Making analytics-driven competencies a reality was a tremendous opportunity for Indian retailers today. Future Group had a head start in this direction, and some of the business results they saw in this partnership were simply outstanding. Manthan's 12-year endeavour had been focused on simplifying the sophisticated technologies and statistical sciences needed in understanding customer behaviour and realizing its potential in easy-to-use, business friendly analytical applications.

[11]

To explain simply what retail analytics could do, and to enhance the relationship between retailer and its customer, Rakesh Biyani, (Founder and CEO of Future

Group) added, "Without analytics, forecasting and tracking down consumer behaviour, it's not going to be possible to run a business which keeps growing on efficiency terms". [16]. The founder of a retail analytics firm which works for Future Group, Atul Jalan, commented that, "With analytics, I can at least come to you and say I see you come here and thank you. That you buy *atta, daal and chawal* from us. How come you haven't bought this from us?" Future Group is the first Indian and one of the top 20 customers of Manthan to join with the stalwarts such as e-commerce company eBay and another dozen or so Fortune 100 companies [16].

Unlike Shoppers Stop and Future Group, most of the retailers are lagging behind by not giving due importance to analytics as a tool, likely to be used by them in expanding their network in the coming retail scenario. Consequently, instead of doing a scientific assessment of the catchment areas, they end up in the rat race of mindless retail expansion spree. As, prudently explicated by Pankaj Mishra, head of Consumer Insight and Consumer Intelligence, Spencer's Retail:

In our future expansion, we would do more of primary research to understand market potential value of the catchment areas. Such analysis helps us in deciding where to open, which format to go for and how many stores to open. Consumption expenditure analysis, category-wise analysis, market potential value analysis was also some of the research exercises undertaken before a robust expansion strategy was drawn up.

[11]

In similar lines, Kishore Biyani advocated for monitoring demand rate at stores, which made the group to push sales in many cases by up to 300%. He further added, "Close monitoring on point-of-sales data coupled with quicker review of the reorder points helped us achieve a new level of consistent sales. Analytics is also playing a more important role in future store planning." [11]. On June 2015, as stated in Forbes, true to his past feats for a keen eye for consumer insight through the knowledge of each and every customer of his stores, he revealed that his strategic thrust is to transform Future Group (one of the largest conglomerates) from just a retail company to an empowered analytics company. Please refer to Figure 2.1 for different types of customer analytics [17].

Different types of customer analytics [17] is given in Figure 2.1.

2.8 CHALLENGES AND PITFALL – RETAIL ANALYTICS

In the face of exuberance all around, Himanshu Chakrawarti, COO, Landmark Retail remarked that usage of analytics is still at its infancy. He further added, "Analytics in Indian retail is still largely limited to studying consumers and transactions." [11]. In contrast, sectors like banking in India have matured more in using analytics and even using predictive modelling. But it is heartening that Indian retailers now understand the importance of analytics and are investing significantly in it. Landmark, the bookstore retail chain catering to music and gifts under the conglomerate Tata Group, too has set up an internal analytics teams which are trying to understand issues like cannibalization when opening new stores, identifying ideal locations depending on

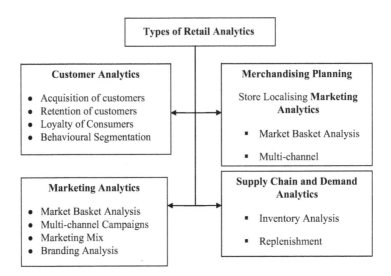

FIGURE 2.1   Analytical Solutions in Retail Industry.

the address of its regular customers, pinning down consumers who might drop out due to changes in buying habits and come up with solutions which will facilitates with offers and changes in merchandise.

The challenge is more for conglomerates like Future Group, who, with their recent acquisition of retail business of Bharti Retail, are planning astronomical targets of achieving at least Rs 1 lakh sales from its one-crore-customers. Biyani sought to push his company in the directions of traditional international retailing giants like Target (American) and Tesco (UK). The game changer is employing retail analytics to predict consumer wants even before they themselves realize. His growing appetite for knowing customer inside and out is apparent in the following illustration of one of his customers a 38-year-old Chandrakant Dhawan (name changed):

> Every month, Dhawan and his family visit the Big Bazaar outlet in Mumbai's Vile Parle to stock up on groceries and other household commodities. During the festive season, his shopping basket includes a few gifts, and at the start of the academic year, he buys stationery for his children. In all, he spends about Rs 60,000 a year at Big Bazaar, which is owned by the Future Group. Biyani, however, is not satisfied with Dhawan's spends. He wants more.

[18]

Customer analytics is like a trump card. He said he wants to use this trump card to reach an exponential growth in the coming years through a turnover of near about to 1,000 billion to which he added, "Unlike in the past, when we were chasing mindless growth, what we want now is profitable growth. We will not grow through debt, but through cash flows." [19].

But to apply data science by churning crores of customer records, and then forecasting their behaviour is indeed no mean feat. This unfolds more of hindrances than solutions, as comprehended by Jayadevan PK, ET Bureau, "Future Group's stores such as Food Bazaar, Big Bazaar, Home Town and Nilgiris see some 300 million footfalls every year and the company has a database of three-crore people who are on its loyalty programme [23,24,25]. It wants to expand this database to include seventy-eight-crore customers and use analytics to sell more to them" [12].

2.9 WAY AHEAD

The retail industry had undergone drastic change over the last couple of decades, and its projected global market size is estimated to be $20,002 billion USD by 2017. The rapid market growth is continuing but is hindered by thin margins and a hypercompetitive environment. Highly informed and digitally savvy customers are seeking a more personalized shopping experience. This has also added to the pressure. Retailers need to sift from handling simple predictable demands to varied and unique tastes by churning terabytes of data to be able to apprehend customers' requirements more precisely [20]. Further, to induce today's post-recession reluctant consumer to spend dollars require retailers to forge relationship based on engagement, personalization and relevancy. As a result, retail analytics is highly critical in helping retailers in effectively collecting, analyzing and acting on both customer and organization data in real time across all the channels they function in. With the acknowledgement of retail analytics as an effective tool to increase customers' share of wallet, acquiring a higher margin, increasing cross sales and reducing wasteful investments, majority of the retailers are still struggling to figure out the suitability of various analytical approaches. As such, they are witnessing several bottlenecks like overwhelmingly large number of options; inefficiency in digesting all the data fetched by multitude point-of-sales systems, online portals and internal transaction processes [21]. Like trajectory of retail growth, application of analytics is also likely to undergo its own learning curve.

However, retailers like Spencer's are scaling this learning curve with a fervent thrust on analytics by using data analysis to improve sales in some of its underperforming stores. It is studying customer lapses, regular customers and occasional customers, to understand the real pain points of the stores, and the purchase drivers of consumers in catchment areas of their ailing stores. "From the research, we could draw up turnaround strategies for the stores and have seen a success rate of almost 98%", claimed Mishra [15]. For Spencer's, it is studying underperforming stores, but for Shoppers Stop it is about segmenting their 1.5 million First Citizen members to identify store promotions and buyers of luxury product, and then inducing them for repeat purchases. As Bhatia said:

> The BTL and luxury segment is growing at over 60% and the frequency of these customers' visits is significantly higher than normal customers — about three times the industry benchmark. So, rather than communicating to the entire base of First Citizen members for a BTL brand communication, we now target offers, schemes and new launches to this segment.

[15]

To make the learning curve smooth for the retailers, retail analytics consultant companies like Openbravo are quite upbeat as well, as Sunando Banerjee, Channel Business Manager for Asia Pacific & Middle East excitedly explained:

> We view India as an important market with unlimited opportunities for growth, especially in the retail segment which was projected to grow to $792.84 billion by the end of 2017. India is the fifth largest retail destination globally. We are excited to offer our complete commerce solution, which enables our customers to maintain their competitiveness in this retail wave. Our breakthrough solutions will enable their business to be truly agile. It will help our customers effectively adapt to rapidly changing business challenges.
>
> [22]

But the real challenge is not to have a team to run analytics solutions, but as comprehended by Devangshu Dutta, CEO of retail consultancy Third Eyesight, that implementing these solutions is the real challenge, "What is harder is getting the organization to react to the insights. If there is a short-term opportunity, but the retailer is unable to source the goods from the supplier, it is as good as not having thedata" [18].

2.10   DISCUSSION QUESTIONS

1. What value does analytics bring to retail?
2. How to zero in on actionable consumer insights?
3. Which retail analytics should be matched to which specific retail scenario?
4. What are the challenges encountered by Indian retailers in the analytics?

REFERENCES

1. Rao, S. S. (2013). *Diaper-beer Syndrome*, retrieved on January 20, 2018, from https://www.forbes.com/forbes/1998/0406/6107128a.html#63dd57726260
2. Whitehorn, M. (2006). *The Parable of the Beer and Diapers*, retrieved on September 23, 2020 from https://s/www.theregister.co.uk/2006/08/15/beer_diapers/
3. Kotu, V. & Deshpande, B. (2014). *Predictive Analytics and Data Mining: Concepts and Practice with Rapidminer*, Morgan Kaufmann, ScienceDirect, 2015.
4. Agarwal, R. (2015). *Category Management: Definitions, Significance and 8-Steps Process*, retrieved on March 12, 2018, from https://goo.gl/9QcZXD
5. Chain Drug Review [CDR]. (2015). *It's Time to Apply Analytics to Category Management*, retrieved on January 23, 2018, from https://goo.gl/e2smGb
6. Chiplunkar, R. M. (2011). *Product Category Management*. New Delhi, India, Tata McGraw Hill.
7. Dotactiv. (n.d.). *What is Category Management?*, retrieved on February 20, 2018, from https://www.dotactiv.com/wha0074-is-category-management
8. ECR Community Follow [ECRa]. (2010). *ECR Europe Forum '05. Use The ECR Scorecard to Benchmark and Improve*, retrieved on March 23, 2018, from https://goo.gl/ckZqwB

9. Salmon, K. (n.d.). *Seven Facets of Modern Category Management*, retrieved January 20, 2018, from http://www.indiaretailnews.com/index.php/best-practices/category-management/203336-seven-facets-of-modern-category-management

10. ECR D-A-CH Hamburg [ECRb]. (2007). *Category Management – PraxisorientierteEinstiegshilfe und Nutzenbetrachtung.* Hamburg, VortragKlafsak/Klüsener, retrieved on November 12.

11. Analytics India Magazine [AIM]. (2015). *Future Group Announces Strategic Partnership with Analytics Firm Manthan*, retrieved on March 12, 2018, from https://goo.gl/sw9fvd

12. IBM Knowledge Center [IBMKC]. (n.d.), *Predict Churn in the Insurance Case Study*, retrieved on February 20, 2018, from https://goo.gl/S6GKNp

13. Frankenfield, J & Drury, A. (2020). *Data Analytics*, Retrived on November 20, 2020 from https://www.investopedia.com/terms/d/data-analytics.asp

14. Freedman, M. (2020). *How Businesses Are Collecting Data (And What They're Doing With It)*, retrieved on November 10, 2020 from https://www.businessnewsdaily.com/10625-businesses-collecting-data.html

15. Sreeradha, D. B. and Writankar, M. (2010). *Analytics Playing Critical Role in Retail Business*, retrieved on January 23, 2018, from https://goo.gl/2A2BEa

16. Jayadevan, P. (2015). *Future Group Banking on Analytics to Battle E-commerce Companies*, retrieved on February 12, 2018, from https://goo.gl/yGTgSa

17. FICO. (2015), *Which Retail Analytics Do You Need?|FICO®*, retrieved on March 20, 2018, from https://www.fico.com/en/latest-thinking/white-paper/which-retail-analytics-do-you-need

18. Srivastava, S. (2015). *Future Group's Ambitious Reboot*, retrieved on January 12, 2018, from https://goo.gl/634U4T

19. Pinto, V. S. & Kamath, R. (2015). *Kishore Biyani's Limitless Ambitions*, retrieved on March 20, 2018, from https://goo.gl/YSRMND

20. Sugandha, P. (2017). *7 Big Trends of 2017 In Retail Analytics*, retrieved on March 20, 2018, from https://www.happiestminds.com/blogs/7-big-trends-of-2017-in-retail-analytics/

21. HCL Technologies. (n.d.), *What is Retail Analytics? HCL Technologies*, retrieved on January 20, 2018, from https://www.hcltech.com/technology-qa/what-is-retail-analytics

22. Openbravo. (2014). *Open bravo to Showcase New Commerce Platform with Retail Analytics at India Retail Forum*, retrieved on January 20, 2018, from http://www.openbravo.com/about/news/Openbravo-to-showcase-new-commerce-platform-with-retail-analytics-at-India-Retail-Forum/

23. Anonymous (n.d.-a). *Anticipate And Connect To Your Customers' Retail Needs*, retrieved on October 25, 2020 from https://www.nielsen.com/eu/en/solutions/retail-analytics/

24. Anonymous (n.d.-b). *Big Data Analytics - What it is and why it matters|SAS India*, retrieved on September 23, 2020 from https://www.sas.com/en_in/insights/analytics/big-data-analytics.html

25. Anonymous (n.d.-c). *How to Measure Retail Performance? 5 Essential Metrics*, retrieved on November 23 from https://erply.com/how-to-measure-retail-performance-5-essential-metrics/

3 Multi-Agent Paradigm for B2C E-Commerce

Bireshwar Dass Mazumdar
Department of CSE, IERT Allahabad, India

Shubhagata Roy
Department of Operations & IT, IBS Hyderabad, India

CONTENTS

3.1 BUSINESS PERSPECTIVE

3.1.1 NEGOTIATION

A regular form of contact between agents with different goals is referred to as negotiation. Negotiation is a method by which two or more agents, each aiming to achieve an individual target or purpose, achieve a collective agreement.

DOI: 10.1201/9781003125129-3

First, the agents express their views, which can cause clashes or disagreement, and then proceed to progress towards consensus by offering compromises or finding alternatives. The key features of negotiation include (a) terminologies used by the participating parties, (b) protocols adopted by the parties as they negotiate, and (c) the judgement process used by each agent to assess its roles, compromises and their conditions. Protocols in negotiation, i.e., mechanisms, may be measured according to several types of parameters. The selection of protocol would then depend on what characteristics the protocol maker wishes to have the overall framework [28]. Fundamentally, the primary purpose of bargaining is to reach an understanding of certain points of dispute. We have taken up the following concepts in this chapter [60,61]:

(i) Negotiation is a method of interaction aimed at settling a disagreement in interests between two or more parties with the help of a given protocol and agents' techniques [30].
(ii) Typically, the protocol specifies the sequence of steps agents need to take during negotiation, while the techniques of the agents are a part of their thinking process (which also requires collecting and evaluation knowledge and providing components of generation) [4,6].
(iii) Negotiation is the practice of negotiating with each other through a group of agents to obtain consensus on a matter of mutual concern. The purpose of negotiation, as can be deduced from the aforementioned description, is to reach an agreement that fits the preferences or restrictions of the agents, but such meetings do not necessarily end up in an agreement (and an agent can obtain zero or negative utility from this).
(iv) Non-agreement can arise as a result of a lack of time, an unavailability for the participants of suitable alternatives (which may result from a lack of information about the inclinations of the participants), or an incompatibility between the agents' strategies [9,18]. However, both parties are generally committed to enacting the substance of the agreement if an agreement is possible and the agents are genuinely willing to accomplish it [8].

3.1.1.1   Types of Agent-to-Agent Negotiations

An agent deals with the world as well as the other agents in general. Negotiation or an agent-to-agent interaction may include receiving a tangible entity from the other agent, getting the other agent to conduct an activity or altering other agent's perceptions or requirements. The various issues are given below for agent-to-agent negotiation:

Competition

This negotiating class is the easiest possible. Various applications have been designed and implemented using opposing agents. The apps cover electronic trading, auctions and can employ solutions focused on game theory [79].

Coordination

Agent-to-agent collaboration is a mechanism by which agents aim to organize their activities to ensure success in the overall scheme. The agents involved are usually a part of a Multi-Agent structure and the communication operation may seek to sequence the access of agents to common resource or monitor the transfer of items and information between the agents. Coordination techniques also focuses on rectifying issues related to distributed restriction satisfaction and its kinds [57,58]. Supply chain management [24] is a prototypical example of teamwork.

Co-operation

As in traditional software creation, as the scale and complexity of a system increases, the system is typically broken down into modules for better management. Similarly, decomposing an agent system into a Multi-Agent system might be required. Co-operation in Multi-Agent scheme like this is directed at achieving a single overarching purpose. While each agent may have its own purpose, the agents may forfeit advancement towards their own objectives in order to accomplish a machine goal instead of each agent attempting to optimize its own utility function. Co-operation can entail the solution of a problem of distributed restriction satisfaction or a problem of distributed optimization [77].

Collaboration

By maintaining coordination between agents, we mean the mechanism by which agents who are not a priori team members are able to determine that teaming up will progress their individual goals [38].

3.1.1.2   Negotiation Strategies

Social welfare

In a given solution, social security is the sum of all agents' payoffs or utilities. It tests the agents' global good. Through comparing the solutions that the mechanisms lead to, it can be used as a criterion to compare alternative mechanisms. The criterion is somewhat subjective when calculated in terms of utilities, since it involves inter-agent utility comparisons and currently the utility function of each agent can be defined only up to positive affine transformations) [18,46].

Pareto efficiency

Another solution measurement parameter that takes a global view is Pareto Efficiency. Again, by comparing the solutions that the mechanism leads to, alternate mechanisms can be tested according to Pareto Efficiency. A solution x is effective for Pareto, i.e. Pareto is ideal if no other x_0 solution exists, so that at least one agent is better off in x_0 than in x and no agent is worse off in x_0 than in x. Pareto Efficiency thus tests global good, and it does not entail questionable comparison of inter-agent utility. A subset of Pareto effective solutions is social welfare optimizing solutions. Once the total of the pay offs is maximized, the payoff of another agent decreases [52].

Individual rationality

Involvement in an agreement is personally rational to an agent, if the agent's payoff in the agreed solution is no less that the payoff that the agent will get from not engaging in the agreement. When engagement is independently rational for all agents, a system is considered to be independently rational. Solely, the individually rational mechanisms are said to feasible: the self-interested agent does not partake in the negotiation if the negotiated solution is not personally acceptable for that agent.

Stability

The system should be structured to be stable (non-manipulability) for self-interested agents, i.e., they should encourage each agent to behave in the desired way. This is since, in such a case that a self-interested agent is in ideal situation acting in some other way than wanted, it will do as such. Sometimes, it is conceivable to plan components with predominant techniques. This implies that a specialist is best off by utilizing a particular methodology regardless of what systems different operators use [28].

3.1.1.3   Negotiation Types

Auctions

In an auction, the bidding is initiated by one or more agents termed as auctioneers, and some other agents termed as bidders make bids according to the protocol implemented (which might allow one or many rounds). A contract between the auctioneer and the effective buyer is then typically the product of the auction [36].

Bilateral negotiations

Bilateral negotiation comprises two sides, a service/good seller and a customer, finding a mutually agreeable compromise on the terms and conditions of a trade. Bilateral negotiation typically involves multi-attribute bids (price/cost, delivery date, and so on) [12,14,29,33].

Decision-making by the opponent's behaviour

Agents specifically think for their opponents' goals and actions using the techniques and then determine the acceptable response of their behaviour. A significant method for evaluating strategic relationships between agents is the non-cooperative game theory [12,14,29,33].

Multi-attribute negotiations

Multi-attribute negotiation is an agreement comprising several issues which must be rectified simultaneously [12,14,29,33]. In this case, agents can have different interests on issues, and by trading some that are not so important, both parties may reach greater consensus on issues that are more important to them.

Issue-by-issue negotiation

Negotiation on issue by issue is often based on the negotiating paradigm of Rubinstein, where agents may select either sequential negotiation with sequential implementation or simultaneous negotiation with simultaneous implementation.

Cooperative multi-attribute negotiation

On multi-attribute negotiation that concentrates on the viewpoint of cooperative game theory on the principle of unbiased division and the creation of the division procedure. Knaster and Steinhaus first formulated this method based on the principle of [12,14,29,33]. Another unbiased division procedure termed "adjusted winner" was proposed by Brams and Taylor, which implements an equal result.

Contracting

Contracting entails arranging the reallocation of jobs between agents; it entails one agent offering to contract any of his duties to another agent while promising any incentives. Contracts were implemented in areas such as energy markets, distribution of bandwidth, preparation and timing of processing, and electronic exchange of financial instruments [12,14,29,33].

3.1.2 CUSTOMER RELATIONSHIP MANAGEMENT (CRM) AND CUSTOMER ORIENTATION (CO)

Customer relationship management (CRM) refers to the methodologies and equipment that help enterprises coordinate the management of customer relationships. CRM processes that help to recognize and attract their potential clients, produce quality sales leads and organize as well as conduct marketing strategies with specific priorities and goals; CRM processes that help build individualized customer experiences and offer the highest level of customer support to the most productive clients; CRM processes that provide workers with the knowledge they need to know their customers. Tools/equipment for customer relationship management include software and browser-based applications to collect and organize customer information [67]. For example, an organization might use a database of customer knowledge to aid in creating a survey of customer feedback as a part of their customer plan, or determine the potential product their consumers may be interested in [44,45].

Customer orientation is the collection of sales principles that specifies that an organization's goal is customer desires and fulfilment. It reflects on complex relationships between the businessman clients as well as rivals or opponents in the industry and its stakeholders. This requires a continuing transition in corporate practices. It is "The Corporation that is observed from the point of view of its ultimate outcome, which is from the point of view of the consumer," (Peter F. Drucker, 2004). Customer orientation relies on customer listening (e.g., "I wish to explore what type of offer will be more suitable to a customer") and conversation (e.g., "I wish to have consumers convey their needs to me"). Customer oriented salespeople, perhaps at the cost of instant sales, appear to display habits that increase long-term customer loyalty.

There are seven main patterns that clearly suggest an attitude towards customers [46,48]:

1. Thinking and discussing frequently about customers to learn about them.
2. Continually assessing the views of your clients.

3. Resolving priority concerns in favour of the client.
4. Giving in, sacrificing and bringing value to the client.
5. Making amends for the mistreatment of clients.
6. Using a policy of "whatever it takes" to meet special needs.
7. Redesigning policies and redeploying personnel when service efficiency gets in the way. (Drucker, 1994).

There are three forms of consumer orientation:

1. Profit-centred
2. Knowing customers
3. Partnerships with consumers

There are some basic (private) and some general (public) criteria for each orientation that are general to other orientations. The public and private criteria in the three orientations follow below:

Profit-centric orientation

The aim in the orientation is on gathering and evaluating the customers' prior purchases and preference details. The consumer who adds even more to the benefit and the consumer who has strong pricing expectations are maintained and dealt for the future. It then allows for the parameters: history records, requirements and capacity.

Customer understanding

The requirements and expectations of existing and prospective consumers contribute to the perception of the need of the consumer. Greater understanding of customer's conditions and behaviour in latent levels amounts to sales leveraging. Demands, match and priorities are the three criteria of this orientation.

Customer relationship

The entity or collective partnership between the buyer and seller makes the difference in the company's sales and also rewards the consumer. When there is a strong match between them, the partnership becomes strong and connected. A good fit is defined as the difference between the requested item and the actual item supplied. The promptness also governs the relationship in the sense of fit. The three criteria that constituted the consumer relationship are also a good fit choice and skill [21,42,43].

3.1.3 BROKER AND BROKERING

The middle agent (broker agent) scans its marketing database for a request for products given by buyer agent that can satisfy such a request when a buyer agent enters request for products. Requests are satisfied by the middle agent when the advertising of the seller agent is sufficient close to the definition of the buyer agent's requirement. The relationship between the vendor and the client is based on restrictions imposed on agents [39]. The broker's efficacy is fully dependent on the market. Agents involved in the same thing have to match up. When a selling agent is found, the marketplace must supply it with a list of possible buyer agents and notify the broker agent of the presence of this of this new selling agent to all potential buyers [47]. Therefore, the broker is the agent who serves as a mediator between buyers and sellers. By assessing the profile of the different seller agents, the broker agent determines the requirement of the buyer and then chooses the best seller agent and ultimately negotiates between the buyer and seller and this method is known as brokering. There are primarily two forms of the brokering process [70]:

1. Merchant brokering

The agent seeking a good merchant (seller) to buy the commodity is engaged in merchant brokering. Delivery time, warranty, pricing and gift services are involved in merchant brokering process problems for choosing the right seller representative. Also, many merchants choose not to judge their offers on price alone. There is therefore a step to expand these agents to take several attributes into account. The agent seeking a good merchant (seller) to buy the commodity is engaged in merchant brokering. The significance of the various characteristics can vary between consumer agents [36].

2. Product brokering

Having ascertained a need, the product brokering stage involves an agent determining what product to buy to satisfy this need. The main techniques used by the brokers in this stage are feature-based filtering, collaborative filtering and constraint-based filtering. Feature-based filtering involves selecting products based on feature keywords. Collaborative filtering involves giving an agent personalized recommendation based on the similarities between different users' preference agents. Constraint-based filtering requires an agent defining restrictions (e.g., price range and date limit) [36].

Broker position in different prospects:

A tabular presentation to define the role of broker as coordinator (in MAS) and market perspective in various scenarios of seller buyer in Table 3.1.

3.1.4 BUSINESS MODEL

The business model consists predominantly of two components: Financial model and Ease model. The different definitions and terms in these two models are discussed below:

Financial Model

Price-based problems are known as a financial model. Thus, all qualities integrated with price reconsidered by agents. Of course, the meaning of the various characteristics will differ between buyer and seller agent according to the price. The assessment is based on a cumulative score based on weighted score of these individual qualities, measured for each seller and

TABLE 3.1
Broker's Role and Market Perspective

Applications of Business	• Electronic market, providing B2C • Electronic commerce trading facilities. • Any kind of one-to-one promotion, with smart assistance.
Buyer's perception	• Generalized connections with clients. • Customized support and notification for clients. • Navigation and reviewing of the variety of offers and demands by assistance and a single view. • Propagation of requirements.
Seller's perception	• Communicating the deals to potentially interested clients only. • Clarity in interactions. • Obtaining details on the current interests of the consumer in the business in general and on the supplier's deals.
Market perception	• Enhancement of the mediation standard. • Flexibility to respond to ongoing shifts in offers and demands. • The gained expertise (combined knowledge capitalization and sharing mutual memory and recommendations, form of ML) is made accessible to all consumers.
Agent's perception	Smart agent technology that allows several features: • Autonomy: for dynamically documenting the advancement of the environment; • Co-operation: for communicating the skills available in the broker domain; • Delegation: for customer assistance in the monitoring the request and reporting results; • Own skill: for accomplishing a goal or a subgoal; • Reasoning: for evaluating its own abilities as well as of others; • Learning: to grow with improved outcomes through the capitalization and exchange of knowledge [73].

buyer. The buyer and seller acquire these weights, defining them with a specific profile under which the weights are given [1].

Ease Model

In the ease model, problems other than expense, such as shipping time, warranties and gift services, are considered. Further, many merchants choose not to judge their offers on price alone. Consequently, agents consider several ease-based utility attributes. Of course, between buyer and seller agent, the meaning of the various characteristics can differ. The analysis is based on a combined score based on the weighted score of these individual characteristics, measured for each seller and buyer. The purchaser and seller acquire these weights, defining them with a clear profile in which the weights are provided [51].

3.2 COMPUTATIONAL PERSPECTIVE

This comprises of different methods of computation that are evolved from multi-agent systems:

3.2.1 MULTI-AGENT SYSTEM

3.2.1.1 Agent: Definition and Characteristics

An agent is an embedded computer device residing in a certain setting that is capable of versatile, independent action in that setting to achieve its projected goals. The strong and weak concept of agency [28] is a common portrayal of agents. Agents are independent computational beings that can be seen as interpreting their environment by sensors and responding to their environment by means of effectors. Agents are computing beings which actually means they exist physically in the context of programmes operating on computing machines. Agents are independent which implies that they have control over their actions to some level and can function without the interference of humans and other mechanisms. Agents follow goals or execute activities in order to achieve their projected goals and these goals and activities may be both complimentary and contradictory in general. The common types of agents are described below [10]:

Buyer Agent (Buyer): An agent that wants to obtain certain goods from another agent. When the buyer purchases products, the buyer gains consistency.

Seller Agent (Seller): These products are sold to the buyer by this agent. It gives preparation time and other supplies to trade these goods.

Broker Agent (Broker): The broker agent is the agent who serves as a facilitator between buyers and sellers. By analyzing the profile of the different seller agents, the broker agent determines the requirement of the buyer agent and then chooses the best seller agent and eventually negotiates between the buyer and seller agent.

Coordinator Agent (Coordinator): The coordinator agent has a base of survey knowledge which comes with system coordination, promotes communication of knowledge and is responsible for the creation and implementation of customer contentment surveys.

Some important characteristics of agents are:

Intelligent

The agents follow their targets and conduct their roles in such a manner that certain success metrics are optimized. It would not mean they are omniscient or omnipotent if we say that agents are knowledgeable, nor would it imply that they never underperform. Instead, it suggests that they function flexibly and rationally, under a range of environmental conditions, provided the knowledge they have and their visual and effectual skills.

Interacting

In following their purposes and conducting their duties, the agents can be influenced by other agents or even by humans. Communication may take place implicitly by means of the environment in which they are incorporated (e.g., through watching each other or through taking activity that affects the state of the environment) or specifically through a common language (e.g., through presenting knowledge that is of concern to other agents or that confuses other agents). It focuses specifically on teamwork as a mode of co-operation that is especially relevant with regard to the accomplishment of goals and the execution of tasks. The object of co-operation is to obtain or prevent states of operations which are regarded by one or more agents as favourable or unfavourable. Agents have to specifically take into account the dependencies between their operations in order to organize their priorities and responsibilities. Two simple differing patterns of teamwork are *Collaboration* and *Competitiveness*. Cooperative agents attempt to do what people do not, and either struggle or excel together as a team. Contrary to this, some agents operate against each other in the case of competitiveness when their purposes differ. Competitive agents attempt, at the cost of others, to optimize their own profit, so one's success means others' loss. An agent is a software program that, on behalf of its creator, works flexibly to accomplish clear goals [30]. To achieve this, the programme must possess the following characteristics:

Autonomy: Capable of determining what steps to take without continuously going back to its user (i.e., functioning without direct human interference or any other interference and maintaining power over its action and internal state).

Social ability: Capable of coordinating with other agents (i.e., in order to accomplish its tasks, it cooperates with humans or other agents).

Reactive: Capable of reacting adequately to the predominant circumstances in complex and unpredictable situations.

Proactive: Capable of behaving in contemplation of potential priorities such that the expectations of its owners are fulfilled (i.e., takes leading action. It does not simply behave in reaction to its setting, but by taking action, it is able to demonstrate goal directed actions).

In addition, an agent may be mobile, if necessary, with the potential to move between various nodes on a computer network. It should be honest, ensuring the assurance that false facts would not be intentionally shared. It can be benignant; it always attempts to do what is expected of it. It can be rational, always functioning in order to achieve its objectives and never restricting the achievement of its objectives, and it can learn to respond to its environment and to the needs of its users [50].

3.2.1.2   Multi-agent Systems: Salient Features

Artificial Intelligence when distributed is a branch of AI that involves networks composed of several individual entities that communicate in a domain. This research has primarily been divided into sub-disciplines: distributed problem solving (DPS) and Multi-Agent Systems (MAS) [35,49,75]. By integrating their expertise, information and skills, DPS focuses on designing strategies using the combined effort of multiple agents. It is also used to solve large problems by decomposing them into smaller subtasks; each delegated to a separate person and may thus be called a top-down strategy that is closely coupled. On the other hand, a MAS is a loosely linked bottom-up technique that attempts to include principles for the development of complex structures consisting of several autonomous agents and emphasizes on the synchronization of the agents' actions in those frameworks [35,49,75]. The agents in MAS will have separate even opposing priorities in theory. Collaboration helps the multiple agencies to function more quickly and to accomplish tasks that they are unable to execute independently. More precisely, the following benefits apply to the use of MAS [35,49,75].

- The presence of several agents will speed up a system's operation since the computations can be carried out in parallel by the agents. In fact, this is the case for domains where the overall mission can be broken down into several individual subtasks that can be performed and managed by different agents.
- Usually, a high level of robustness is exhibited in MAS. A single failure will cause the whole device to crash in single-agent schemes. A MAS on other hand, gracefully deteriorates if one or more agents fail, the device will still be operational and the workload will be taken over by the remaining agents.
- MAS modularity allows one, if necessary, to incorporate additional agents to the scheme and thus has a high degree of scalability. It is also much harder to incorporate additional features to monolithic structure.
- MAS can simultaneously make observations and execute actions at many sites, and can thus take advantage of geographical distribution.
- MAS usually have a better performance-cost ratio than other programmes with single agents. One robot with all the required job capabilities is indeed much more costly than using several, cheaper robots with a subset of these abilities.

3.2.2 Cognitive and Social Parameters

The preceding parameters are determined as cognitive. Their meanings are mentioned below:

Belief

The belief refers to knowledge about the world that agent has, desires correlate to the world condition that the agent has opted to fulfil. Belief is regarded as an informative mentality. Viewed from a temporal perspective, the views of an agent derive from a background of experiences; perceptions and messages obtained as an instance. Dependencies on other deliberate principles may also play a role by internal mechanisms of derivation or of building inference. In addition, perceptions influence the agent's potential actions by their effect on other strategic notions (e.g., motives or aspirations) that form the basis of actions. Beliefs are linked to agents' history. In the contextual explanation of the other motivational attitudes, their relation to the future is discussed [2,3].

Desire

Desires may refer to the world's desired state of events (including the other agents), but also to the acts (desired) to be done [6,11,25,27,30,31].

The wishes of an agent are thought of as the states of the world which the agents need to bring in [2,3,33,36]. Desires reflect the roles delegated to the agent and so relate to the aims or priorities it can achieve.

Preference

The preference of an agent plays an important role in social realistic thinking, in which an action is to be chosen in order to satisfy the purpose given [17,26,27,52].

Intention

Intention is essentially the aim an agent wishes to accomplish; the intention of an agent would propose commands on what to do [69,70,78]. Intention is a central mannerism of agents requiring a particular kind of self-dedication to acting [5,21,66].

Commitment

The individual purpose of an agent towards a state of affairs requires the commitment of agent to act towards the state's accomplishment [17,20,21,52].

Performance

An agent's efficiency can be calculated with regard to the mission or tasks it executes. Three aspects of performance metrics are widely used: productivity (the role is well done), efficacy (the task is performed in such a manner that performance is maximized according to any input), and perceived efficiency (the agent is perceived by one or more stakeholders such as the general public, the administration, the board of directors, or the media as a well performer) [29].

Capability

The capability desired by an agent is the ability to focus on his decisions in the light of other agents' activities around it [18,29].

Trust and Reputation

Parameters/features that reflect the output of agents in a business domain are widely used for trust and reputation [15,16,54].

Trust: There are several meanings of trust that rely on the domain of the problem. Significant and applicable meanings provided by various researchers include [30,35]:

- Trust is a collection of beliefs that contribute to behavioural intentions that entail possible failure due to the absence of influence over those on which one relies.
- Trust is characterized as
  dependence on an object's features, or the occurrence of an incident, or a person's actions in order to attain a desired but unknown object, or the occurrence of an incident or a person's actions in a risky position in order to attain the desired but not so certain objective,

[25,26,72]

- Usually, this trust consists of three dimensions of trust: intellect (compatible with ability), morality (integrity and honesty), and goodwill (benignancy) [13,79].

Rotter also described trust as "a belief maintained by an individual or group that it is possible to depend on the world, pledge, verbal or in written declaration of another individual or group." Again, trust is characterized as a perception specific expectation that defines actions.

Zucker described trust as collection of mutual social expectations that are central to social activity and to determine, encouraging people to respond to each other without defining contractual information directly [41]. Similarly, Korsgaard et al. asserted that trust is the confidence that group members have in their leader's goodwill and loyalty (that is integrity and benignity), while Hart and Saunders described trust as the faith that another party will act as planned, coupled with expectations of the goodwill of the other party. This trust is made up of a sense of the integrity of the partners, transparency (willingness not to hide information), care (not taking undue advantage) and dependability [29,38,40].

McAllister describes trust as the degree to which an individual is assured of, and able to act on the basis of, another's terms, conduct, and choices, "that is as a belief-based behavioural purpose" Kumar, Ramaswami et al. describe belief as reliability based on procedural justice perceptions-fairness in the management of a relationship, rules and procedures and distributive justice as the presumed fairness.

Rousseau et al. described that belief deals with the desire to recognize vulnerability based on optimistic assumptions of another's actions or conduct. Rousseau et al. also acknowledged, along with Lewis and Weigert, that trust varies considering the history and essence of the agreement between the parties [64,65].

Dwyer et al. characterizes trust as a collection of values related to interchange in a partner's capability and desire to participate in the social exchange. Moorman et al. characterized trust as "a desire to rely on an exchange partner in whom one has faith." Morgan and Hunt consider trust as faith in the dependability and morality of another person. Ganesan often describes trust as a desire to rely on one another, based on values or perceptions derived from the knowledge, reliability and benignity of the partner. In the sense of e-commerce, Gefan (2002) describes trust as a single dimension construct concerned with a customer's evaluation that the supplier is reliable, based on Luhmann's (2006) concept of trust as a process that reduces social complexity and contributes to a readiness to rely on a supplier. This willingness is extracted from the assumption that its responsibilities would be fulfilled by the seller [42,61].

Reputation: Reputation is perceived on the basis of two consumer ratings [56,75]. The reputation concept of Histos [56,75] is based on customer witness details; the broker and third-party agent's most recent experience with the agent being assessed. Thus, value of reputation of any user is a worldwide measure that is exchanged by all observers [72].

3.2.3 MAS COMMUNICATION

Agents are basically a kind of shared code procedure and, therefore, agree with the classic concept of a two-part distributed computing model: elements and connectors. Consumers, suppliers and facilitators of contact messages that are shared through connectors are components.

3.2.4   FOUNDATION FOR INTELLIGENT PHYSICAL AGENTS (FIPA)

FIPA is a global non-profit community of businesses and establishments that share the initiative to develop standardized agent technology requirements. FIPA is designed not only as a single-application technology, but also as a generalized technology for various application fields, and not only as an individual technology, but also as a collection of simple technologies that developers can combine to build complex applications with a high level of interoperability.

The following set of principles is at the centre of FIPA ():

1. Agent innovations have a modern framework for addressing old problems and new ones.
2. A large degree of maturity has been achieved by certain technologies of agent.
3. Standardization is necessary for certain agent technology to be of use.
4. It has been shown that standardization of generic technology is feasible and that other standardization for an agent produces successful outcomes.
5. It is not a primary concern to standardize the internal mechanics of the agents themselves, but rather the framework and language needed for accessible coordination.

The communication of agents in FIPA is focused on the passing of messages, where agents interact by formulating and sending each other individual messages. By setting forth the encoding, grammar and pragmatics of the texts, the FIPA ACL defines a basic message language. A specific method for the internal transport of messages is not laid out in the standard. Instead, FIPA specifies that messages transported between platforms should be encoded in a textual form, because different agents may operate on different platforms and use different networking technologies. The agent is believed to have some way to convey this textual kind. The ACL syntax is very similar to the commonly used language KQML in communication. However, there are fundamental distinctions between ACL and KQML, considering syntactic resemblance, the most apparent is the presence of a formal semantics for ACL that can eradicate all complexity and uncertainty from the use of the language. Through defining contact protocols, the specification facilitates typical types of inert-agent conversations, which are patterns of messages shared by two or more agents. These protocols vary from basic query-request methods to better known net negotiation method for contracts and auctions in English and Dutch. Other elements, including agent-software integration, agent agility and protection, ontology service, and human-agent communication, are defined in other sections of the FIPA standard. Even so, they have not yet been taken into account in the application of JADE [60,67].

FIPA reference model is given in Figure 3.1.

FIPA-compliant Agent Framework, comprises the DF (Directory facilitator), ACC (Agent Contact Channel) and the AMS (Agent Management System). These three agents are all enabled synchronously at the start-up of the agent platform. It is possible to break the agent platform into many hosts (given that the firewall is absent between them). In order to implement multi-domain applications, a set of FIPA-compliant (Directory Facilitator) DFs can be initiated at runtime.

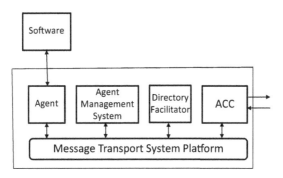

FIGURE 3.1 FIPA reference model.

Agent Communication Channel (ACC)

The ACC is an agency that offers a service on an agent platform directly to the agents. In order to carry out its message transport tasks; the ACC can access information provided by other agent platform services such as AMS and DF.

Agent Management System (AMS)

For each Agent platform, this agent is eccentric and obligatory. It monitors and handles the agent platform and activities of agents. In other words, it handles an agent's enrolment and revocation into its portal. In addition, the white-pages service is yet another significant service that the AMS offers to the agent community. It is a list of registered agents on the AP who are recognized by their GUID (Global Unique Identifier: the identifier which uniquely locates the agent inside the community). In order to obtain information about platform users, any agent may inquire the AMS.

Directory Facilitator (DF)

A DF agent helps other agents with the yellow pages service. This is helpful in acquiring details regarding the different services including the agents that provide them. An agent domain is created by all agents registered at a given DF. A separate agent domain is handled by each DF.

Performatives of FIPA

Performative is defined as the form of the communicative act of message. Using FIPA ACL messages (), agent communication is implemented. As given in the Table 3.2, FIPA used the following performative messages. SUBSCRIBE messages are the ones used by buyer and seller agents. INFORM messages are used to reply to the REQUEST or SUBSCRIBE texts. FAILURE messages are being used by the buyer agents to provide information about the failed outcome of a negotiation to the seller agent or broker. Ultimately negotiating agents use CFP, PROPOSE, ACCEPT-PROPOSAL, REJECT-PROPOSAL and REFUSE messages. The variety of communication acts of FIPA (performatives) are listed below.

TABLE 3.2
FIPA Communication Acts (Performatives)

The FIPA Communicative Acts

FIPA Communicative Act	Explanation
Accept Proposal	The act of approving a request, previously submitted to execute an operation.
Agree	The practice of agreeing to undertake any action, perhaps in the future.
Cancel	The act of one agent telling another agent that the former no longer has the intention that the latter carries out some operation.
Call for Proposal	The action of inviting proposals to carry out a given action.
Confirm	The sender advises the recipient that a given proposition is valid where it is understood that recipient is unsure about the suggestion.
Disconfirm	The sender tells the recipient whether a given proposition is false or not, where it is understood that the receiver assumes that the idea is real.
Failure	The action of informing the other agent that an act has been performed, however it failed.
Inform	The sender tells the receiver that a given proposition is valid.
Inform If	An agent's macro action to tell the receiver whether a given proposition is true or not.
Inform Ref	A macro action that permits the sender to notify the recipient of a certain item the sender assumes that it refers to a particular descriptor (e.g., a name).
Not Understood	The act's sender (for instance, I) tells the recipient (for instance, j), it sensed that j executed some operation which i failed to comprehend. A relevant particular case is that j is told by i that i did not understand the text that j had just sent to i.
Propagate	The sender plans that the recipient handles the embedded message as sent instantly to the recipient and wants that the recipient to recognize the agents denoted by the provided descriptor and to send the acquired propagate message to them.
Propose	The act of sending a plan to carry out certain activities, provided certain preconditions.
Proxy	The sender wants the recipient to pick target agents represented by a given definition and transmit an embedded message to them.
Query If	The act of questioning another agent if a given proposition is valid or not.
Query Ref	The act of questioning other agent for the item addressed to by a referential statement.
Refuse	An act of disapproving to carry out an action and clarifying the refusal's reason.
Reject Proposal	The act of declining a proposal to carry out an operation at the time of negotiation.
Request	The sender puts forward a request for the receiver to undertake an action. One significant category of uses of the request act is to make an appeal to the receiver to carry out another communicative act.
Request When	The sender needs the recipient to take some action when a given proposal becomes relevant.
Request Whenever	The sender needs the recipient to carry out an action instantly when a proposition turns out to be true and subsequently each and every time when proposition turns to be true again.
Subscribe	The action of requesting a constant intent to inform the sender of the value of a reference, as well as to notify again each and every time the object is recognized by the changes in reference.

3.3   MACHINE LEARNING: FUNCTIONS AND METHODS

Machine Learning is a continual mechanism in which the discovery determines development, either by automated or by manual methods. In an exploratory research situation, Machine Learning is quite useful, where there are no fixed ideas of what would make an interesting result. Machine Learning is the quest for new, useful and non-trivial knowledge in vast quantities of data. It is a joint endeavour between humans and machines. The best outcomes are obtained by balancing the expert knowledge of human specialists in explaining challenges and priorities with the automated search capabilities. In operation, Machine Learning's two main objectives tend to be estimation and explanation. To forecast uncertain or possible values of other variables of interest, estimation requires the use of certain variables or fields in the set of data. Explanation, on the other hand focuses on identifying patterns that illustrate the data which humans can understand. It is also to put the tasks of Machine Learning into one of two groups [77,80]:

1. Predictive, which generates the system model as defined in the provided set of data.
2. Descriptive, which generates new, non-trivial outcomes dependent on the set of data available.

The purpose of Machine Learning is to generate a model, represented as an executable code, on the predictive end of the spectrum, that can be utilized to perform categorization, predictive analytics, approximation or other related tasks. The aim is to obtain an interpretation of the analyzed structure on the descriptive end of the spectrum, by discovering trends and connections in broad data sets. For specific Machine Learning applications, the significance of prediction and explanation may differ quite considerably. Machine Learning has its roots in numerous fields, of which Statistics and Machine Learning are the two most important. Statistics had its origins in Mathematics, so, focus was laid upon Mathematical rigour, a need to show that something makes sense on theoretical grounds, before bringing it into practice. The Machine Learning culture, on the other hand, is very much rooted in computer experience. This has resulted in a mindset that is practical, a desire to try something without asking for a standardized proof of efficiency to see how well it works.

3.3.1   SUPERVISED AND UNSUPERVISED LEARNING

Supervised Learning

1. **Classification** – Discovery of a function for predictive learning that categorizes a data object into one of the numerous predefined groups.
2. **Regression** – Discovery of a function for predictive learning that maps a piece of data to prediction variable of real value.

Unsupervised Learning

1. **Clustering** – A basic descriptive activity under which a finite range categories or clusters is identified in order to define the data.

2. **Summarization** – An auxiliary descriptive activity that incorporates methods to find a concise description for data's group or subgroup.
3. **Dependency Modelling** – Seeking a local model in a data set or a part of a data set that defines major dependencies between variables or between the values of a function.
4. **Change and Deviation Detection** – Exploring the most critical developments in the data collection.

3.3.2 DECISION TREE (DT)

DT is one of the numerous methods used for creating a model for classification. Concentrating on the data presented, a tree-shaped structure model is created using inductive reasoning. Each node of the tree is a differential equation to define the data input. The calculation would concentrate on a single attribute to decide if the data imported is greater than, equal to or less than a certain value. Any of these nodes will subsequently assign the imported data into various categories. A typical methodology that offers both classification and predictive functions synchronously is the decision tree. Data is categorized with a series of questions and laws (Chein et al., 2011). The decision tree theory is very suitable for performing medical projections and data analysis description in this field, incorporating the use of related models to project similar results. ID3, C4.5, classification and regression trees (CRAT), chi-squared automated interactive detector (CHAID) models, and the C5.0 algorithm are the major algorithm of decision trees analysis model. C5.0 could be used quite efficiently in the basic handling of the vast data sets. It is also known as Boosting Trees, as it uses the Boosting approach to improve simulation precision. It is much faster in speed and more effective in memory than C4.5 [73].

3.3.3 NEURAL NETWORK

A neuron is the fundamental part of a neural network. This is a basic virtual system that takes many inputs, totals them, imposes a (nonlinear, usually) transfer function, and produces the outcome, either as a model projection or as a source to other neurons. A neural network is a device connected in a systematic way by several such neurons. In Clementine, the neural networks used, that are also known as Multilayer beliefs, are feed-forward neural networks. The neurons are organized in layers in such networks (they are seldom called units). There is usually one input neuron layer – the input layer, one or more than one internal processing unit layers – the hidden layers, and one layer for output neurons – the output layer. The preceding layer and the subsequent layer are entirely interconnected to each layer. To produce projections, information flows from the input layer to the output layer via processing layers. The network learns to deliver better predictions by tuning the connection weights during the training to equate projections to target values for particular records.

RBFN

A special sort of neural network is Radial base Function Network (RBFN). It is made up of three layers: an input layer, a hidden layer (also known as a receptor layer), and a layer of output. The layers of input and output are identical to those of a preceptor for multi-layers.

Quick Method

A single neural network is trained when the swift strategy is followed. By default, the network has one concealed neuron layer (3, $(n_i+n_o)/20$), where n_i is the number of neurons-input and n_o is the number of neurons-output. The network is trained using a backpropagation approach.

Dynamic Method

The topology of the network varies during training when the dynamic method is chosen, with neurons inserted to boost efficiency until the network reaches the desired precision. For dynamic training, there are two phases: discovering the topology and testing the final network.

3.3.4 SENSITIVITY ANALYSIS (SA)

Analysis of sensitivity is an approach that analyzes and reflects the degree of sensitivity of the result of the model can be distributed and altered to various conditions of difference [73]. Generally, it at first determines the sensitive variables in the analysis that influence the objects. It then confirms the degree of effect on the aim and goals of the analysis of a certain responsive element. By obtaining variations on sensitive factors or information about the changing trend, this approach can verify variations and also the changing trend of the goals and objectives in the study. Sensitivity analysis is performed to reduce network complexity by deleting the variables that have no or less influence on network training and to understand the degree of influence of each variable network training. The higher the degree of sensitivity, the larger the influence it has on the results of the artificial neural networks [73].

3.3.5 FEATURE SELECTION

Hundreds, or even thousands, of variables are often involved in the Machine Learning problems. As a result, a lot of time and resources spent in the process of model-building entails examining of increasing variables to use in the model. It may take more time than is practical to adapt a neural network or a decision tree to a set of variables this large.

The collection of features helps the variable range to be minimized in size, providing a more accessible range of modelling attributes. There are some advantages of introducing feature selection to the analytical procedure:

- Streamlines and narrows the spectrum of the characteristics that is important in constructing a predictive model.
- Minimizes the processing time and memory demands for the creation of a predictive model, so that attention can be drawn to the most relevant subset of predictors.
- Tends to lead to models that are more precise and/or parsimonious.
- Reduces time for scores to be generated since only a subset of predictors is based on the predictive model.

Selection of features consists of three steps:

1. **Screening** – Unimportant and problematic predictors and cases are excluded.
2. **Ranking** – Sorts and assigns ranking to the remaining predictors.
3. **Selecting** – Determines the significant subset of characteristics to be included in future models.

The algorithm mentioned here is restricted to the situation of supervised learning in which the target variable is estimated using a series of predictor variables. Any variable can be, either, categorical or continuous in the analysis. Common target variables determine whether or not a client churns, whether a person would buy or not, and whether or not there is a presence of disease.

The phrases traits, causes and traits are also used interchangeably. In this document, while addressing feedback to the feature selection algorithm, we use variables and predictors, with features relating to the predictors that are currently chosen for used in a later modelling procedure by the algorithm.

3.4 CONCLUSION

In this chapter we have illustrated a variety of notions/concepts relating to modern intelligent computing methods to implement the various functionalities of e-business. The concepts of brokering customer orientation, customer relationship management and negotiation have been outlined and described to make the content meaningful and relevant. Agent characteristics, the multi-agent device model and its communication protocol from a computational point of view have also been elaborated. The functions and methods of Artificial Intelligence, concepts of supervised and unsupervised learning, decision tree, neural network and sensitivity analysis have also been explained to understand their applications in e-commerce.

REFERENCES

1. Abdul-Rahman, A. and Hailes, S. (2000). *Supporting Trust in Virtual Communities: Proceedings of the Hawaii's International Conference on Systems Sciences*, Maui, Hawaii.
2. Bell, J., (1995). Changing attitudes In Intelligent Agents, *Post-Proceedings of the ECAI-94 Workshop on Agent The ories, Architecture and languages*, Wooldridge M. and Jennings N. R., eds. Springer, Berlin, pp. 40–50.
3. Bellifemine, F. *Developing Multi-Agent Systemswith JADE*, John Wiley & Sons, Hoboken; NJ, 2007
4. Blau, P.M. *Exchange and Power in Social Life*. Wiley, New York, 1964.
5. Bratman, M.E., (1990). *What is intention? In Intentions in Communication*, Cohen P.R., Morgan J. Pollack, eds. MIT Press, Cambridge, MA. pp. 15–31.
6. Brazier, F., Dunin-Keplicz, B., Treur, J. and Verbrugge, R., (1997). Beliefs, Intentions and DESIRE.
7. Preist, C., Byde, A. and Bartolini, C., (2001) *"Economic Dynamics of Agents in Multiple Auctions,"* *Proceedings of First International Conference on Autonomous Agents*, pp. 545–551.

8. Sierra, C., Faratin, P. and Jennings, N.R., (1997). A Service-Oriented Negotiation Model between Autonomous Agents, *Lecture Notes in Artificial Intelligence*, 1237, 17–35.

9. Carter, J., Bitting, E. and Ghorbani, A. (2002). Reputation Formalization for an Information-Sharing Multi-Agent Sytem, *Computational Intelligence*, 18(2), 515–534.

10. Castelfranchi, C. and Falcone, R. (1998*). Principles of Trust for MAS: Cognitive Anatomy, Social Importance and Quantification.* In: *Proceedings of the International Conference on Multi-Agent Systems (ICMAS'98)*, Paris, France, pp. 72–79.

11. Catholijn, M.J., Valentin, R. and Jan, T. 2006. An Agent Architecture for Multi-Attribute Negotiation Using Incomplete Preference Information.

12. Chan, H.C., Cheng, C.B. and Hsu, C.H. (2007). Bargaining Strategy Formulation with CRM for an e-Commerce Agent, *Electronic Commerce Research and Applications*, 6, 490–498.

13. Chee, C.N. (2004). *Three Critical Steps to Customer-centric Business Orientation.* MetaCore Asia Pte Ltd Retrieved on October 2004, from www.metacore-asia.biz.

14. Deutsch, M. 1958. Trust and Suspicion, *Con:ICT Resolution*, 2(4), 265–279.

15. Esfandiari, B. and Chandrasekharan, S. (2001). On How Agents Make friends: Mechanisms for Trust Acquisition: Proceedings of the Fourth Workshop on Deception, Fraud and Trust in Agent Societies, Montreal, Canada. pp. 27–34.

16. Aımeur, F.M.O.E., Brassard, G. and Onana, F.S.M. *Blind Negotiation in ElectronicCommerce* In *Montreal Conference on eTechnologies* (pp. 1–9). 2005

17. Faratin, P., Sierra, C. and Jennings, N., (2003). Using Similarity Criteria to Make Issue Trade-offs in Automated Negotiations, *Journal of Artificial Intel*, 142(2), 205–237.

18. Fatima, S.S., Wooldridge, M. and Jennings, N.R. (July 2003). *Optimal Agendas for Multi-Issue Negotiation.* In *Second International Conference on Autonomous Agents and Multiagent Systems (AAMAS-03)*, Melbourne, pp. 129–136.

19. Fisher, R., Ury, W. and Patton, B. (2011). *Getting to Yes: Negotiating Agreement Without Giving In.*

20. Frederick, F.R., (1996) *The Loyalty Effect*, Harvard Business School Press, Cambridge, MA.

21. Garg, S.K. and Mishra R.B., (2008(to appear)). A Hybrid Model for Service Selection in Semantic Webservice Composition, *International Journal of Intelligent Information Technologies*, 4 (4), 55–69.

22. Giffin, K. 1967. The Contribution of Studies of Source Credibility to a Theory of Interpersonal Trust in the Communication Process, *Psychological Bulletin*, 68(2), 104–120.

23. Giffin, D. (2004). Social Presence: Experiments in e-Products and e-Services, *Omega*, 32, 407–424.

24. Gutman, R. and Maes, P., (1998). *Cooperative vs. Competitive Multi-Agent Negotiation in retail electronic commerce.* In *International Workshop on Cooperative Information Agents* (pp. 135–147). Springer, Berlin, Heidelberg.

25. Ha, S.H. Bae, S.M. and Park, S.C. (2002). Customer's Time-Variant Purchase Behavior and Corresponding Marketing Strategies: An Online Retailer's Case, *Computers & Industrial Engineering*, 43, 801–820.

26. Hake, R. ed. (1996)., The British Computer Soc, Wiltshire, UK.

27. Hart, P. and Saunders, C. 1997. Power and Trust: Critical Factors in the Adoption And Use Of Electronic Data Interchange, *Organizational Science*, 8(1), 23–42.

28. He, M., Jennings, N.R. and Leung, H. (2003). On Agent-Mediated Electronic Commerce, *IEEE Transactions on Knowledge and Data Engineering*, 15(4), 985–1003.

29. Leea, J.H. and Parkb, S.C. (2005). Intelligent Profitable Customers Segmentation System Based On Business Intelligence Tools, *Expert Systems with Applications*, 29, 145–152.

30. Jonker, C.M., Robu, V. and Treur, J. (2007). An Agent Architecture for Multi-Attribute Negotiation Using Incomplete Preference Information, *Autonomous Agent and Multi-Agent System*, 15. doi:10.1007/s10458-006-9009-y.
31. Jung, J. and Jo, G. 2000. Brokerage between Buyer and Seller Agents Using Constraint Satisfaction Problem Models, *Decision Support Systems*, 28, 293–304.
32. Kang, N. and Han, S. (2002). Agent-Based e-Marketplace System For More Fair And Efficient Transaction, *Decision Support Systems*, 34, 157–165.
33. Karl, K. and Iouri, L. *Multi-agent Negotiation under Time Constraints on an Agent-based Marketplace for Personnel Acquisition*, 2003.
34. Korsgaard, M.A., Schweiger, D.M. and Sapienza, H.J. 1995. Building Commitment, Attachment, And Trust In Strategic Decision-Making Teams: The Role Of Procedural Justice, *AMA*, 38(1), 60–64.
35. Kraus, S., Sycara, K. and Evenchil, A. (1998). Reaching Agreements Through Argumentation: A Logical Model And Implementation, *Artificial Intelligence*, 104, 1–69.
36. Krulwich, B., The Bargain-finder Agent: Comparison Price Shopping on the Internet," *Bots, and Other Internet Beasties*, J. Williams, ed., pp. 257–263, Macmillan Computer Publishing, New York, 1996.
37. Luhmann, N. *Trust and Power*. Wiley, London 1979.
38. Subramani, M. and Walden, E. *"Economic Returns to Firms from Business-to-Business Electronic Commerce Initiatives: An Empirical Examination,"* In *Proceedings of the 21st Int'l Conference Information Systems*, pp. 229–241, 2000.
39. Sim, K.M. and Chan, R. 2000. A Brokering Protocol For Agent-Based e-Commerce, *IEEE Transactions On Systems, Man, and Cybernetics Part C: Applications and Reviews*, 30(4), 474–484.
40. Bichler, M. and Segev, A. A Brokerage Framework for Internet Commerce CMIT Working Paper 98-WP-1031, n.d.
41. Martin, L. Griss Software Agents as Next Generation Software Components. *Chapter 36 in Component-Based Software Engineering: Putting the Pieces Together*, G. T. Heineman & W. T. Councill, May 2001 Addison-Wesley, Boston, MA, 2001.
42. Mazumdar, B.D. and Mishra, R.B. 2009. Multiagent Paradigm for the Agent Selection and Negotiation in a B2c Process, *International Journal of Intelligent Information Technologies*, 5(1), 61–82.
43. Mishra, R.B. 2009. Rule Based and ANN model for the evaluation of Customer Orientation in CRM, *IE(I)*, 90, 28–33.
44. Murch, R. and Johnson, T.*Intelligent Software Agents*, eds. Chapter 14, pp. 131–137, Prentice Hall PTR, Upper Saddle River, N.J 1999.
45. Jennings, N.R. 2001. An Agent-Based Approach for Building Complex Software Systems, *Communications of the ACM*, 44(4), 35–41.
46. Jennings, N.R., Faratin, P., Lomuscio, A.R. S., Parsons, C. S. and Wooldridge, M. 2001. Automated Negotiation: Prospects, Methods and Challenges, *The International Conference on Group Decision and Negotiation*, 10(2), 199–215.
47. Nehemiah, M. *Armstrong Kadyamatimba Acomprehensive Agent–Mediated e-Market Framework ICEC* 2003. Pittsburgh, PA ACM 1-58113-788-5/03/09
48. Faratin, P., Sierra, C. and Jennings, N.R. 2002. Using Similarity Criteria to Make Trade-Offs in Automated Negotiations, *Artificial Intelligence*, 142(2), 205–237.
49. Stone, P. and Veloso, M. *A layered approach to learning client behaviors in the Market*, (n.d.)
50. Wurman, P.R. 2001. Dynamic Pricing in the Virtual Marketplace, *IEEE Internet Computing*, 5, 36–42, Mar./Apr.

51. Panzarasa, P., Jennings, N.R. and Norman, T.J. (2002). Formalizing Collaborative Decision-making and Practical Reasoning in Multi-agent System, *Journal of Logic and Computation*, 12(1), 55–117.

52. Perry, P.Y.L. and Henry, C.B. *Chan A Markov-decision-based Price Comparison Problem for Mobile Agent-based Internet Commerce System (MAGICS).* In *Proceedings of the IEEE International Conference on E-Commerce Technology* 0-7695-2098-7/04, 2021; Aiming, C., Meacham, H. and Dayal, U., Martin Griss Multi-Agent Co-operation, Dynamic Workflow and XML for E-Commerce Automation, 2000.

53. Rotter, J.B. 1971. Generalized Expectancies for Interpersonal Trust, *American Psychologist*, 26, 443–450.

54. Russell, S.W. 2001. Customer Relationship Management: A Framework, Research Directions, and the Future, *Haas School of Business*, 43, 89–105.

55. Sabater, J. and Sierra, C. (2005). Review on Computational Trust and Reputation Models, *Artificial Intelligence Review*, 24, 33–60.

56. Salvatore, G., Domenico, R. and Giuseppe, M.L. *Sarn´ MAST: An Agent Framework to Support B2C E-Commerce*, (n.d.)

57. Sandholm, T.W., "Distributed rational decision making." In *Multiagent System: A Modern Approach to Distributed Artificial Intelligence*, 201–258, 1999.

58. Schurr, P.H. and Ozanne, J.L. 1985. In: Uences on Exchange Processes: Buyers' Preconceptions of a Seller's Trustworthiness and Bargaining Toughness, *Journal of Consumer Research*, 11, 939–953.

59. Shoham, Y. (1993). Agent Oriented Programming, *Artificial; Intelligence*, 60(1), 51–92.

60. Suwu, W. and Das, A., (2001). *An Agent System Architecture for E-Commerce, 1529-4188/01* IEEE, pp. 715–719.

61. Takayuki, I. and Mark, K. *A Multi-Issue Negotiation Protocol among Competitive*, n.d.

62. Tang, T.Y., Winoto, P. and Niu, X. Investigating Trust between Users and Agents in A Multi Agent Portfolio Management System: a Preliminary Report, (2003).

63. Liang, W.-Y. The Research of Intelligent Negotiation Agent-Application for B2C E-commerce Proceedings of the International Multiconference of Engineers and Computer Scientists 2009 Vol IIMECS 2009, March 18–20, 2009, Hong Kon ISBN: 978-988-17012-2-0IMECS 2009

64. Wilkes, J. (2008) "Utility Functions, Prices, and Negotiation" Technical report HP Laboratories, HPL-2008-81, www. Hpl.hp.com/techreports/2008/HPL-2008-81.pdf.2008

65. Von Wright, G.H. *Freedom and Determination*. North Holland Publishing Co, Amsterdam, 1980.

66. Wu, W., Ekaette, E. and Far, B.H. (2003). Uncertainty Management Framework for Multi-Agent System, *Proceedings of ATS*, 122–131.

67. Wu, H.J. (2005). An Agent-Based CRM Model for Multiple Projects management, *IEEE*, 851–855.

68. Xiang, L. and Chengqing, Y. (2018). *A Novel Multi-Agent Negotiation Model for E-Commerce Platform*, International Conference on Intelligent Transportation, Big Data & Smart City (ICITBS).

69. Che, Y.-K. (1993). Design Competition through Multidimensional, the RAND, *Journal of Economics*, 24 (4), 668–680.

70. Chen, Y.M. and Wang, S.-C. 2007. An Agent-Based Evolutionary Strategic Negotiation for Project Dynamic Scheduling, *The International Journal of Advanced Manufacturing Technology*, 6.

71. Yu, B. and Singh, M.P. (2001). *Towards a Probabilistic Model of Distributed Reputation Management*. In *Proceedings of the Fourth Workshop on Deception, Fraud and Trust in Agent Societies*, Montreal, Canada. 125–137.

72. Zacharia, G. (1999). Collaborative Reputation Mechanisms for Online Communities. Master's thesis, Massachusetts Institute of Technology.

73. Zeng, D. and Sycara, K. (n.d.) Bayesian learning in negotiation. International Journal of Designing Agents with Multi-attribute Preference Models for I Nikos

74. Zhang, X., Lesser, V. and Podorozhny, R. (2005). Multi-Dimensional, Multistep Negotiation for Task Allocation in a Cooperative System, *Autonomous Agents and Multi-Agent Systems*, 10, 5–40.

75. Zhao, X., Wu, C., Zhang, R., Zhao, C. and Lin, Z. (n.d.) A Multi-Agent System for E-Business Processes Monitoring in a Web-Based Environment, TCL Group Corporation. Department of Information Science, Peking University, Beijing 100871, China.

76. Zhao, Y., Zhou, Y. and Deng, W. (2020). Innovation Mode and Optimization Strategy of B2C E-Commerce Logistics Distribution under Big Data, *Sustainability*, 12, 3381. doi:10.3390/su12083381.

77. Zhibin, X., (2008) "Factors which affect the dynamics of privately-owned Chinese firms: An interdisciplinary empirical evaluation" Ph.D. Thesis.

78. Zucker, L.G. 1986. Production of trust: institutional sources of economic structure, 1840–1920, *Research in Organizational Behavior*, 8, 53–111.

79. http://media.wiley.com/product_data/excerpt/24/04712285/0471228524-1.pdf

80. http://www.fipa.org/

81. Gefan. (2002). Customer Loyalty in E-Commerce. *AIS Educator Journal*, 3(1), 27–51, doi:10.17705/1jais.00022.

82. Luhmann. (2006), *Journalism Studies*, 7(4), 644–655. doi: 10.1080/14616700600758066.

83. Chein et al. (2011). *Developmental Science*, 14(2), F1–F10. doi: 10.1111/j.1467-7687.2010.01035.x21499511.

84. Peter F. D. (2004). *Management Decision*, 42(10), 1269–1283.

4 Artificial Intelligence and Machine Learning
Discovering New Ways of Doing Banking Business

Puspalata Mahapatra and Sarita Kumari Singh
KSCE, KIIT DU, BBSR, Odisha

CONTENTS

DOI: 10.1201/9781003125129-4

STRUCTURE OF THE CHAPTER

The present chapter aims at providing indispensable information about the way AI is developed and adopted in banking sector. It aims to impart some basic idea on the area of practical AI application and how this technique is used and helpful for the banking sector. Here through this chapter attempt has been made to explore about the banks who have started implementing the AI and ML solution while doing their business and at the same time highlighting the benefits they avail of it.

Section 4.1 is the Introduction, which gives a brief description of Artificial Intelligence with ML, AI application in finance area with the special focus on banking sector. Section 4.2 summarizes the areas where AI can be applied and how it works in that particular area and how it is useful for both banks and clients. Section 4.3 deals with the adoption of AI technology by Indian banks as case study and the companies who are providing such technology. Section 4.4 contains benefits and influence of AI and ML on banks with respect to different parameters of Key Performance Indicator (KPI) like profitability, performance and reduction of number of frauds. Lastly, Section 4.5 presents concluding remarks along with the future of AI implemented banking industry. Figure 4.1 shows the conceptual framework of AI application on banking sector.

4.1 INTRODUCTION

In the era of progressive innovation, AI turned into the trendy expression and rising star. We as a whole need to know and comprehend the utilization of AI in various zones including banking sector. The financial business has consistently developed with the occasions to grasp new difficulties and to get accustomed with the buyer practices. Innovation plays a conspicuous as well as progressively significant part in this development and technology plays an obvious and increasingly important role in this evolution. Inventions such as the Automated Teller Machines (ATM) and credit cards launched in the 1960s, Internet banking services in the 1990s, mobile banking in 2000s and now services based on AI and Robotics Process Automation (RPA), have all fundamentally changed the functioning of banking sector. A significant driver in banking industry change is the purchaser interest to be better associated with their cash. This interest is presently supporting another type of computerized banking administration that is coming in the middle stage. A significant inquiry right now is in what capacity banks can profit by the new kinds of client communication empowered by advanced administrations fuel by man-made brainpower. Banking is an industry or domain that is extremely diversified and complex. To simplify complex banking functions, the banking industry requires a constant supply of advanced technological solutions. Realizing the importance and profound impact of AI and ML in the banking sector this chapter tries to highlight the uses of

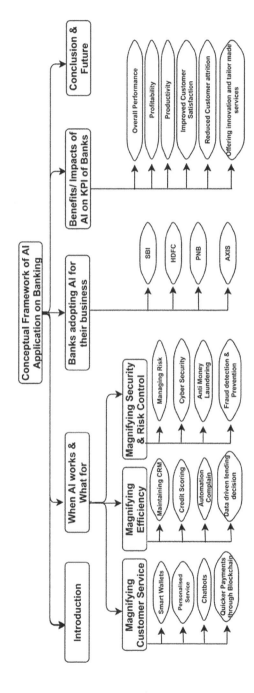

FIGURE 4.1 Conceptual Framework of AI Application on the Banking Sector. *Source:* Author's Self Compiled.

AI in banking industry in-depth including the benefits and impact of adopting the application of AI. The web has given us quicker admittance to more data. Circulated figuring and IoT have prompted gigantic measures of information, and interpersonal interaction has empowered the vast majority of that information to be unstructured. With Augmented Intelligence, we are putting data that topic specialists need readily available and backing it with proof so they can settle on educated choices. One of the key highlights that differentiate people, from others on the planet is likely knowledge. Human capacity to comprehend, apply its information and improve their abilities has assumed huge part in their advancement and building up the human progress on this planet. Simulated intelligence is what, which makes machines act all the more wisely. Computer based intelligence resembles an enlarged insight. It is accepted that AI ought not endeavour to supplant human specialists, yet rather broaden human capacities and achieve errands that neither people nor machines could do all alone. Man-made consciousness (AI) is one of the front computerized change systems which can spread in the territory of accounts today. In spite of the fact that different areas like company, insurance, mutual asset companies, wealth administrators are receiving the AI in their tasks yet banking industry in India is the pioneer in embracing it and has end up being the early adopter in examination with different areas.

As the name recommends, AI is the capacity to duplicate something applying information and skills by a machine or a computer so when a machine/PC mirrors a human brain by speculation for people it is otherwise called AI. As AI is now executed and applied both in assembling and administration area which incorporates showcasing, Advertising, Finance, Aerospace route, Agribusiness and uniquely banks likewise, so its effect and territories of use must be distinguished. Banks are receiving both AI and ML simultaneously as there exists a huge relationship between these two creative and novel innovations. Simulated intelligence makes the machines capable to play out the errand all the more keenly and applies Machine Learning and different methods to take care of the genuine issues. Most AI work presently includes ML in light of the fact that clever conduct requires extensive information, and learning is the least demanding approach to get that information.

ML is just a subset of AI which helps banks bringing numerous benefits through analyzing piles of financial data. AI carries a few advantages to restore the monetary area, especially identified with helping banks to gather, sort out and break down the hills of information in budgetary administrations. AI is a development of man-made consciousness which permits PCs to gain from information without programming performed by people. Banks utilize AI to grow more significant discussion with its clients through noting genuine issues and dealing with their budgetary exchanges by means of chatbots [1].

Indian finance areas combined with banking areas have ended up being the early adopters of AI in contrast with different sectors. Unmistakably, the Indian banking area, amongst others, has encountered many means of addressing innovative turns of events and utilization of AI and ML. The importance or effectiveness of AI and ML can be imagined in every single corner of economy, business and industry, and is additionally reflected in many banks of India in various modes of utility. The usage of AI can be reflected in type of Internet banking, versatile banking, making the money related exchanges simpler and client situated activity. In spite of the fact that the advancement of AI and ML is in growing stage and fulfilment is yet to come, the Indian banking area has begun selecting AI for both back-office and just as giving client care.

Presently banks all over the world understand the need of appropriation and use of AI not exclusively to meet the client's budgetary need, but additionally to infer an upper hand in a globalized world. As we realize that banks contribute a central piece of Indian economy and treated as soul of it, so there is a need that each money related exchange regardless credit or money ought to be finished with most extreme consideration and with appropriate documentation. Hence, for prudent steps banks essentially use PCs and embrace all its activity through ATMs, online banking, telephone banking, mail and mobile banking. All the tasks done by the banks through PCs are conceivable on the grounds that it utilizes AI and ML. Many of today's banks are turning for the use of AI in place of process automation, and they are applying AI for pre-screening, application processing, underwriting and disbursal of loan by banks. As the choice and preference of customers are changing, in order to match the pace of changing demand of customers the banking industry are also adopting new and innovative methods which is evident from the implementation of AI and ML in its operation [4]. The application of AI is very evident in the banking industry and use of AI is not only limited to modernizing it but has scaled the banking sector to a greater height. As per a 2018 report distributed by the World Economic Forum, as a team with Deloitte, 76% of Chief Experience Officers in the financial business concur that AI is a main concern since it is basic for separation.

In spite of many challenges for the banks, either in the form of cyber threats, cybercrime, lack of training, lack of commitment to upskill human resources, demand for skilled workforce such as proficient and experienced engineers, the banking sector is slowly adopting the AI and ML in its operational activities [5]. Banks are actively adopting new-age technologies for better growth prospects and to serve new-age customers. From accounting to sales to contracts and cybersecurity, AI is helping banks transform operations across the board [6,7]. According to open content review of monetary assistance experts, 80% of the banks are profoundly mindful of possible advantages of AI application beginning from front office and enemies of instalments extortion in the centre office. The application of AI is just not limited to retail banking service but extended or spread to investment banking and other financial service like mutual fund and merchant banking. There is a developing need and request to utilize AI and the Indian financial sector is bit by bit moving itself towards utilizing AI. Banks are investigating and actualizing innovation in different manners. Man-made consciousness is improving and more astute step by step. The appropriation of AI in banking has grown far more than different areas. This has happened in light of the fact that the financial area actually has parcel of human intercession in the tasks. Indian financial area is investigating the approaches to improve client administrations with the assistance of AI.

So, it tends to be referenced that AI offers banks a serious separation which thus results in improved consistency, quality client support, client maintenance and accomplishing generally speaking operational proficiency. It is being seen that the Indian financial area is embracing AI forcefully because of its generous advantages from multiple points of view. As per Fintech India report by PwC in 2020, the worldwide spending in AI applications contacted $5.1 billion, up from $4 billion out of 2015. There is an unmistakable fascination for the Indian financial area, too. The financial area saw a surge in the utilization of chatbots in this manner, decreasing human interface, cutting down working costs and improving effectiveness.

According to the McKinsey Global Institute out of 13 industries, financial services ranked third in AI adoption, followed by the high-tech, telecommunications and automotive and assembly industries. Banks requires the adoption of AI and ML in order to deliver high level customer service, to retain the customers and to understand the personal banking habits and needs. There is a tremendous scope for the banks to reduce costs, increase profitability and to become more competitive by adopting AI and ML altogether for providing many of their services. The importance and usefulness of AI can be realized in the economy, business and industry including banking through its different form of its application. It is used in online banking, mobile banking and it also offers high level of security to the banks. In case of mobile banking, AI helps to make transactions easier and safer also. Banks with these help of AI handles customer-oriented operations without hiring qualified professionals. It helps either in the form of predicting creditworthiness of customers or for customer recommendation. The adoption of AI is helpful especially for preventing financial frauds, catching the criminals and detecting the money laundering. When contrasted with elective areas, Indian banking area investigating and golf stroke AI in, to see the changed ways that past the fundamental applications. Banks additionally actualizing the AI innovation in carrying more effectiveness to its back-office and diminishing the illegal tax avoidance cheats and NPAs. Banks can take up the AI-based technological application in many ways like maintenance of customer data base, verification of signature, cheque book reorder facility, credit and interest rate control, credit evaluation, portfolio, risk assessment, evaluation of employee performance and investment forecasting etc.

4.2   AI IN THE BANKING SECTOR: WHERE IT WORKS AND WHAT FOR

During the last decade the very term AI came into reality and became essential part of the fast-moving sector including the Indian banking Sector. "Several routine and manual tasks in banking industry which were earlier performed by the humans are now being replaced by the automated machines (AI) with advance technology," [10]. Forward-thinking bank managers are actively exploring the new and innovative technology AI along with ML through different applications to get a competitive advantage on the market. As per the research findings if one innovative technology that's paying dividends to banking and finance industry it is none other than AI and ML. AI has shaped the world of banking sector in a way which can meet the customers demand, personalized service in a smarter, safer and convenient way. The innovative and advance technology AI has made profound impact on finance sector. After the introduction of AI and Fintech the journey of banks has been shifted from digital transformation to use of AI. It has been observed that AI with ML technology has changed the way of interaction of banks with its customers. Banks, through the help of AI, are driving the personalized way of journey and powerful weapon like AI aid in providing an affective omni channel personalized strategies to their customers. Banks want to perform all its transaction very meticulously for why it invests in new technology and one of them is AI. Nowadays, AI has entered and adopted in almost all area of bank's operations as well as into the work of every department. Sometimes even the customers use and get the benefits of AI application without realizing the presence of AI.

As shown in Figure 4.2, the uses of AI in banking areas can be grouped into three areas basically like Artificial Intelligence has already entered in to the core of finance business including bank and its impact is clearly manifest in many areas from customer service to enhancing the productivity and reducing the financial frauds. AI is helping the banks in streamlining and optimizing the areas ranging from financial risk management, fraud detection, credit decisions, prediction of risk, anti-money-laundering process and anticipates the needs of customers.

   i. Magnifying customer service and experience which includes chatbots, Personalized financial service, Voice banking, Robo advice, Biometric Authentication, smart wallet and quicken payment through blockchain.

   ii. Magnifying efficiency of banks which includes credit scoring, Automation Complain Management, Maintaining CRM and KYC along with Data driven Lending Decisions.

   iii. Magnifying Security and risk control which includes Fraud detection and prevention, Anomaly fraud detection including anti money-laundering, risk control and management and cyber-risk.

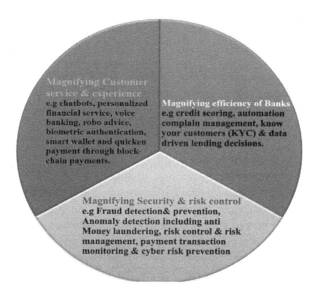

FIGURE 4.2   Use of AI in Banking Sector. *Source:* Author

4.2.1   AI AND CUSTOMER SERVICE

"AI is manifested in intelligent performance and behaviours by machines, computers or robots that are used to assist humans and businesses," [9]. According to a report published by World Economic Forum (2018) in collaboration with Deloitte, about 76% of banking industry chief executive officers agree that AI is a top priority because it is critical for providing smart customer service through its chatbots, personalized financial services, smart wallets, voice assisted customer support, blockchain expedite payment etc. Banks requires the adoption of AI and ML in order to deliver high level customer service, to retain the customers and to understand the personal banking habits and needs of the customers to get a better customer experience. Through the use of AI, banks are using their customer experience and also increasing the number of customers. The big banks like SBI, PNB and HDFC are adopting AI powered tools such as chatbot, natural language processing (NLP) and Cognitive computing to offer personalized service to customers, round the clock support to users, and to do the analysis of transaction and loans. 'Personetics', one of the London based company through its chatbots, identify patterns in information and can do predictive analysis. Through this analysis it can guess what will the next likely interaction from customers' side. AI not only help banks to provide innovative customer service, but also helps to determine creditworthiness, streamlining the lending process and improve customers experience for borrowers.

4.2.1.1   Chatbots

Chatbot is AI software which simplifies the interactions between user and machines or computers in a natural language. It helps banks to enhance the customer experience, improve the customer engagement, magnify the operational efficiency and reduce the typical customer service cost. "The financial sector in India has seen tremendous investments into chatbots and AI to augment customer service," [11]. AI-driven chatbots are widely adopted and are fairly easy to deploy and can be used in various areas of activities like online customer support, phone interaction, answer product and company related queries. It generally deploys these tools 24/7 to engage and interact with customers. Renowned platforms of chatbots in 2020 include Mobile-money, Chatfuel and Its Alive. Allahabad Bank is also developing and applying its own mobile app chatbot named "Empower".

4.2.1.2   AI and Personalized Banking

The banks using the existing data through digitization process, deliver meaningful and powerful personalized service to their customers. Through AI application banks are focusing on understanding customer needs on the basis of their requirements, taste, moods and resources. This creates a win–win situation for both banks and clients, but it drives a competitive advantage to the first mover banks. AI truly shines when it comes to exploring new ways to provide additional benefits and comfort to individual users. These Apps, by tracking the personal data like income, recurring expenses, spending habits and working experience, can suggest financial tips and optimized plans to customers. Some of the biggest US banks like Bank of America and Wells Fargo, through their mobile banking apps provide different services to their clients like sending reminders to pay electric bills, plan their financial transactions and connect with their banks in a streamlined way.

4.2.1.3   Smart Wallets

Digital wallets, otherwise known as smart wallets, refers to make digitization payment through AI application by one party to another party through digital currency for goods and services. In the current scenario digital payments is the future real world payment technology. In order to reduce the dependence of physical cash payments and to increase the reach of money at higher level banks are implementing AI technology. Adoption of AI application in the banking industry promoted the use of smart wallets and digital wallets such as Google, Apple, PayPal and others have developed their payment gateways. Through the digital wallets banks are storing the user's payment information and passwords for making payment.

4.2.1.4   Voice Assisted Banking

Now a days the presence of AI technology influence customers to get accustomed with voice command and touch screen banking service as a result of which voice assisted and physical presence banking are vanishing away. It helps to process queries to answer questions, provides the necessary information and helps the customers to get various banking services.

4.2.1.5   Robo Advice

For banks, regulations play an important role and AI also helps the banks in this regard. All the collected data are carefully checked, organized and analyzed before forwarding for further decisions. Without the interference of AI, the entire work would be labour intensive which results in time consuming and resulted/prone to mistakes. This kind of solution provided by AI can be to some extent called as RPA. HDFC Mutual Fund and Investment bank Axis Securities with the partnership of Robo advisory start-ups like Artha Yantra using a methodology named as Personal Financial Lifecycle Management for their business transaction.

4.2.1.6   AI Backed Blockchain for Expedite Payments

It is a digital record of transaction where the individual records called blocks are linked together in single list called chain and it is used for recommending transactions made with cryptocurrency such as Bitcoin. Through the AI assisted blockchain the banks have replaced the expedite payments with sluggish payments. Blockchain offers the advantage of real time payment process, speed-up of payment procedure and increased satisfaction level of customers.

4.2.2   AI AND MAGNIFYING EFFICIENCY OF BANKS

Banks are adopting AI as a tool to reduce cost and improve efficiency. "The banks cannot afford to wait, to get on their AI journey as they have to compete in a future which is packed with innovative and advanced technology,"[10]. On the basis of literature it is well accepted that investment in the right AI technology can improve workforce productivity and increase bank's operational efficiency and profitability.

4.2.2.1 Determining Credit Scoring and Lending Decisions

According to the International Data Corporation report, financial companies will spend $11 million to operate with AI and ML by 2020. By the estimate AI-based developments, including underwriting and AI credit scoring, financial sector will be able to increase their GDP by as much as 10% in less than a decade (Volodymyr Soffinskyi, Chief data scientist at Datrics). Many companies like Zestfinance and Lenddo have developed their AI tool for credit scoring and through the ML they are trying to determine the creditworthiness of individual customers or how likely a particular customer can be defaulter. These companies look at potential applicants on the basis of variables like Internet browsing habits, geolocation, social media accounts; ML then turns all these data into credit score which afterwards are used by banks to determine the credit score of the individual customer. On the other hand, one of the start-up companies, Upstart, is using the modern science data to automate the loan process. This company focuses on young adult's education, SAT score, GPT, Job history; field of study and by using ML predicts their creditworthiness. Now a days, AI is proved to be a greater solution for banks to provide individual credit score on the basis of more data. AI application takes into consideration many factors like current income, employment status, work experience, current credit history educational background on the basis of which bank grants loans to clients. ML provides best technological solution by developing the risk scoring models. These models predict on forecast about the difficult against credit supply to a particular client.

4.2.2.2 AI and CRM

AI works for maintaining customer relationship by giving advice and empowering them to take more judicious financial decisions. On the basis of integrated data AI develop tailor made products and services and identify areas of interest that are most important and useful to each customer at a given moment. AI as an advance and innovative technology helps the banks to maintain strong and long-lasting customer relationship either through budgeting tool or technology driven interaction. It also assists the banks to improve the performance in terms of improved customer satisfaction, reduced customer attrition, enhanced customer relationship, increased occurence of deposits and increased number of innovative and tailor-made products for the clients.

4.2.3 Magnifying Security and Risk Control

The inclusion of AI in process have decreased the probability of human error to all most zero in banking sector and its fruitful for maintaining high level security to both loan and fund security of banks. From the loan perspective, AI helps to identify the risk associated with loan and reliability and creditworthiness of borrowers. At the same time, banks, due to its application, can be aware of cybercrimes and instantly spot malware on a network.

4.2.3.1   Detection and Prevention of Financial Fraud

AI is highly effective at and helpful in preventing financial fraud and catching criminals. It reveals the money laundering, credit card fraud and anomaly fraud which have a significant impact on the profitability position of banks. It is being observed that credit card fraud is growing exponentially due to expand of online and e-commerce transactions which compel the adoption of AI. The application of AI in preventing fraud and money laundering plays a vital role and through this application bank analyses clients' behaviour, buying habits, location and use of Internet banking etc and when some sort of deviation seems to happen, then the security mechanism gives the information about fraud. Application of AI technique in this regards results decreasing number of credit card fraud and other anomaly frauds.

4.2.3.2   Reducing Money Laundering

AI in conjunction with AL assists to reveal and prevent one distinct type of financial crime such as money laundering. Plaid which works with CITI, Goldman Sachs through its complex algorithms analyzes the interactions under different conditions and variables and builds multiple unique patterns. Plaid works as a small gadget which connects the banks with its client's app and helps to ensure secure financial transactions. Financial institutions like banks have set up some technical weapons like AI and ML to prevent money laundering and other financial frauds. AI-based organization modelling and customer segmentation is more effective to bring the greater accuracy with respect to financial frauds. AI using ML is proved to be very influential in identifying sources of complex transactions and finding their irregularities and abnormalities. It helps to find out suspicious financial transaction, irregular network of transaction and fraud transactions. Through this technique the bank as vendors can identify fraudulent payments that appear legitimate and lawful payments that seems to be fraudulent. Ayasdi and SAS are two examples who are offering AI enabled anti money-laundering solutions. They are purportedly offering solutions to their client Banks to reduce money laundering and financial frauds. These companies build their data warehouse platform, identify the changes in customer behaviours and analyse these data for patterns related to fraudulent money transfer. Ayasdi AML includes core competency like auto feature engineering, intelligent segmentation, organization insights, Intelligent Event Triage and Contextual Alert Information in order to offer customers more accurate results with respect to AML.

4.2.3.3   Cybersecurity

Now a days, the banks feel it necessary to take initiative to reduce and eliminate cybersecurity and financial frauds for which AI is the vital role provider so far. The AI as a digital technique enhances online financial security. Banks everyday undertake large volume of digital financial transaction either in the form of transfer money, cheques deposited, bills payments and grant of loans etc. for which strict cybersecurity along with fraud detection technique is very much required. In this regard two renowned companies have proved themselves as pioneers like Shape's solutions who protect customers from account hijacking and also help to detect credential stuffing attacks.

4.2.3.4 AI: Managing and Controlling Risk

For financial service sector including banking, unnoticed risks can be proved to be fatal and dangerous to the organizations. So, a detailed and minute forecast prediction about future financial risk is very much required for the protection of the banking transaction. For this reason, financial markets use ML which is a subset of AI to conserve manpower, identify risk and to ensure better information for future planning. The role of AI is just like a potent weapon with respect to risk management in financial service including bank, insurance and mutual fund. AI with its enormous processing power handles piles of data within very short period of time. Cognitive computing manages data and algorithms analyze the risk history and accordingly identify and forecast about the future issues and risks. Crest Financial, a US leasing company employed AI for risk analysis without relying on traditional data science methods and experienced a remarkable improvement in this area with high amount of risk reduction. The companies like KENSHO (Cambridge) software offers analytical solutions using a combination of cloud computing and NLP provides answers to complex financial questions. Ayasdi creates cloud-based and machine intelligence solutions for banks like enterprises to solve complex challenges in the fintech space, Ayasdi AI and ML understand and manage risks, anticipates needs of customers and also aid in anti-money-laundering process. It is not much surprising that AI has become one of the technical pedestals on which total banking companies rely on. It is not only foremost innovative technique but has changed the method in which the customers deal with banks and vice versa. Like Blockchain, AI in the banking industry is a revolution in technology which makes the work of banks easier, effective and in turn increases the quality and speed of service. AI and ML are proved to be the poised agitator for the banking industry.

4.3 AI APPLICATIONS IN INDIAN BANKS: SOME SELECTED EXAMPLES

"The Indian financial area is investigating the ways by which it can saddle the intensity of AI to improve the procedures and upgrade the customer service in the long run," [8]. According to a McKinsey Global Survey (2018), the adoption of AI has been a key topic of interest for organizations, including banks. Most respondents in the study, who have implemented AI in a specific area, reported that it helps for achieving moderate or significant value from that use and only 21% of the respondents reported implant AI into multiple business process.

> The rudimentary applications which AI include brings smarter chatbots for customer service, personalizing services for individuals and even placing an AI robot for self-service at banks. Beyond these basic applications, banks can implement the technology for bringing in more efficiency to their back-office and even reduce fraud and security risks.
>
> [13]

Despite the need expressed by Indian bankers about AI adoption, most of Indian bankers admitted that due to low risk appetite and huge investment the banks are not showing interest to adopt mass usage.

Though many of the Indian banks are actively adopting leading age technology for their better growth, development and prospects to serve modern age customers but few of them have been chosen and discussed here. It is estimated and forecasted by analysts and experts that by the end of 2030, AI will save the Indian banking Industry an average of $1 trillion. At the same time, narrative science expects that nearly 32% of the participating banks have incorporated predictive analytics, recommendation engines, voice recognition and response times in their processes. As shown in Figure 4.3, Business Insider Intelligence report (2020) says 75% of respondents banks with over $100 billion in assets giving their consent that are currently implementing AI strategies, compared with 46% at banks with less than $100 billion in assets as shown in Figure 4.4. The respondent banks are saying that size of the cost savings opportunity is $199 billion for front office (conversational banking), and as much as $217B for middle office (anti-fraud) banking. But according to McKinsey Global Institute, application of AI technologies in banking could generate more than $250 billion in value across the sector. This section discusses which banks look to adopt and integrate AI and how they have applied AI in their existing system.

As indicated by joint examination directed by the National Business Research Institute and narrative science of numerous Indian banks, very nearly 12 are applying the AI and ML and who have been featured because of their AI activity in the course of the most recent couple of years. The rundown incorporates SBI, Bank of Baroda (BoB), Allahabad Bank, Andhra Bank, YES Bank, HDFC, ICICI, Axis, Canara Bank,

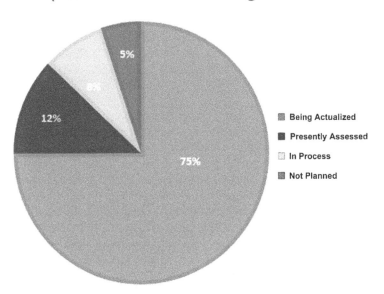

Implementation of AI Strategies in Banks

- Being Actualized
- Presently Assessed
- In Process
- Not Planned

5%
8%
12%
75%

FIGURE 4.3 Execution of AI techniques in banks having more than $100 billion assets.
Source: Author

Implementation of AI in Banks

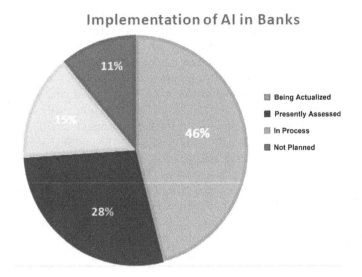

FIGURE 4.4   Execution of AI techniques in banks having more less than $100 billion assets.
Source: Author

City Union Bank, Punjab National Bank, IndusInd Bank. The Banks who have adopted or are on the verge of adopting the AI technology can implement it in three broad areas: either in front office or Middle office or in the back-office business activities. The rudimentary applications AI include bring smarter chatbots for customer service, personalizing services for individuals and even placing an AI robot for self-service at banks. Beyond these basic applications, banks can implement the technology for bringing in more efficiency to their back-office and even reduce fraud and security risks.

4.3.1   STATE BANK OF INDIA

SBI proves that a public sector bank where the government holds more than a 50% stake can promote innovation in technology and leadership through an ecosystem of partnerships. SBI is the 43rd largest bank worldwide and largest Indian public sector bank with 23% market share and 25% of market loan and ranked 236th in the Fortune Global 500 list of the world's biggest corporations of 2019. Indian banks, including state-owned SBI have started adopting AI as a tool in a big way to improve efficiency, profitability, reduce operational costs, detect human committed fraud and reduce cyber risks. As shown in Figure 4.5 State Bank of India, the India's largest lender has implemented different apps and AI enabled software and one of them is SBI Intelligent Assistant (SIA), a smart chart assistant. SIA offers instant solutions to banking queries, efficiently resolves doubts of NRI customers in the chat box like a bank representative. SBI is as of now utilizing an AI-based arrangement created by Chapdex, the triumphant group from its first public hackathon, "Code for bank". On the front work area, it utilizes SIA chatbot, an AI-controlled visit partner. SIA which

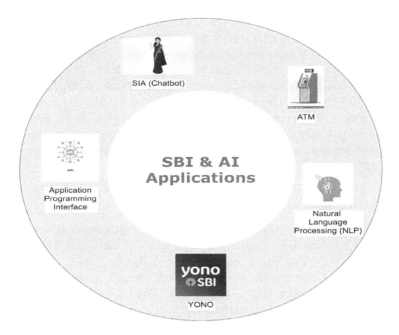

FIGURE 4.5 AI technology used in SBI. *Source:* Author's Self Complied.

is very fluent in providing the answers on all banking products, services and answering all queries like how to open an account, how to avail other customers' service. This helps the customers to process the transactions in many regional languages across the multiple customer channels. It is experienced that due to adoption of SIA, the SBI could be able to manage to get new customers for different banking products.

SBI started using analytics in 2014 and got training to use the AI from IDBRT and Manipal University 2016 for commencing the use of integrated analytics, AI and ML to address many of business operational problems. Some of the techniques used by SBI are NLP. Geolocation analysis (GLA), String Matching, Network Analysis, Identification of Fraud prone branches, Early warning system and predictive analysis etc. SBI is trying to redesign the customer journey from physical to digital. It has three major technology programmes with about 500 projects which are risk management, customer relationship management and YONO (You Only Need One), its mobile app. The bank has 30 million mobile banking customers and 47 million Internet banking customers, but there is yet a huge potential to be tapped. It is adopting YONO platform which includes sanction of pre-approved paperless loan within five minutes which enables overseas customers to easily open accounts. It has made a symbiotic relationship based on collaboration. SBI is going to bring prudence in lending with early warning signals on bad loans and for fraud prevention applying latest innovation YONO, a mobile app. This App was launched a year ago that packs banking services with lifestyle shopping features, with plans to extend it beyond individual customers to the agriculture and corporate sectors. Fintech provides technology solution and proves win-win situation to both of them. SBI's improved loan portfolio performance attributed to risk management and fraud detection technology programmes. It has deployed early warning signals for recognizing NPAs, and data analytics to analyze behaviour patterns for small loans or personal loans. According to SBI chief technology officer Shiv Kumar Bhasin (2019), SIA is the first of its kind banking application in AI and conversational banking and it will enhance customer service several notches above. "Payjo's expertise in the conversation domain helped us build SIA as a superior chatbot in the global banking space," said Bhasin. SBI has built an application programming interface (API) layer over its banking solution.

4.3.2 HDFC BANK

HDFC Bank (1994) has a registered office in Mumbai, and has the bank's distribution network at 5,500 branches across 2,764 cities as of 30 June 2019. The bank also installed 430,000 POS terminals and issued 23,570,000 debit cards and 12 million credit cards. HDFC Bank is India's largest private sector bank in India by market capitalization as of March 2020. As shown in Figure 4.6. HDFC Bank offers a different scope of monetary items and banking services to clients through a developing branch and ATM organization and advanced channels, for example, Net banking,

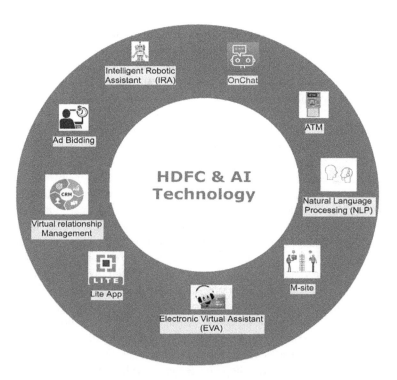

FIGURE 4.6   AI technology used in HDFC. *Source:* Author.

Phone banking and mobile banking. The bank operates in a highly automated environment which is reflected online connectivity among all branches, speed funds transfer facility, multi branch facility provided to its retail customers and ATMs. Bank has made huge investment for acquiring best technology like AI, IoT, Flexcube core banking software, Finware retail banking business which is scale-able and web-enabled. The bank uses Net and mobile banking to enable the existing customers to experience banking through their choice device. It provides digital marketing and analytics to create a seamless experience across different platforms. It has moved to digital innovations for ensuring superior digital capability of the Bank across the industry and maintains Virtual Relationship Management (VRM) for fulfilling all the financial needs of Customers through Voice Channels and to adopt the banking products on digital platforms.

With respect to AI, chatbot EVA (Electronic Virtual Assistant) was developed by Bengaluru-based Senseforth AI Research, and it can collect information from a number of sources and provide answer within fractions of seconds and also handles real banking transactions. From the day it was received it has tended to over 2.7 million customer questions, connected with more than 530,000 novel clients, and held 1.2 million discussions. It eliminates the need to search, browse or call. EVA additionally gets more brilliant as it learns through its customer interactions. Going ahead, "EVA would have the option to deal with genuine banking transactions too, which would empower HDFC Bank to offer the genuine intensity of conversational banking to its customers," the bank expressed in an organization news discharge. As per Nitin Chugh, Country Head, HDFC Digital Banking EVA will supplement their advanced stages in improving customer experience. HDFC is likewise testing Robotic applications like HDFC's IRA (Intelligent Robotic Assistant) robot which gives off an impression of being in innovative work, not in far reaching use while different banks have tried different things with in-store robots to help control customers or guests as it were.

Solutions like our mobile banking App, AI-based OnChat has been developed for customers who enjoy good connectivity. Customers of HDFC who struggle with limited connectivity issues have LITE App and m-site to avail banking services, whereas customers with no connectivity or feature phones have missed call commerce, SMS/Toll Free Banking at their service. HDFC key advancements in Artificial Intelligence space incorporates HDFC Bank OnChat (AI put together online business chatbot with respect to Facebook), Programmatic Ad Bidding (AI-based promotion offering instrument for computerized showcasing), Ask EVA (AI-based FAQ and customer administration assistant) and IRA (Intelligent Robotic Assistant at branches). This assistant is able to meet, greet and guide customers as per their requirements. The domain of AI extends to recruitment, customer service, core banking, employee training and engagement, operational efficiency, analytics and e–commerce. The other additional initiative under AI adopted by HDFC is it's chatbot 'OnChat' and NLP, wherein user can interact, confirm and pay for services within chat itself without any additional download app. Banks also tapped upon AI for Ad bidding which helps customers for increasing the conversion rate by five times. This initiative helped in reducing the overall cost of acquisition for digital products and in improving overall profitability. HDFC bank's approach to AI is holistic and it has implemented AI solutions through a strong testing and learning-driven approach either to customer experience, customer support, process automation, HR and security or fraud detection areas. HDFC does not want to just create gizmos but believes in the principle "Generating Customer Value" out of AI. To put it across bank is applying AI which will help to manage both internal and external customers much more effectively and help to reduce operational costs exponentially in the near future.

4.3.3 AXIS BANK

Axis Bank, founded in 1993, is the third-largest private sector bank in India, having approximately 20 million customers, 59,000 employees, 18% customer growth. Axis Bank has a physical presence in over 2,100 cities and towns across India, with a concentration in eight metropolitan areas. According to Rajiv Anand, Executive Director, Axis Bank is intending to provide 24×7 assistance, instant gratification and convenience to customers in an intuitive and native way.

It is India's third-biggest private area bank which has dispatched an advancement lab called "Thought Factory" a year ago to present the imaginative improvement through AI innovation answers for the banking area. It has innovation team working in innovation hub located at Bengalure through which the bank engages with start-ups in a short-term duration of 3 months. The Axis Bank management has two objectives for adopting AI into its customer service pipeline (1) To handle increased number of customer service through automated channels (2) To lower down customer complain by providing satisfied customer service. To achieve these two objectives, it has launched its AI chatbot solution, named "Axis Aha!" Through Axis Aha! Customers are comfortable to transfer their funds, order chequebooks, pay bills, use fund prepaid cards, block transactions on existing cards, set or reset the PIN for a card, can change a card's credit limit, download their bank statement, apply for a loan or card. The chatbot could also be helpful to customers for giving answers for the questions or complaints about Axis Bank's products and services. Axis Aha! offers many more such interesting features, serving to be a conversational assistant for almost all your banking and finance related needs. But Axis Aha! is still in its initial phase of integration within Axis Bank's broader customer service ecosystem. Axis Bank recently also has launched to avail conversational banking an AI and NLP enabled app only to answer FAQs and to get in touch with loan and other products and to address the queries. Axis Aha! used a combination of NLP for classification, NLU (Natural Language Understanding) for customer data, and deep learning for extracting and summarizing raw data and to leverage both ML and rules-based techniques to understand and respond to customers' needs. Figure 4.7 shows the different areas in which AI technology is used at Axis Bank.

The other basic territory where Axis Bank utilizes AI is operational danger and AML for why there is a critical improvement in proficiency, time and cost savings. Bank has a powerful credit hazard model because of which reality 80% of the dubious transactions are from 5% customers recognized as high danger by the AI-empowered neural organization. Bank has likewise begun Robotic cycle mechanization (RPA)

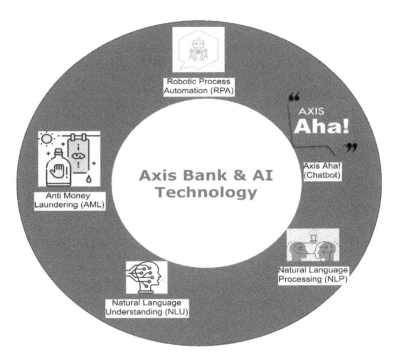

FIGURE 4.7 AI technology used in Axis Bank. *Source:* Author.

for most cycles, including account upkeep and adjusting, advance payment, mass exchange cycles and ATM uphold. Through the execution of AI bank is attempting to lessen the turnaround time (TAT), the bank has actualized AI across 125+ cycles and intellectual mechanization across 90 cycles, which required tedious physical work. It is encountered that with the utilization of RPA there is obvious decrease in TAT, time spent in investment account opening has diminished by 90%, on current records by 92%, and on different cycles by 50% to 80%.

According to Sameer Shetty, Head of digital banking (Axis Bank) fraud has been declining due to the rise of improved authentication and security systems and he even stated that Axis has had no digital banking identity fraud incidents, due to multi-layered defence system that incorporates video customer authentication and AI. Through the implementation of AI Axis' cross-references customers' identifying information with India's national identification number system, that is the world's largest biometric identity programme. Axis verifies that the number the customer presents is the same as what they have in the national database in order to confirm their identity with the objective to reduce the fraud and anti-money-laundering. This instant verification system has made synthetic identity fraud nearly impossible, as the instant cross-referencing with government databases means that any made-up identification number will be discovered immediately. The on boarding system is supplemented by an AI platform that looks for signs of account takeovers, like mismatched location data or unusual transactions.

4.3.4 Punjab National Bank

According to the reports published at the end of 30th June 2020, PNB is the second largest Public sector Bank (PSB) of the country next to SBI. Punjab National Bank is India's first Swadeshi bank, which commenced its operations on 12 April 1895 from Lahore, and during the long history of the bank, nine banks have been merged with PNB. Its current market e-modelling ion stands at Rs 31,478.56 Cr. It serves 8.9 crore customers and has country wide presence through 6,081 branches including five foreign branches and 6,940 ATMs.

The Indian financial area is starting to embrace AI for both the back-office and client confronting purposes. As per the information given by RBI, among state run banks in India, PNB bested in the quantity of loan fraud cases across India with 389 cases throughout the last five monetary years. After the scandalous bank fraud that the nation saw for the current year, Punjab National Bank (PNB) on May 6th, reported its arrangements to depend on AI for reconciliation of accounts and join examination for improving the audit frameworks as it looks to tidy up the cycle and counter fraud sooner rather than later. Internal audit measure is likewise being expanded to give higher load to the off-site observing instrument and lessen reliance on actual examination and audit to distinguish the dangers. This choice was taken after the greatest bank fraud where two junior officers at a solitary branch had wrongfully directed USD 1.77 billion (Euro 1.43 billion) in fraudulent loans to organizations, constrained by Nirav Modi and his uncle Mehul Choksi.

PNB has implemented its own chatbot "PIHU" i.e., PNB Instant Help for You for enhancing customer experience and has used resolution of customer queries (FAQs) regarding bank digital frauds, credit and debit cards. PIHU will enhance customer service experience and reduce customer complaint and queries. PNB managing director Sunil Mehta said in a statement that, "The 'business e-modelling' brought alive by changes at PNB is essential to ensure that the bank continues to grow and compete with its peers better," and elaborated on several steps that would reduce human intervention. PNB has looked to set up a start to finish exhaustive answer for Early Warning Signals (EWS) and smart exchange checking with the goal that ideal remedial move can be made in case of an expected fraud. The bank plans to use progressed abilities, for example, AI, web crawling and Optical Character Recognition (OCR) to get early admonitions on a unique premise, in light of cautions created utilizing borrower's data gathered from different internal and outside sources. Utilizing AI and ML, the arrangement would have clever realities extraction capacity from sources as assorted as news, online media, government information bases, rating offices, intelligence organizations, SEBI, RBI and other global controllers. It would likewise be fit for finding the connections among borrower's connected gatherings. A last score would be allocated based on seriousness of triggers and risk categorization of the client. By getting to various information focuses to set up the credibility and monetary soundness of the borrower, the software would hurl cautions consistently to help the bank officials take information driven choices about tolerating or dismissing an exchange. The bank has intended to redistribute the gracefully, execution and upkeep of such a EWS framework, and has just revealed a notification welcoming application from intrigued sellers. By utilizing AI to make a

360-degree profiling of the borrower, PNB plans to help the anticipation, early recognition and brief revealing of frauds to the RBI and insightful offices. This will be a bit nearer to understanding a zero-resistance strategy of the Indian financial framework towards unscrupulous practices. The bank expanded its digital Base with over 35% ascent in internet banking users and over 45% in mobile banking Users. It successfully overhauled the Core Banking Solution (CBS) stage to Finacle 10.x adaptation for better client experience. Finacle is a centre financial item created by the Infosys that gives widespread digital financial usefulness to banks. In August 2015, bank dispatched number of imaginative portable applications to encourage computerized exchanges, for example, PNB MobiEase, PNB Rewards, PNB Fin Literacy, PNB Yuva, PNB ATM Assist, PNB m-banking, PNB Kitty and so on. Further, PNB M-Passbook was dispatched in FY'18 for clients to get to their record explanation on cell phones. ¾ SWIFT was coordinated with CBS, wherein all outward instalment SWIFT messages are naturally produced through CBS with no manual mediation. Figure 4.8 shows the different AI technology used in PNB and PNB MetLife.

According to Samrat Das, CIO, PNB MetLife:

> PNB MetLife has introduced two key innovations which is first-of-its-kind firstly, Virtual Reality (VR) based customer service platform – conVRse which was built in partnership with LumenLab MetLife's innovation centre in Singapore. Second is a secure digital hub called Infinity that allows you to create a digital legacy by enabling you to share important documents and memories with your nominees in case something were to happen to you. If we look within the MetLife system, we have MetLife Japan with some interesting

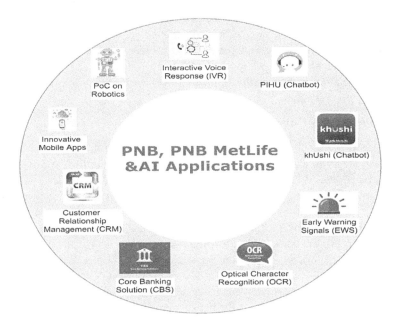

FIGURE 4.8 AI technology used in PNB, PNB MetLife. *Source:* Author.

work in the field of robotics for Surrender Cash Value process called The Proof of Concept (PoC) on Robotics. This is helping solve for one off requests for Cash value certificates which were manually processed by extracting data from multiple sources and building a statement. Through this process, the team was able to reduce the time spent by ~50% with 91% of transactions automated and further configuration can take this to 100%.

PNB Metlife has likewise dispatched chatbot named khUshi, which is a customer administration application, fuelled with AI utilized for getting insurance related queries. PNB has marked a long-term contact with Mphasis to set up contact communities in Noida and Mangalore. Mphasis will offer start to finish Customer Relationship Management (CRM) administrations that incorporate inbound telephone banking, outbound calling and protests management. The extent of the administrations incorporates uphold for all financial items and administrations including deposits operations, core banking processes, lending services, Internet banking, account and card-related services. PNB plans to improve nature of its customer administration and empower wise customer commitment through ideal use of information. The IT organization will actualize Interactive Voice Response (IVR) framework and a far-reaching CRM arrangement Advisor360 which will take into account the bank's customers, branches and satisfaction prerequisites across 13 territorial circles in India. The administrations will be made accessible in different dialects (English, Hindi, Malayalam, Kannada, Tamil and Telugu) through Mphasis' focuses in north and south.Based on the review, it is inplied that there are numerous reasons and zones why and where the AI-empowered innovation can be actualized. These reasons are accomplishing improved development and advancement, to give improved customer administration, to adjust to the cutting-edge business climate or to increment cultural advantages through financial area nearly constrained the banks to embrace AI which is another age innovation for doing their business. The most widely recognized AI application on which a large portion of the bank are embracing and actualizing independent of their size is their particular chatbot, RPA and NLU.

4.4   AI AND ITS IMPACT ON BANKS' KPIs

Banking is an extremely diversified and complex industry or domain which requires a constant supply of advanced technological solutions in order to simplify complex banking functions. AI has colossal advantages, for both banks and their clients. The major reason for adoption of AI by big global banks is to stay competitive in the digital era. As shown in a recent analysis conducted by Forbes, the implementation of AI in various banking processes will save the industry more than $1 trillion by 2030. As a result, the banking industries are expected to benefit the most from AI system in the near future. AI has numerous advantages to bring to the table for the financial area, be it Android application advancement or iOS application improvement, the AI can acquire progressive changes in the financial business.

Recently, top level managers of the banks are realizing that either to improve the operational efficiency, to enhance the employee productivity for taking effective decisions to face the demand for customized solutions, or to manage vast amount of data at a high speed in the adoption of technology like AI and ML in their business operation becomes necessary. [2]) explored the significant positive impact of AI on the overall performance of banking system and banking network in the Middle East. Application of AI also augment the decision-making process either with respect to lending and risk taking, evaluating the credit score and underwriting which will help the analyst to take critical decision. This section is trying to highlight the critical positive impacts of AI application on the different parameters of overall performance of banks. Among several future banking trends, AI is creating the most impact in the Indian banking sector. To stay ahead in the competition, banks today are struggling to reduce operational costs, meet goals and exceed customer expectations through customer experience which is possible with the presence of AI.

Early adopter banks of AI and ML are showing high-impact business results in fraud detection, manufacturing performance optimization, preventative maintenance and recommendation engines. On the basis of extensive literature, it is unearthed that AI along with ML yields many benefits to the daily operation of banking industry. AI's greatest impact is yet to come, but the combination of big data with ML algorithms has already yielded benefits to the financial world daily operations. The traditional banking business is now moving to be replaced by AI by the use of blockchain, Big data and cloud computing. The impact of AI on the banking industry is undoubtedly manifest in many areas of bank with respect to different KPI parameters which are like Profitability, Productivity, Improved customer satisfaction, Reduced customer attrition, Increasing deposits and CRM. From the bank's prospective KPI is a quantifiable worth that exhibits how successfully it is accomplishing key business destinations at different levels to assess their targets.

4.4.1 IMPACT OF AI ON PROFITABILITY

AI as a part of digitalization is expected to increase the profitability in the long run due to lower cost structure. It requires fewer branch and limited personnel as majority of the work is automated. Banks which rely on innovation technology like AI, blockchain, Cloud computing will be able to generate huge profits or revenues in turn it will get reflected in the profitability position of banks. Artificial Intelligence in credit scoring can save time and total costs of the institution and many banks were helped by AI to increase profits. Active development of this area is taking place which increases the total profit of the loan sphere. Thus, now the decisions to grant a loan are made more efficiently, and the bank does not lose money on unscrupulous borrowers. AI significantly increase profit in any sphere. AI contributes to the profitability of banks in three different ways:

1. By taking over repetitive assignments from bank workers and improving the proficiency of outstanding bank staff thereby reducing the remuneration.
2. AI execution could likewise add to revenue generation.
3. Improving the accuracy forecast and reducing the risk cost.

It was proved by Orgun Kaya (2019) there is 80% correlation between profitability and level of AI patent activity. So, it is inferred that the bank's profitability is positively correlated with stronger use of AI in different banks.

4.4.2   IMPACT OF AI ON PRODUCTIVITY AND EFFICIENCY OF BANKS

Banks also tap into AI for ad bidding, which helps customers increase the conversion rate by five times. This initiative helped in reducing the overall cost of acquisition for digital products and in improving overall profitability. Productivity for a bank is a combination of business per employee, profit per employee, employment generation and number of branches. There is a direct impact of digitalization and banks productivity where under digitalization AI and ML forms a vital segment. The application of AI can increase the productivity and competitiveness with respect to customer service and offering of products and services.

> The focus of business in most industries is efficiency and sustainability and the banking industry is no different in this regard. This sustainability is all based on proper decision making and AI is unmatched in this process as it takes the human bias out of decision trees.
>
> [12]

The digital revolution brings extraordinary gains in the productivity of banking industry. Manmade consciousness gives banks a colossally groundbreaking set of instruments that change and smooth out a portion of their most key monetary cycles. A combination of elements including massive, distributed computing power, the decreasing cost of data storage, and the rise of opensource frameworks is helping to accelerate the application of AI in banking sector. Improving security, following guidelines, and effective compliance are on the whole advantages of AI strategy which helps to enhance the productivity and is also necessary to stay ahead of the competition. AI can help banks' finance teams, re-imagine and restructure operating models and processes and through the processing huge volume of data helps for increasing the productivity and efficiency of banks. The software bots used in RPA can be coded to deal with rules and some exceptions, but it's the added layer of ML across the more complex challenges and frequently changing tasks that make the combination of RPA and AI particularly powerful.

4.4.3   IMPACT OF AI ON IMPROVED CUSTOMER SATISFACTION

There are mainly five attributes which play a major role in providing customer satisfaction: better customer experience, ease of banking, accessibility, security and protection, and cost effectiveness. Different AI-driven tools and strategies have high potential to fulfil these five attributes of customer satisfaction. If we talk about enterprise risk management, AI is more beneficial to detect and prevent fraud risk, fincrime risk and operational risk. As AI applications are being utilized to give progressed technologic security and insurance to information and money of the bank clients. Blockchains are one of the famous cybersecurity systems which enable financial transactions in chains of computer code. Blockchain technology provides direct transaction along with greater reliability and prolonged data storage, transparency, quick-handling, cost reduction and easy maintenance. Because of this, almost every bank has adopted blockchain technology; especially to maintain two things: KYC records and their authentication, and to make payments because of its special feature minimum TAT. In the financial area, chatbots are filling in as virtual specialists with various symbols and character which are basically used to know the reactions and personal conduct standards of clients by changing over their content and feelings into a valuable information base, which helps the banks in providing better customer experiences to its customers. While Online payments, electronic clearing services, immediate payment service (IMPS), national automated clearing house, unified payments interface (UPI), prepaid payment instruments (PPIS), national electronic funds transfer (NEFT), social media banking which forms a part of AI provides higher accessibility to its customers. ML and deep learning techniques are specifically designed to cater niche problems in banking sector.

4.4.4 AI Helps in Offering Innovative and Tailor-Made Services

Utilizing deep learning for customer analytics makes it simpler to consolidate bits of knowledge from different information sources; for example, exchanges and Internet banking logs. It assists with understanding a customer in a better way and makes customized proposals and shrewd customer aides, making the business more responsive and proficient.

For banks, improving the client experience is basic. "For low-complexity tasks, consumers considered the problem-solving ability of AI to be greater than that of human customer service and were more likely to use AI." [14] Alexa and Google Home are currently normal family unit mates, permitting purchasers to appreciate extraordinary collaborations. Also, individuals have generally expected similar degree of administration from their banks. Simulated intelligence driven advances can convey profoundly customized client encounters. Intelligent voice and chatbots, not accessible in a pre-AI period, are changing and reshaping how banks cooperate and speak with customers. Like an Alexa for banking that can provide individual computerized aides, assist buyers with getting to an abundance of data on planning, putting something aside for retirement, and then some custom-made to their financial requirements. With better understanding and more personalization, banks can more accurately respond to market needs, creating a fitting customer experience and gaining a competitive advantage. Every customer has distinct needs according to their spending, habits, activities, behavioural characteristics and income generation. AI develops a better understanding of customers and their behaviour. This enables banks to customize financial products and services by adding personalized features and intuitive interactions to deliver meaningful customer engagement and build strong relationships with its customers.

4.4.5 AI Helps in Reducing Customer Attrition

Customer churn (or customer steady loss) is a propensity of customers to surrender a brand and quit being a paying customer of a specific business. Customer retention is one of the primary growth pillars for any organization. AI helps the banks for increasing the number of customers, retaining the existing customers and reducing the customer churn at a time. Reduced customer churn is possible because AI helps to understand the behaviour, attitude, perception and buying and saving behaviour of customers in a better creative way and create personalized recommendation to the banks. AI through the use of accurate algorithms makes the business more responsive and efficient and through which the churn probability predictions improve customer retention. Also due to precise AI algorithms, churn probability predictions improve client maintenance. This is critical as clients every now and again mix without evident notice signs. On the opposite side, maintenance exercises can be exorbitant, now and then substantially more so than the worth a potential client may bring. Therefore, AI can play a major role in reducing the customer attrition and in bringing more loyal customers for the banks.

4.4.6   IMPACT OF AI ON OVERALL PERFORMANCE

ML, blockchain and data analytics are some of the technologies which have the ability to impact the overall performance of the banks. AI has the potential to increase the performance of banks by mitigating risk, reducing NPA and Fraud, assessing the credit score and enhancing quality customer services which have the significant impact on the earnings of the banks. AI is changing financial services, offering more prominent benefit to clients through chatbots and personalization, limiting dangers and costs, improving worker profitability and guaranteeing higher administrative consistence. Despite the fact that these are just the unassumed beginnings of AI usage, clearly before long it will turn into the operational hub of the financial business. As AI does all the routine and tedious work of the employees more accurately and effectively, the employees can deploy their time on taking important business decisions which helps in improving the overall performance of banking sector. AI application can manage the risk which is very much crucial for the better performance of banks. So, it can be cited that the application of AI enabled technique can add significant economic value which in turn impact the overall performance of the banks.

Through this write-up much has been talked about, AL and ML and finally it can be concluded this can be treated as an improved productivity tool for the Indian banking sector. AI has got a bright and promising future in India. AI can provide large incremental value to many sectors, which may be energy, retail, manufacturing, healthcare, education, agriculture, insurance and banks. That will also mean increase in the opportunity for jobs in all these sectors, each for AI experts and others.

4.5   CONCLUSION AND FUTURE OF AI

To conclude, AI is gaining popularity day by day and banks are exploring and implementing this technology in transforming the way customers are assisted. The universe of banking is moving quicker than any time in recent memory, with AI driving the path in getting ocean change in the financial business. Various AI technologies have been applied in banking in fields such as core banking, operational performance, customer support and analytics. The introduction of new banking services by modern day banks is helping them to grow and expand. AI is simply going to turn out to be more significant and omnipresent pushing ahead and will surely keep on having exceptionally huge effects on present day culture. AI as a tool plays a significant role for the growth and development of the banks by helping in almost all areas of activities like mitigating the risk, protecting from the fraudulent activities, serving the customers quick queries through chatbots, helping algorithm-based marketing etc. Adoption of AI application by the banks will be the key to gain a competitive edge by offering fast, secure personalized banking experience to their customers. Banks to achieve the highest level of result in terms of employee productivity, overall performance, profitability, reduced cost and less customer churn, needs to perform its activities in collaboration with machine. Many of the Indian banks are now finding solace in the new days technology like AI, IoT, Cloud computing, blockchain and many more. By the use of AI banks can provide magnifying customer service and experience as well as strengthen the security and control risk in a more effective manner. AI helps in magnifying efficiency of banks by providing credit scoring, Automation Complain Management, maintaining CRM and KYC and Data driven lending decisions in cost efficient, accurate and faster manner. In excess of 36% of huge monetary organizations are as of now putting resources into these advances, and just about 70% report that they are planning to apply it soon. In India, banks having large market capitalization and turnover like State Bank of India, HDFC, Axis Bank, PNB, etc have already applied AI in many areas of its functionaries starting from chatbots to CRM and fraud detection. Application of AI in banking sector has shown a huge benefit in terms of increasing profitability, efficiency and customer satisfaction, reducing cost and customer attrition as well as helps in achieving all the parameters of Key Performance Index. With AI-driven robotization, banks will use machine abilities to upgrade activities, decrease manual mistakes, let workers centre around and will be cost-effective.

The future of Artificial Intelligence in banking sector is very bright and with the introduction of AI, it makes it even easier for a customer to do transactions from any place and at any time without waiting in long queues at the bank. The AI technology is constantly evolving, and no one among us really knows how AI will surprise us next, but at the same time all the banks need to take advantages of the power of AI in order to stay competitive. The future of AI in banking looks much clearer, which will help the banks in increasing its revenue multi-fold times. Although there are certain fears like job loss and process opacity, reduced customer loyalty is associated with the increase in implementation of AI in future but we should be more adaptive and prepared for the obvious change coming in the near future.

REFERENCES

1. Adam, M., Wessel, M., and Benlian, A. (2020) "AI-Based Chatbots in Customer Service and their Effects on User Compliance", *Electronic Markets.* doi:10.1007/s12525-020-00414-7
2. Alzaidi, A. (2018) "Impact of Artificial Intelligence on Performance of Banking Industry in Middle East", *International Journal of Computer Science and Network Security,* http://paper.ijcsns.org/07_book/201810/20181021.pdf.
3. Hassija, T. and Srivastava, P. (2020) "Impact of Artificial Intelligence in Customer Satisfaction for Banking Industrys", *International Journal of Advanced Science and Technology,* Volume 29, issue 9s, pp. 1947–1962.

4. https://www.idrbt.ac.in/assets/publications/Best%20Practices/2020/AI_2020.pdf

5. https://www.managedoutsource.com/blog/6-ways-artificial-intelligence-is-changing-the-banking-sector/

6. https://www.mckinsey.com/~/media/mckinsey/industries/advanced%20electronics/our%20insights/how%20artificial%20intelligence%20can%20deliver%20real%20value%20to%20companies/mgi-artificial-intelligence-discussion-paper.ashx

7. Kumar, S. and Akalya, A. (2020) "Impact and Challenges of Artificial Intelligence in Banking", *Journal of Information and Computational Science*, Volume 10, Issue 2, pp 1101–1109.

8. Lakshminarayana, N. and Deepthi, B. R. (2019) "Advent of Artificial Intelligence and its Impact on Top Leading Commercial Banks in India – Case Study", *International Journal of Trend in Scientific Research and Development*, Volume: 3, Issue: 4, e-ISSN: 2456 – 6470.

9. Prentice, C., Lopes, S., and Wang, X. (2020) "The Impact of Artificial Intelligence and Employee Service Quality On Customer Satisfaction And Loyalty", *Journal of Hospitality Marketing and Management*, ISSN: 1936–8623.

10. Sahdev, S., Sharma, M., Kaur, N. and Siddiqui, L. (2020) "Banking 4.0: The Influence Of Artificial Intelligence On The Banking Industry and How Ai Is Changing The Face Of Modern Day Banks", *International Journal of Management*, Volume 11, Issue 6, pp. 577–585.

11. Salunkhe, R. (2019) "Role of Artificial Intelligence In Providing Customer Services With Special Reference to SBI and HDFC Bank", *International Journal of Recent Technology and Engineering (IJRTE)*, Volume-8, Issue 4, November 2019, ISSN: 2277–3878.

12. Smith, A. and Nobanee, H. (2020). "Artificial Intelligence: In Banking A Mini-Review", *SSRN Electronic Journal*. doi:10.2139/ssrn.3539171.

13. Vijai, C. (2019) "Artificial Intelligence in Indian Banking Sector: Challenges and Opportunities", *International Journal of Advanced Research*, ISSN: 2320-5407. doi:10.21474/IJAR01/8987.

14. Xua, Y., Shiehb, C., Escha, P., and Ling I. (2020) "AI Customer Service: Task Complexity, Problem-Solving Ability, And Usage Intention", *Australasian Marketing Journal*. doi:10.1016/j.ausmj.2020.03.005.

5 Analysis and Comparison of Credit Card Fraud Detection Using Machine Learning

Saloni and Minakhi Rout
School of Computer Engineering, KIIT Deemed
to be University, Bhubaneswar, Odisha, India

CONTENTS

5.1 INTRODUCTION

A credit card is a plastic card consisting of a thin rectangular slab including a magnetic strip which is issued by the financial institution to their customers. These cards are provided to the customers so that they can buy items without paying by cash or cheque. The financial institution pre-sets the limit of their cards before giving it to customers as per their monthly income, and fraud is defined as wrong activity carried out by illegitimate persons by misrepresenting themselves either for money or property gain. Therefore, credit card scams are nothing but the gaining of confidential information like password, CVV number, etc. by the intruders. So, we need credit card fraud detection technique is required to protect the cardholders from false activity.

India is on its way to becoming a developed country. To achieve this, the Government of India (GoI) has launched several initiatives, and one of these is the Digital India Campaign. The main intention of government through this initiative is to digitally empower the nation. One of its main tasks includes the promotion of a cashless economy, which can be operated by making transactions with debit card, credit card, net banking, UPIs etc. as modes of payment, rather than going for regular cash or cheque payments. GoI and RBI have focused immensely on digitalizing the

DOI: 10.1201/9781003125129-5

transactions. These have come in handy at the time of crisis which includes the ongoing COVID-19 pandemic, and demonetization by GoI in 2016.

The government and the other financial institutions have recommended to opt for digital transaction because of its several advantages. One of the most important benefits of digital transaction is that it saves time. Customers no longer have to visit ATMs and stand in a queue to withdraw money. Whenever they want to make payment, they just have to swipe the card and enter the PIN or need to provide the OTP while doing online shopping. Another important reason for the promotion of electronic transaction is to trace the flow of black money and charge tax defaulters.

This transforming technology comes with some disadvantages too; cybersecurity being one of them. Online transactions are done on compromise of our sensitive information. Any sort of data breach can result in huge loss for both the service provider as well as the customer. This is one of the major issues of the contemporary world, where intruders make use of the slightest loophole in the system to carry out fraud transactions. So, we are in a dire need of being able to keep a check on the techniques being used to identify the loopholes and detect the fraudsters associated.

This threat is globally recognized, and it can be carried out in ways like skimming, phishing, stealing of credit card etc. Different sources can be responsible for the same. This can be done by the customer or bank/credit card service provider, or by a third party. A customer who makes payment using their credit card and fails to repay the amount falls into this category. Bank/credit card service providers create transactions by charging for crossing the limits or late payments or cash withdrawals from the customer. But the major threat is that of third parties. In this case, if the third party is able to obtain sensitive data of the card holder, results can be abysmal.

The rest of this chapter is as follows: Section 5.2 presents research that consists of similar kind of problem statements in this area. Section 5.3 presents the proposed method for the implementation of research work whereas Section 5.4 consists of results and finally the conclusion and future scope is presented in Section 5.5.

5.2 RELATED WORK

Thulasyammal Ramiah Pillai et al. [1] have used MLP to identify fraud. They have tuned parameters such as activation function, number of neurons and number of hidden layers to compare the performance of the model. They have found that logistic activation function with 10 and 100 neurons and 3 hidden layer models, and in case of hyperbolic tangent activation function when the node is 1,000 and number of hidden layers is 1, 2 and 3, give the most sensitive scores.

Mohamad Zamini et al. [2,3], have proposed a deep learning model with auto-encoder to detect credit card fraud. In [2] the author has suggested to use an unsupervised method for fraud detection, for which they have used an auto-encoder having 3 hidden layers and a k-means clustering. The implementation results show that their proposed method has outperformed when compared with other models. In [3] the authors have used different methods, such as K-nearest neighbour (KNN), Genetic Programming (GP), Self-Organizing Mapping (SOM) along with auto-encoder for extraction of relevant features and Softmax to determine whether the class label belongs to fraudulent or non-fraudulent.

Aji Mubarek Mubalaike et al. [4], have suggested the deep learning model which provides an efficient result in the determination of fraud transactions. They have used Ensemble of Decision Tree (EDT), Stacked auto-encoders (SAE) and Restricted Boltzmann Machines (RBM) for classifications. On comparative analysis the results shows that the RBM provides better results.

Abhimanyu Roy et al. [5], have done analysis on the data set using various deep learning topologies such as Artificial Neural Networks (ANN), Recurrent Neural Networks (RNN), LSTM and GRU. After the implementation it has been observed that LSTM and GRU perform better than ANN.

Dilip Singh Sisodia et al. [6], proposed different sampling methods to handle imbalance data sets apart from SMOTE. At the end of the experiment, they have observed that SMOTE ENN detects fraud in better way. Also, in [7] Yu Xie, et al has discussed about different methods for feature extraction.

Dr V Ceronmani Sharmila et al. [8], have used anomaly techniques for the detection of fraud in credit card. They have used Local Outlier Factor (LOF) and Isolation Forest Algorithm (IFA) algorithm for anomaly detection.

However, in [9], E. Saraswathi et al., have proposed the model which has used ANN and Self-Organizing Mapping (SOM) for the efficient detection of fraud.

Yang Wang et al. [10], have proposed model for privacy preservation by using distributed deep learning framework. They have used Report-NoisyMax algorithm to select the large absolute gradient to guarantee its privacy.

5.3 PROPOSED METHOD

All the experiments are conducted in the Python 3.7.7 programming language. The software operating environment is Jupyter notebook 6.0.3 which is a part of Anaconda platform. This research experiment has implemented deep learning architecture like LSTM, GRU, CNN, and Multilayer Perceptron (MLP) by using Keras library with Tensorflow library as back end. Some other libraries which have been used are numpy, scipy, pandas, matplotlib, matplotlib, seaborn, sklearn, imblearn. All the data sets have been split in the ratio of 20:80. Figure 5.1 shows the flowchart of the experiment.

The experiment has been done on three publicly available data sets which are the German data set, the Taiwanese data set and the European data set. The European and Taiwanese data sets have been downloaded from Kaggle website, and the German data set has been downloaded from UCI repository. The German credit card data set consists of 25 features and 1,000 transactions out which only 300 are fraudulent. The Taiwanese credit card data set has 25 features and 30,000 transactions, out of which 6,636 are fraudulent, and the European credit card data set consists of 31 features and 2,84,807 transactions, of which 492 are fraudulent. These data sets are all highly imbalanced.

After collecting the raw data, the pre-processing step has been applied to these data before feeding it into the deep learning-based classifiers algorithm. The pre-processing of data involves basically three steps, which are Data Cleaning, Data Reduction and Data Transformation. In this proposed method, initially it checked whether there are any missing or inconsistent values in these collected data sets or not. And it has found that there were no missing values present in any of the three

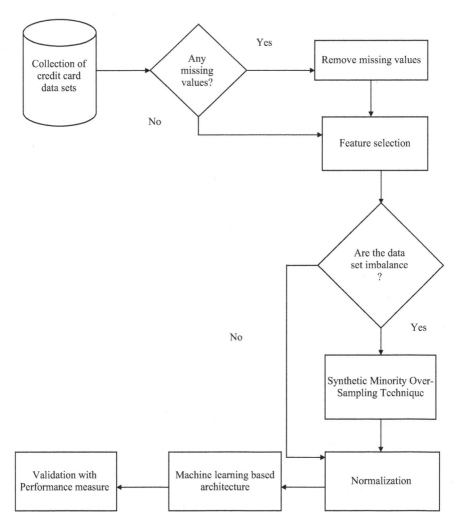

FIGURE 5.1   Flowchart of proposed model for credit card fraud detection.

data sets. Then, univariate feature selection has been applied on these data sets in which only 75% features were selected, which means in European data sets only 22 features and in Taiwanese and German data sets only 18 features got selected. Feature selection is important because it helps in reducing training time, improving accuracy and limiting the over-fitting problem of the model.

Moreover, all the data sets are highly imbalanced as per the statistics observed. The European data set has only 0.00173 fraudulent transactions, while the Taiwanese data set has 0.2212 and the German data sets have 0.3 fraudulent transactions. To overcome the problem of imbalanced data sets we have applied SMOTE. SMOTE helps to balance the class distribution.

Furthermore, all the collected data sets consist of different numerical values. To make it into the range of 0 and 1, standard scalar normalization technique has been applied. In deep learning, normalization has been considered as the best practice for training a neural network and also helps in speeding up the learning which leads to faster convergence.

After pre-processing, these data sets were feed into different deep learning based architecture such as LSTM, GRU, CNN, and Multilayer Perceptron (MLP) for analysis. For the evaluation purpose different evaluation metrics such as accuracy, precision, recall, F1, MCC score of each model have been computed but our main focus is on the F1 score.

5.4   RESULTS

The research experiment has been performed using deep learning architecture such as LSTM, GRU, CNN, and Multilayer Perceptron (MLP) on the German data sets, then on the Taiwanese data sets and finally on the European data sets. For analysis and comparison of model we have tuned the parameter such as activation function, number of hidden layers and the number of neurons in hidden layers of deep learning architecture. In this experiment relu, sigmoid, tanh and swish activation function and 1 hidden layer and 2 hidden layers have been used while the number of neurons remain constant. The number of epochs used in each implementation is 150. The number of input neuron has been taken as 22 when the model is implemented on European data set while the number of input neuron has been taken 18 when the model is implemented on Taiwanese and German data sets. As the data sets are imbalance so, this experiment has considered F1 score for evaluation of the proposed model. Table 5.1 shows the results obtained from German datasets.

As the implementation has been done using four deep learning architecture, it can be observed from Table 5.1 that the accuracy of training and testing set in most of the cases is good. Moreover, whenever the parameters of the architecture (i.e, the number of hidden layers and activation functions has been tuned), it has observed that there is a slight variation in the results. In all the architectures it has been observed that the architecture with two hidden layers provides better results when compared with architecture with one hidden layer. Also, in each of the architectures it has been observed that the best results are obtained when the architecture is implemented with sigmoid activation function with two hidden layers. Here, from the above table it can be illustrated that the MLP architecture with sigmoid activation function and two hidden layers is providing precision of 0.68, recall of 0.51, F1 score of 0.56 and MCC score of 0.411. While in CNN architecture with sigmoid activation function and two hidden layers the precision is 0.60, recall is 0.57, F1 score is 0.58, MCC score is 0.413. Whereas in LSTM architecture with sigmoid activation function and two hidden layers the precision is 0.54, recall is 0.57, F1 score is 0.55, MCC score is 0.350. In GRU architecture with sigmoid activation function and two hidden layers the precision is 0.49, recall is 0.76, F1 score is 0.60, MCC score is 0.388. But as in this experiment F1 score has been considered as its main evaluation metrics so, among all the four architecture the best F1 score which is 0.60 has been achieved by GRU with sigmoid activation function and two hidden layers. Figure 5.2 represents the ROC curve on German data set which is obtained by the GRU architecture using sigmoid

TABLE 5.1

Results from the German Data Set

Model Name	NH	Activation Function	NN	Precision	Recall	F1	MCC	Tra	Tea	ROC
MLP	1	Relu	10	0.58	0.11	0.18	0.147	0.7450	0.7088	0.759
	2	Relu	10	0.70	0.27	0.39	0.315	0.7350	0.7437	0.773
	1	tanh	10	1.00	0.03	0.05	0.132	0.6900	0.7075	0.774
	2	tanh	10	0.61	0.30	0.40	0.281	0.7350	0.7325	0.773
	1	sigmoid	10	0.66	0.41	0.51	0.380	0.7500	0.7613	0.778
	2	sigmoid	10	0.68	0.51	0.56	0.411	0.7850	0.7650	0.794
	1	swish	10	0.49	0.15	0.23	0.1349	0.7500	0.6989	0.589
	2	swish	10	0.55	0.24	0.34	0.2168	0.7700	0.7144	0.659
CNN	1	Relu	10	0.67	0.01	0.02	0.049	0.7150	0.7013	0.665
	2	Relu	10	0.71	0.02	0.04	0.084	0.7100	0.7038	0.617
	1	tanh	10	0.67	0.06	0.11	0.131	0.7150	0.7088	0.709
	2	tanh	10	0.52	0.19	0.28	0.165	0.7500	0.7033	0.728
	1	sigmoid	10	0.64	0.20	0.31	0.230	0.7950	0.7262	0.752
	2	sigmoid	10	0.60	0.57	0.58	0.413	0.7650	0.7575	0.786
	1	swish	10	0.60	0.01	0.02	0.051	0.7150	0.7013	0.669
	2	swish	10	0.71	0.02	0.04	0.084	0.7100	0.7038	0.617
LSTM	1	Relu	10	0.53	0.19	0.27	0.1728	0.6600	0.6733	0.594
	2	Relu	10	0.40	0.31	0.35	0.121	0.7350	0.6550	0.604
	1	tanh	10	0.48	0.49	0.48	0.259	0.8650	0.6862	0.712
	2	tanh	10	0.56	0.53	0.55	0.360	0.7750	0.7362	0.768
	1	sigmoid	10	0.42	0.33	0.37	0.147	0.8350	0.6650	0.644
	2	sigmoid	10	0.54	0.57	0.55	0.350	0.7350	0.7225	0.751
	1	swish	10	0.54	0.19	0.28	0.179	0.7000	0.6787	0.658
	2	swish	10	0.39	0.33	0.35	0.109	0.7150	0.6425	0.541
GRU	1	Relu	10	0.75	0.02	0.04	0.0929	0.7100	0.7022	0.455
	2	Relu	10	0.58	0.18	0.27	0.1935	0.7200	0.7000	0.623
	1	tanh	10	0.67	0.15	0.25	0.190	0.7100	0.7237	0.665
	2	tanh	10	0.59	0.21	0.31	0.757	0.7500	0.7488	0.216
	1	sigmoid	10	0.54	0.47	0.50	0.309	0.7700	0.7100	0.763
	2	sigmoid	10	0.49	0.76	0.60	0.388	0.7650	0.6925	0.752
	1	swish	10	0.48	0.05	0.09	0.07	0.6700	0.6900	0.484
	2	swish	10	0.84	0.07	0.12	0.184	0.7100	0.7163	0.757

NH = Number of hidden layers, NN = Number of neurons, Tra = Training Accuracy, Tea = Testing Accuracy.

activation function and two hidden layers and Figure 5.3 represents the statistics of different parameters used for the evaluation of model using 2 hidden layers.

After the implementation on the German data sets, the implementation has been done on the Taiwanese data sets. Table 5.2 shows the results obtained from the Taiwanese data set.

Here, also from Table 5.2 it can be seen that in each of the architecture it has been observed that the best results are obtained when the architecture is implemented with sigmoid activation function with two hidden layers. From the above Table 5.2 it can be illustrated that the MLP architecture with sigmoid activation function and two

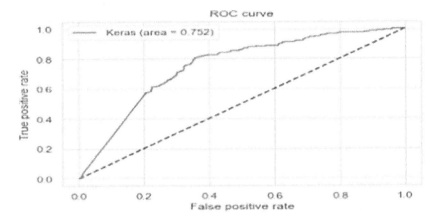

FIGURE 5.2 ROC curve for GRU model using sigmoid activation function and 2 hidden layers.

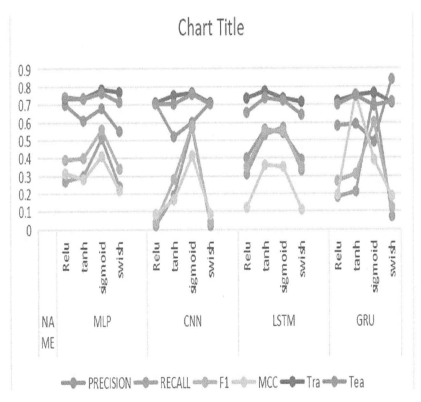

FIGURE 5.3 Graphical representation of performance of all models using 2 hidden layers on the German data sets.

TABLE 5.2
Results from the Taiwanese Data Set

Model Name	NH	Activation Function	NN	Precision	Recall	F1	MCC	Tra	Tea	ROC
	1	Relu	10	0.62	0.002	0.003	0.028	0.7792	0.7788	0.621
	2	Relu	10	0.27	0.00056	0.00054	0.002	0.7797	0.7788	0.633
	1	tanh	10	0.38	0.40	0.39	0.209	0.7787	0.7788	0.700
	2	tanh	10	0.40	0.39	0.40	0.228	0.7787	0.7788	0.710
	1	sigmoid	10	0.61	0.32	0.42	0.341	0.7787	0.7788	0.317
	2	sigmoid	10	0.60	0.33	0.43	0.339	0.7787	0.7788	0.496
	1	swish	10	0.16	0.06	0.08	0.04	0.7783	0.7788	0.387
	2	swish	10	0.17	0.36	0.23	0.11	0.7787	0.7788	0.428
CNN	1	Relu	10	0.68	0.02	0.03	0.844	0.7937	0.7809	0.739
	2	Relu	10	0.66	0.18	0.28	0.266	0.7933	0.7978	0.718
	1	tanh	10	0.61	0.32	0.42	0.3378	0.7527	0.8038	0.706
	2	tanh	10	0.58	0.34	0.43	0.3365	0.7283	0.8006	0.694
	1	sigmoid	10	0.67	0.28	0.39	0.3424	0.8003	0.8095	0.732
	2	sigmoid	10	0.65	0.39	0.49	0.402	0.8178	0.8179	0.758
	1	swish	10	0.22	1.00	0.36	0.003	0.7363	0.7363	0.622
	2	swish	10	0.66	0.26	0.38	0.3283	0.7983	0.8070	0.721
LSTM	1	Relu	10	0.19	0.01	0.02	0.007	0.7437	0.7687	0.499
		Relu	10	0.17	0.02	0.03	0.02	0.7160	0.7582	0.495
	1	tanh	10	0.67	0.37	0.47	0.399	0.8227	0.8196	0.753
	2	tanh	10	0.66	0.38	0.49	0.405	0.8213	0.8196	0.749
	1	sigmoid	10	0.63	0.40	0.49	0.401	0.8120	0.8161	0.746
	2	sigmoid	10	0.64	0.41	0.50	0.407	0.8200	0.8176	0.749
	1	swish	10	0.20	0.07	0.10	0.013	0.4240	0.7183	0.536
	2	swish	10	0.20	0.13	0.16	0.022	0.6697	0.6623	0.480
GRU	1	Relu	10	0.29	0.15	0.19	0.037	0.7210	0.6844	0.515
	2	Relu	10	0.23	0.39	0.29	0.013	0.7050	0.4872	0.500
	1	tanh	10	0.64	0.35	0.45	0.369	0.8073	0.8115	0.736
	2	tanh	10	0.65	0.40	0.49	0.406	0.8240	0.8186	0.755
	1	sigmoid	10	0.62	0.42	0.51	0.4123	0.8237	0.8181	0.752
	2	sigmoid	10	0.63	0.43	0.51	0.4130	0.8167	0.8176	0.750
	1	swish	10	0.22	1.00	0.36	0.003	0.7723	0.7788	0.500
	2	swish	10	0.65	0.39	0.49	0.402	0.7640	0.7788	0.758

hidden layers is providing precision of 0.60, recall of 0.33, F1 score of 0.43 and MCC score of 0.339. While in CNN architecture with sigmoid activation function and two hidden layers the precision is 0.65, recall is 0.39, F1 score is 0.49, MCC score is 0.402. Whereas in LSTM architecture with sigmoid activation function and two hidden layers the precision is 0.64, recall is 0.41, F1 score is 0.50, MCC score is 0.407. And in GRU architecture with sigmoid activation function and two hidden layers the precision is 0.63, recall is 0.43, F1 score is 0.51, MCC score is 0.4130. But as in this experiment F1 score has been considered as its main evaluation metrics so, among all the four architecture the best F1 score which is 0.51 has been achieved by GRU with sigmoid activation function and two hidden layers. Below Figure 5.4 represents the ROC curve on Taiwanese data set which is obtained by the GRU architecture using sigmoid activation function and 2 hidden layers. Moreover, Figure 5.5

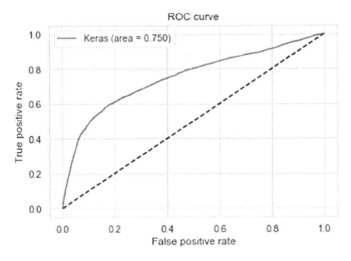

FIGURE 5.4 ROC curve for GRU model using sigmoid activation function and 2 hidden layers.

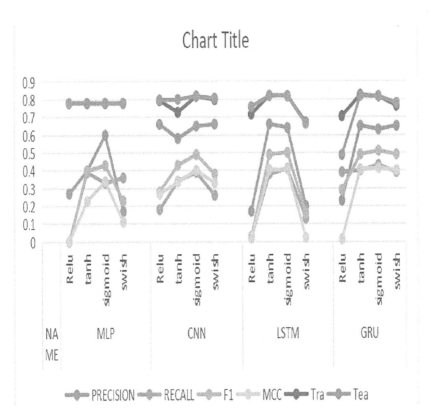

FIGURE 5.5 Graphical representation of performance of all models using 2 hidden layers on the Taiwanese data sets.

represents the statistics of different parameters used for the evaluation of model using 2 hidden layers.

In addition to the German data set and the Taiwanese data set the implementation is also carried out in the European data set. Below Table 5.3 shows the results from the European data set:

From Table 5.3 it can be seen that here also, in each of the architectures it has been observed that the best results are obtained when the architecture is implemented with sigmoid activation function with two hidden layers. From Table 5.3 it can be illustrated that the MLP architecture with sigmoid activation function and two hidden layers is providing precision of 0.87, recall of 0.79, F1 score of 0.83 and MCC score of 0.829. While in CNN architecture with sigmoid activation function and two

TABLE 5.3
Results from the European Data Set

Model name	NH	Activation Function	NN	Precision	Recall	F1	MCC	Tra	Tea	ROC
MLP	1	Relu	10	0.85	0.81	0.83	0.825	0.9983	0.9981	0.905
	2	Relu	10	0.84	0.81	0.83	0.824	0.9985	0.9986	0.953
	1	tanh	10	0.84	0.81	0.83	0.824	0.9906	0.9973	0.938
	2	tanh	10	0.84	0.81	0.83	0.824	0.9867	0.9966	0.940
	1	sigmoid	10	0.85	0.81	0.83	0.825	0.9983	0.9981	0.905
	2	sigmoid	10	0.87	0.79	0.83	0.829	0.9984	0.9986	0.970
	1	swish	10	0.86	0.79	0.83	0.825	0.9985	0.9985	0.967
	2	swish	10	0.87	0.79	0.83	0.829	0.9984	0.9986	0.970
CNN	1	Relu	10	0.84	0.42	0.56	0.5958	0.9984	0.9989	0.753
	2	Relu	10	0.83	0.78	0.80	0.8039	0.9992	0.9993	0.889
	1	tanh	10	0.85	0.79	0.82	0.8186	0.9993	0.9994	0.954
	2	tanh	10	0.83	0.80	0.82	0.8151	0.9992	0.9994	0.967
	1	sigmoid	10	0.88	0.75	0.81	0.8137	0.9989	0.9994	0.958
	2	sigmoid	10	0.83	0.80	0.82	0.8151	0.9991	0.9994	0.966
	1	swish	10	0.84	0.73	0.78	0.7811	0.9989	0.9993	0.871
	2	swish	10	0.83	0.80	0.81	0.8136	0.9993	0.9994	0.912
LSTM	1	Relu	10	0.87	0.55	0.68	0.694	0.9985	0.9984	0.500
	2	Relu	10	0.84	0.69	0.76	0.760	0.9984	0.9984	0.902
	1	tanh	10	0.86	0.66	0.74	0.929	0.105	0.0012	0.929
	2	tanh	10	0.84	0.79	0.82	0.815	0.4649	0.3992	0.923
	1	sigmoid	10	0.84	0.79	0.81	0.814	0.9992	0.9994	0.929
	2	sigmoid	10	0.84	0.79	0.82	0.8153	0.9980	0.9980	0.946
	1	swish	10	0.86	0.72	0.78	0.789	0.9982	0.9982	0.922
	2	swish	10	0.84	0.78	0.81	0.807	0.9994	0.9994	0.922
GRU	1	Relu	10	0.83	0.36	0.50	0.542	0.9984	0.9988	0.910
	2	Relu	10	0.82	0.39	0.53	0.566	0.9985	0.9985	0.908
	1	tanh	10	0.89	0.73	0.80	0.802	0.0017	0.0013	0.925
	2	tanh	10	0.84	0.78	0.81	0.809	0.1816	0.0659	0.931
	1	sigmoid	10	0.95	0.80	0.87	0.874	0.9995	0.9995	0.947
	2	sigmoid	10	0.96	0.82	0.89	0.868	0.9996	0.9996	0.950
	1	swish	10	0.87	0.72	0.79	0.792	0.9981	0.9981	0.909
	2	swish	10	0.86	0.78	0.82	0.817	0.9981	0.9981	0.909

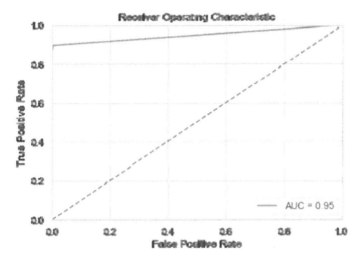

FIGURE 5.6 ROC curve for GRU model using sigmoid activation function and 2 hidden layers.

hidden layers the precision is 0.83, recall is 0.80, F1 score is 0.82, MCC score is 0.8151. Whereas in LSTM architecture with sigmoid activation function and two hidden layers the precision is 0.84, recall is 0.79, F1 score is 0.82, MCC score is 0.8153. And in GRU architecture with sigmoid activation function and two hidden layers the precision is 0.96, recall is 0.82, F1 score is 0.89, MCC score is 0.868. But here also F1 score has been considered as prime evaluation metrics so, among all the four architecture the best F1 score which is 0.89 has been achieved by GRU with sigmoid activation function and two hidden layers. Below Figure 5.6 represents the ROC curve on the European data set which is obtained by the GRU architecture using sigmoid activation function and 2 hidden layers whereas Figure 5.7 represents the statistics of different parameters used for the evaluation of model using 2 hidden layers.

5.5 CONCLUSION AND FUTURE SCOPE

A comparative analysis has been made to determine the fraudulent transaction by using various deep learning architecture such as LSTM, CNN, GRU, MLP. The proposed model was implemented on three publicly available data sets. As all the data sets were highly imbalanced, SMOTE technique has been used to get rid of it whereas F1 score have considered for the evaluation purpose. It has found that, among all the deep learning architectures implemented on three of the data set, the highest F1 score is achieved by the GRU model with sigmoid activation function and 2 hidden layers. On the German data set, the highest F1 score is achieved by the GRU model with sigmoid activation function having 2 hidden layers which is 0.60. While on the Taiwanese data set, the highest F1 score is achieved by the GRU model with sigmoid activation function having 2 hidden layers is 0.51. And on the European data sets, the highest F1 score is achieved by the GRU model with sigmoid activation function and

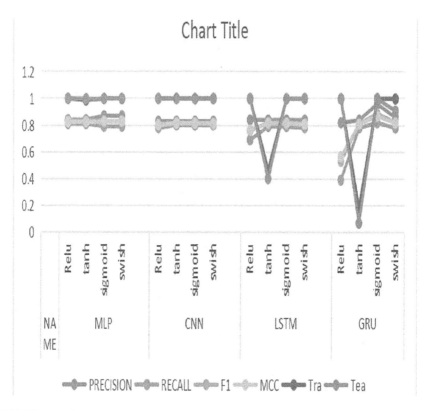

FIGURE 5.7 Graphical representation of performance of all models using 2 hidden layers on the European data set.

2 hidden layers which is 0.89. In future some more deep learning architectures and their parameters can be explored to improve the performance of this proposed model. In this analysis, limited numbers of hidden layers have been used and also the number of neurons in each hidden layer have kept constant. So, further research is likely to vary the number of layers and neurons in each layer to get insight into the effect on performance by increasing the network size.

REFERENCES

1. Pillai, T. R., Hashem, I. A. T., Brohi, S. N., Kaur, S., & Marjani, M. (2018, October). *Credit Card Fraud Detection Using Deep Learning Technique*. In *2018 Fourth International Conference on Advances in Computing, Communication & Automation (ICACCA)* (pp. 1–6). IEEE.
2. Zamini, M., & Montazer, G. (2018, December). Credit card fraud detection using auto-encoder based clustering. In *2018 9th International Symposium on Telecommunications (IST)* (pp. 486–491). IEEE.
3. Kazemi, Z., & Zarrabi, H. (2017, December). *Using deep networks for fraud detection in the credit card transactions*. In *2017 IEEE 4th International Conference on Knowledge-Based Engineering and Innovation (KBEI)* (pp. 0630–0633). IEEE.

4. Mubalaike, A. M., & Adali, E. (2018, September). *Deep Learning Approach for Intelligent Financial Fraud Detection System.* In *2018 3rd International Conference on Computer Science and Engineering (UBMK)* (pp. 598–603). IEEE.

5. Roy, A., Sun, J., Mahoney, R., Alonzi, L., Adams, S., & Beling, P. (2018, April). *Deep learning detecting fraud in credit card transactions.* In *2018 Systems and Information Engineering Design Symposium (SIEDS)* (pp. 129–134). IEEE.

6. Sisodia, D. S., Reddy, N. K., & Bhandari, S. (2017, September). *Performance evaluation of class balancing techniques for credit card fraud detection.* In *2017 IEEE International Conference on Power, Control, Signals and Instrumentation Engineering (ICPCSI)* (pp. 2747–2752). IEEE.

7. Xie, Y., Liu, G., Cao, R., Li, Z., Yan, C., & Jiang, C. (2019, February). *A Feature Extraction Method for Credit Card Fraud Detection.* In *2019 2nd International Conference on Intelligent Autonomous Systems (ICoIAS)* (pp. 70–75). IEEE.

8. Sharmila, V. C., Kumar, K., Sundaram, R., Samyuktha, D., & Harish, R. (2019, April). *Credit Card Fraud Detection Using Anomaly Techniques.* In *2019 1st International Conference on Innovations in Information and Communication Technology (ICIICT)* (pp. 1–6). IEEE.

9. Saraswathi, E., Kulkarni, P., Khalil, M. N., & Nigam, S. C. (2019, March). *Credit Card Fraud Prediction and Detection using Artificial Neural Network And Self-Organizing Maps.* In *2019 3rd International Conference on Computing Methodologies and Communication (ICCMC)* (pp. 1124–1128). IEEE.

10. Wang, Y., Adams, S., Beling, P., Greenspan, S., Rajagopalan, S., Velez-Rojas, M., ... & Brown, D. (2018, August). *Privacy preserving distributed deep learning and its application in credit card fraud detection.* In *2018 17th IEEE International Conference on Trust, Security and Privacy In Computing And Communications/12th IEEE International Conference on Big Data Science and Engineering (TrustCom/BigDataSE)* (pp. 1070–1078). IEEE.

6 Artificial Intelligence for All

Machine Learning and Healthcare: Challenges and Perspectives in India

Sanghmitra Patnaik and Parthasarathi Pattnayak
School of Computer Applications, KIIT Deemed to be
University, Odisha, India

CONTENTS

DOI: 10.1201/9781003125129-6

The right to health is an inclusive right extending not only to timely and appropriate healthcare but also to the underlying determinants of health, such as access to safe and potable water and adequate sanitation, an adequate supply of safe food, nutrition and housing, healthy occupational and environmental conditions, and access to health-related education and information... – Committee on Economic, Social and Cultural Rights, General Comment No. 14 [1]

6.1   INTRODUCTION

Clinical data of each patient play a determinant role in prescribing the methods of treatment for a particular patient. Information leads to the improvement in health-care. With the help of clinical data, ML exercises influence on automatic speech recognition (ASR), computer vision and natural language processing (NLP). Its ability to extract information from data related to healthcare helps to do further research in ML.

The increasing scope for ML in healthcare covers various fields such as diabetic retinopathy, autism and detection of lymph node metastases from breast pathology. In spite of these developments, the application of ML in healthcare has been facing various challenges. Most of these issues are originated from personalized predictions. Instead of supporting healthcare, data are used only to facilitate subsequent analysis.

AI supports ML in the field of large population-level data sets like electronic health records (EHRs), medical imaging and whole-genome studies. This information is useful for high-risk individuals. Current applications can be used, for example, to predict clinical outcomes like in-hospital mortality, final discharge diagnoses of patients and prolonged length of stay, in great numbers. The important issue is to access high quality and large datasets of majority of the people for ML application. It would be useful to understand the behaviour of a particular disease and its treatments. Doing so could help to generate hypotheses for research.

The challenges in the healthcare system need to be identified for better understanding of the application of ML in India.

6.2 HEALTHCARE IN INDIA: CHALLENGES

Some of the measure challenges in healthcare are to find out qualified doctors, nurses and technicians. Infrastructure is also a major problem in healthcare. There are 0.76 doctors and 2.09 nurses per 1,000 population in contrast to the recommendation of World Health Organization (WHO). According to WHO, there should be at least 1 doctor and 2.5 nurses per 1,000 population. There are 1.3 number of hospital beds available per 1,000 population though WHO recommends for at least 3.5 hospital beds per every 1,000 population [2].

Unequal accessibility to healthcare is one of the major problems in India for both preventive and curative health services. The disparity can also be observed in the cases of both rural and urban localities. It can be assessed from Figure 6.1 reflecting the Accessibility of Healthcare across India [3].

Figure 6.1 Shows that, Reflecting the Accessibility of Healthcare across India PwC Analysis, World Bank data (2017).

It is observed that private hospitals prefer to be located in and around Tier 1 and Tier 2 cities. So, patients from rural areas are compelled to take the pain of travelling long distances to get the basic and advanced healthcare services as well. Tata Memorial Hospital provides the fact that there were more than 67,000 new registrations for cancer treatment in 2015. It is also noticed that patients from outside the state of Maharastra is outnumber the patients from Maharastra, where the hospital is located. From Maharastra, the number of patients is less than 23%, while the number of patients visiting from other states like Bihar, Utter Pradesh, West Bengal and Jharkhand constitute 21.7% of the total patients. It reflects the unfortunate condition of healthcare in India.

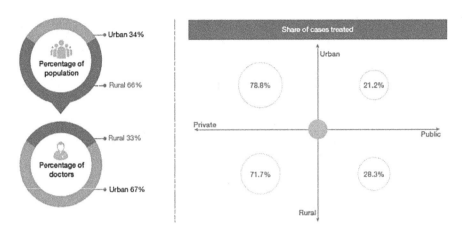

FIGURE 6.1   Reflecting the Accessibility of Healthcare across India.

Affordability represents a serious problem of healthcare in India. It is estimated that 62% out of 70% of expenditure is spent by the patient from one's own pocket which is beyond the reach of a patient. The patient has to depend on loans or selling of assets to meet the hospital costs. 63 million of people faced the challenge of leading a miserable life due to the healthcare expenditure every year [4].

Majority of the people do not seem to be proactive towards basic essential healthcare. It is because of either lack of awareness or absence of accessibility. Usually, they consult a physician only when they at the advanced stage of the disease. It increases the cost of treatment with slim chance of recovery.

Climate sensors can supply data to predict changes in ecosystem and environmental crises. It can be useful to check pollution trends [5] with a greater degree accuracy in comparison to the prevailing systems. It would send alert to the people as well as government to remain alert for tackling emergency situations. The city transportation audits also support with data to identify the locations of injuries due to vehicular accidents [6].

The Universal Health Coverage of Government of India shows a strong commitment to make primary healthcare more accessible to the people. The major challenges faced by healthcare in India look forward to searching an appropriate solution through ML. Here, the analysis shall focus on the avenues where ML can be used to meet the challenges and the steps taken by India to address those issues.

6.3   FRAMEWORKS IN HEALTH MUST CONSIDER MISSINGNESS

Regardless of whether or not exceedingly significant factors are remembered for a social insurance data set, all things considered, numerous perceptions will be absent. Genuinely complete information is frequently illogical because of cost and volume. Gaining from deficient, or missing, information has gotten little consideration in the AI people group (despite the fact that special cases exist), [7] however is an effectively examined subject in statistics.[8] Since human services is a powerful procedure where vitals are estimated and labs are requested after some time by specialists in light of past perceptions there are solid conditions between what factors are estimated and their qualities, which must be deliberately represented to maintain a strategic distance from one-sided results. There are three generally acknowledged arrangements of missing information components (i.e., the estimation instrument deciding if a worth is recorded or not [9].) The primary, missing totally aimlessly (MCAR), places a fixed likelihood of missingness. For this situation, dropping deficient perceptions – known as complete case examination – is generally utilized (though gullibly), and will prompt fair outcomes. Second, the information might be absent aimlessly (MAR), where the likelihood of missingness is irregular contingent on the watched factors. For this situation, regular strategies incorporate re-weighting information with techniques like converse likelihood of editing weighting or utilizing various ascription to in-fill [10]. At last, information might be absent not aimlessly (MNAR), where the likelihood of missingness relies upon the missing variable itself or other absent and imperceptibly factors.

6.3.1   Wellsprings of Missingness Must Be Painstakingly Comprehended

Wellsprings of missingness ought to be deliberately analyzed before sending a learning calculation. For instance, lab estimations are commonly requested as a major aspect of a symptomatic stir up, implying that the nearness of a data point passes on data about the patient's state. Consider an emergency clinic where clinical staff estimates persistent lactate level. In the event that a forced blackout prompted a lot of lactate levels being lost, the information is MCAR. In the event that medical caretakers are more averse to gauge lactate levels in patients with horrible injury, and we record whether patients were conceded with injury, the information are MAR. Be that as it may, if medical caretakers are more averse to gauge lactate levels when accepted to be as of now, at that point the lactate estimates themselves are MNAR, and the estimation of the sign itself is significant. The key component of missing information is that there might be data passed on by the nonattendance of a perception and disregarding this reliance may prompt frameworks that make off base, and even hurtful, expectations.

6.3.2   Incorporation of Missingness

Counting missingness markers gives the most data to making predictions [11]. In any case, learning frameworks without a proper model of missingness prompts issues, for example, incorrect evaluation of highlight significance and frameworks that are weak to changes in estimation rehearses. For instance, troponin-T is normally estimated just when a myocardial dead tissue is viewed as likely. A model learnt by treating troponin-T as MCAR would likely over predict the pace of myocardial localized necrosis on information where troponin-T was all the more consistently estimated. A model prepared with MAR troponin qualities would be increasingly powerful to this. Missingness can reflect human inclinations. We note that information may likewise be missing a result of contrasts in access, practice, or recording that reflects cultural biases [12] frameworks prepared on such information may thus show unjustifiable execution for certain populaces if an AI expert is uninformed of this hidden variety; along these lines, checking frameworks across bunches is important [13].

6.3.3 SETTLE ON CAREFUL CHOICES IN DEFINING OUTCOMES

Acquiring solid results for learning is a significant advance in characterizing undertakings. Results are frequently used to make the highest quality level marks required for administered forecast assignments, however, are urgent in different settings also (e.g., to guarantee very much characterized accomplices in a grouping task). There are three key components to consider with result definitions: making solid results, understanding the significance of a result clinically and the nuance of name spillage.

6.3.4 COMPREHEND THE RESULT IN THE SETTING OF A SOCIAL INSURANCE FRAMEWORK

Clinical definitions are working frameworks utilizing ebb and flow logical comprehension of an infection. As understanding develops, so does the definition. The suggestion for AI is that acceptable prescient execution on names dependent on such definitions is just tantamount to the basic frameworks. For instance, intense kidney injury (AKI) is a significant basic sickness with two late definitions: RIFLE34 and KDIGO35. Thus, it is enticing to utilize the genuine conduct of clinicians as names yet recall that they may not be right. For instance, work that objectives expectation of clinical activities should cautiously consider whether the medications are acceptable marks, and whether "erroneous forecasts" are in truth determining medicines that would have been given by different clinicians instead of medications that would ideally treat the patient [11].

6.3.5 BE CAREFUL WITH MARK SPILLAGE

The data gathered in a person's medical clinic experience is firmly coupled across time, and this can bring about data about the focused-on task result spilling once again into highlights. While abusing such connections among highlights and targets is an objective of learning, data spillage can render an expectation aimless. Consider foreseeing mortality of emergency clinic patients utilizing every single accessible datum up until their moment of death. Such an assignment could prompt a neurotic expectation rule: "On the off-chance that the ventilator is killed in the previous hour, envision downfall." This conventionally takes place when families and their patients decide to pull back thought at a terminal period of sickness. High-limit neural frameworks inspecting the whole EHR may likewise be liable to mark leakage; for instance, a last demonstrative name could use names that show up inside clinicians' underlying theories, affirming clinical consistency in speculations, as opposed to anticipating a determination dependent on pertinent information.

6.4   INCLINED OPPORTUNITIES IN HEALTHCARE

There are some high-sway open doors in human services. Prior to fitting frameworks, objectives ought to be plainly distinguished and approved as worth explaining. Here, we outline potential human services openings into three significant level classes: robotizing clinical errands, offering clinical help and extending clinical limits. The subtleties of how a specialized arrangement is conveyed can change its expectation, and it is subsequently significant to connect with clinical partners at an early stage.

6.4.1   AUTOMATING CLINICAL ERRANDS DURING DETERMINATION AND TREATMENT

There are numerous errands right now performed by clinicians for low-draping organic product for AI specialists. Clinical assignment mechanization includes various work of clinicians. These assignments are very much characterized (i.e., known information and yield spaces), and therefore require minimal measure of area adjustment and investment. The assessment of undertaking substitution is likewise clear: execution perhaps estimated against existing standards. We underline that calculations ought not to supplant clinical staff, but instead are utilized to advance the clinical work process. Clinical jobs will probably advance as these procedures improve, engaging staff to invest more energy with patients.

6.4.2   COMPUTERIZING CLINICAL PICTURE ASSESSMENT

Clinical imaging is a characteristic open door for AI since clinicians experience serious preparing to outline a fixed information space (for example, the pictures) to a yield (for example, the diagnosis). There have been a few late triumphs in applying profound figuring out how to clinical imaging undertakings. For instance, doctor level equality in the discovery of diabetic retinopathy, recognizing harmful and non-threatening skin injuries utilizing namely dermatoscopic images [12], identifying spleen hub metastases from bosom pathology slides, and distinguishing hip cracks put x-beam images [13].

6.4.3   ROBOTIZING ROUTINE PROCEDURES

Robotizing regular clinical procedures stands to diminish the weight set on clinical staff. For instance, organizing triage request in the crisis division is frequently left to staff [14], however it should be possible algorithmically. Likewise, summing up the substance of patients' clinical records is a tedious, yet significant, task. For instance, when emergency clinic personnel are uncertain about patient's ailment status, they may require an irresistible illness interview in which a pro carefully audits all the accessible patient information, and physically sums up unique place of origin into a progression of suggested tests and treatments. Specialists can use work from characteristic language age moving in the direction of producing outlines from organized her information, sparing truly necessary time [15].

6.4.4   Streamlining Clinical Choice and Practice Support

Another arrangement of chances centre around supporting and increasing consideration. Instead of supplanting a very much characterized function, support requires understanding clinical torment focuses and working with clinical staff to comprehend proper information, yield targets and assessment capacities. Open doors for help centre around work that regularly endures because of certifiable requirements on schedule and assets, frequently prompting data misfortune and blunders (e.g., mixed up understanding recognizable proof, defective translations, or off base recall [16]). Within this setting, it is suitable to assess how frameworks improve downstream results couple with clinical info as opposed to no holds barred correlations with clinical staff.

6.4.5   Normalizing Clinical Procedures

Varieties in clinical preparing furthermore experience lead to scopes of treatment decisions that may not be ideal for focusing on the hidden illnesses of a patient's state. For instance, clinical staff might be uncertain which medicine sets or portions are generally proper for a patient. To help such needs, past work has analyzed prescribing both normalized request sets to assist care with staffing rapidly evaluate what drugs they may have missed and default doses to maintain a strategic distance from perilous dosing [17]. Here, notice that robotizing a static, existing, convention is fundamentally simpler than full choice help for complex clinical rules that may change after some time, and there is possibly much incentive in both in-medical clinic and wandering choice support [18], and at-home support.

6.4.6   Incorporating Divided Records

Limited assets can likewise prompt an absence of correspondence and coordination, influencing persistent consideration. For instance, it can take a long time to recognize local maltreatment survivors in light of the fact that each and every unique medicinal visit in disconnection might be reliable with different causes (for example, an affirmation for wounding is reliable with an unconstrained fall). While conceivable without emotionally supportive networks on a fundamental level, AI can be an integral asset (e.g., distinguishing residential maltreatment as long as 30 months ahead of time of the human services system).

6.4.7   Growing Medicinal Capacities: New Skylines in Screening, Analysis and Treatment

As social insurance records become progressively digitized, clinicians are confronted with an ever-expanding measure of novel information for patients and populaces. The outcome is a chance to give the social insurance framework another arrangement of abilities to convey medicinal services in better and more brilliant ways. Significantly, making new limits appropriate contribution with medical teammates and effect ought to be estimated both in development and medical worth.

6.4.8 GROWING THE INCLUSION OF PROOF

While human services is an inalienably information driven field, most clinicians work with constrained proof directing their choices. Randomized preliminaries gauge normal treatment impacts for a preliminary populace, yet various everyday choices are not founded on top notch randomized control preliminaries (RCTs). For instance, most of regularly utilized ICU medications are not thoroughly exactly validated a few examiners have assessed that lone up to 20% of medicines are sponsored by a RCT. Indeed, even in settings where a RCT exists, the preliminary populace will in general be a restricted, centred subgroup characterized by the preliminary's incorporation criteria, yet that partner cannot be illustrative of the different populace to which preliminary outcomes are then applied. At last, RCT results can't mirror the multifaceted nature of treatment variety in light of the fact that, practically speaking, tolerant consideration methods are profoundly individualized. Earlier work found that roughly 10% of diabetes and depression patients and practically 25% of hypertension patients had a one-of-a-kind medication pathway (i.e., zero closest neighbours) in an associate of 250 million patients. One path forward is influence this normally happening heterogeneity to structure regular experiments that estimated the aftereffects of a RCT utilizing less assets, consequently permitting a lot bigger arrangement of clinical inquiries to be explored.

6.4.9 MOVING TOWARDS CONSTANT SOCIAL CHECKING

Phenotyping is a significant objective in healthcare, and wearable information gives a progressing approach to gadgets to gather consistent non-obtrusive information and give important arrangements or alarms once a patient needs consideration. Recent work has concentrated on foreseeing such shifted results as cardiovascular failure frequently gathered data. There are further settings where non-intrusive observing might be the main handy approach to give location. For instance, programmed fall discovery aged patients, or authorizing hand washing consistence in a clinical setting. Critically, earlier difficulties recognized in name spillage, delicate names, bewildering including longing be considered cautiously. In phenotyping interminable conditions, patients are regularly previously being dealt with, thus early discovery may now and then add up to distinguishing a current care. Accuracy medication tries to individualize the treatment of every patient; this is especially significant for disorder—conditions characterized by an assortment of side effects whose causes are unknown. For example, intense kidney injury (AKI) is characterized by an assortment of manifestations portraying kidney disappointment, not a fundamental cause. Two people may have created AKI for various reasons on the grounds that reaper numerous reasons that kidneys can fall flat. More estimation of the two people could uncover the distinction in cause, which may thus recommend elective treatment strategies. By customizing after eventually, one can learn singular explicit care impacts that address the reason for the syndrome [19] in a specific person. This identifies with the thoughts from "N=1" hybrid examinations in trial design [20]. Customized treatment is empowered by developing vaults of longitudinal information, where long haul movements of a person's wellbeing are available [21].

6.5 POPULATION PROTECTION (CROWD SURVEILLANCE)

Data from various digital sources can be analyzed with the help of ML to predict population-level disease diffusion. It can protect people by adopting the method of crowd surveillance. The data from social media will be helpful to monitor spreading of disease like influenza so that appropriate steps can be taken to supply vaccine without delay. One can ascertain the reason for low vaccine coverage [22] and strategies can be adopted accordingly to enhance the coverage area. Illegal online sales of the prescription by global online sellers can be identified by ascertaining information from the available data [23].

Climate sensors can supply data to predict changes in ecosystem and environmental crises. It can be useful to check pollution trends [24] with a greater degree accuracy in comparison to the prevailing systems. It would send alert to the people as well as government to remain alert for tackling emergency situations. The city transportation audits also support with data to identify the locations of injuries due to vehicular accidents [25].

6.6 MARKETING STRATEGY

ML is also very useful for making marketing strategies to promote healthcare. Through information filtering systems, effective decisions can be made to guide health behaviours of the people. ML algorithms offer powerful solutions to content-based analysis ascertained personality information. Past behavioural patterns of the people are utilized to predict their future actions [26]. EHRs with appropriate legal consent can provide information to study unhealthy behaviours of people like buying tobacco-based products, sugar-based drinks and alcohol.

6.7 POPULATION SCREENING

Population screening based on ML is very much helpful for disease protection by resorting to enhanced screening strategies. For example, ML flagging systems help to identify high-risk patients suffering from colorectal cancer on the basis of complete blood count test [27]. Currently, deep-learning image screening is developed for mammography to take rational diagnostic decisions.

6.8 PATIENT ADVOCACY

Patient advocacy emphasized on the application of ethics for the welfare of the people. The big-data analytics [28] will eliminate traditional discrimination and biases. For example, it can study the declining opportunity of health insurance on the part of the individuals belonging to a particular community. However, a judicious application of ML would pave the way for identifying disparities or unjustified data discrimination which in turn, would ensure health justice across society.

6.9 ROLE OF MACHINE LEARNING IN SOCIETY

ML has a potential role to play in society: It can address shortage of healthcare practitioners. At the outset, it would support diagnostic activity, and gradually its scope could be expanded to different levels of healthcare. It would look into matters like fixing appointments for health staff and supplying direct healthcare advice [29].

There are differences of opinion regarding benefits of ML in healthcare. It would have a negative impact on society as some people consider that it will lead to job loss and unemployment. For example, an ML algorithm has the potential to appraise multitudes of images in 24 hours in diagnostic radiology or pathology. In spite of these arguments, one can perceive the merits of ML-based technologies that can generate new jobs. It would also enable health practitioners to devote more of their time to taking care of the patients.

The role of ML in healthcare policy supports the opinion of Alan Turing (1950) who is of opinion that AI, or 'machine intelligence'[30] will emancipate the modern society. Its role can be explored in the field of health governance. ML solutions could offer appraisal of policy statements to help the politicians to draw health policies for the future generation.

6.10   AYUSHMAN BHARAT: A STEP FORWARD

The Ayushman Bharat programme is considered as India's largest government funded healthcare programme. Its objective is to make healthcare accessible and affordable for the common people. It offers yearly INR 5 lakh per family as insurance cover for hospitalization. More than 10 crore families belonging to the vulnerable sections are covered under Ayushman Bharat on the basis of Socio Economic and Caste Census (SECC) database. There is no constraint of age and family size to become the beneficiary of this program. Most of the medical and surgical conditions are covered by the package offered. Patients can avail both pre- and post-hospitalization expenses.

The benefits can be availed in public hospitals as well as targeted private hospitals. In the year 2018, the Union Budget earmarked ~INR1,200 crore for Health and Wellness Centres (HWC). A shift is noticed in the healthcare sector as it enunciates plan to include comprehensive areas like screening and management of Noncommunicable Disease (NCDs). It expands its area to mental health ailments, ophthalmic and ENT problems, dental health, geriatric and palliative treatment and trauma care. NCDs are chronic conditions which claims for ~60% of mortality in India. It has its adverse effects on the poor people due to the high costs of treatment involved.

6.11   THE NATIONAL E-HEALTH AUTHORITY (NEHA)

The National E-Health Authority makes a strong effort to improve the healthcare with the help of technology. It adopts e-health strategies to redefine the health sector. The objective of Integrated Health Information Program (IHIP) is to provide EHR to Indian citizens and interoperability to existing EHR/EMRs. The healthcare sector in India is in need of technological interventions at different levels. Adoption of AI for healthcare applications is expected to grow in coming years. The AI driven healthcare market is presumed to register an explosive CAGR of 40% through 2021. The growing technological innovations prompt India to find out solutions to the prevailing problem of providing healthcare facilities to the common people. AI, Robotics and Internet of Medical Things (IoMT) are identified to help the government in addressing all health-related issues of the people at large.

6.12   CANCER SCREENING AND MACHINE LEARNING

AI is provided with a tremendous scope for interventions in cancer screening and its treatment. Every year, more than one million new cases are registered in India. It is likely to increase with the changing lifestyle and increasing age of population in India. Early detection and management are indispensable for a positive cure of cancer. There is great need of qualitative pathology service for treating cancer which is only available in some selected Indian cities. There are barely 2,000 pathologists who have experience in oncology. There are less than 500 pathologists who could be called expert oncopathologists. ML solutions could assist a general pathologist to go for a quality diagnosis which would bridge the gap of providing essential healthcare. Quality annotated pathology datasets are very much required to bring out a solution. NITI Aayog is developing a national repository to solve the problem. It can be termed as "Digital Pathology".

6.13   "SICK" CARE TO "HEALTH" CARE: MOVING FORWARD

There is a collaborative effort on the part of NITI Aayog to join hands with Microsoft and Forus Health to explore technology for detecting diabetic retinopathy at an early stage. Forus Health developed 3Nethra: a portable device to screen the common eye problems. Aravind Eye Hospital, Narayana Nethralaya and Sankar Nethralaya collaborating with Alphabet Inc's to introduce an AI system to detect diabetic retinopathy. This project is an example of bringing AI supported healthcare solution in India.

It is very much crucial to explore various opportunities offer by ML in healthcare sector. The following analysis focuses on these issues.

6.14   MACHINE LEARNING AND HEALTHCARE OPPORTUNITIES

There are plenty of high-sway openings in social insurance. Before making models, objectives should be plainly distinguished and approved. The potential medicinal services openings can be characterized into three significant level classes: robotization of clinical undertakings, arrangement of clinical help and growing the ambit of clinical limits.

6.14.1   COMPUTERIZING CLINICAL ASSIGNMENTS DURING DETERMINATION AND TREATMENT

There are numerous errands as of now performed by clinicians that current low-draping organic product for AI scientists. Clinical undertaking robotization centres around a class of work that clinicians at present do. These assignments are very much characterized and, in this way, require minimal measure of area adjustment and venture. The calculations ought not supplant clinical staff. It ought to be utilized to upgrade the clinical work stream to engage the staff to invest more energy with patients [31].

6.14.2 ROBOTIZING CLINICAL PICTURE ASSESSMENT

Clinical imaging offers a characteristic open door for AI. The clinicians are to experience serious preparing to plan from a fixed information space (for example, the pictures) to a yield (for example, the finding). There have been a few ongoing occasions of achievements in applying profound figuring out how to clinical imaging undertakings. For instance, doctor level equality in the identification of diabetic retinopathy, recognizing dangerous and non-threatening skin injuries utilizing in dermatoscopic images [32], identifying lymph hub metastases from bosom pathology slides, and distinguishing hip cracks in x-beam images [33].

6.14.3 ROBOTIZING ROUTINE PROCEDURES

Computerization in routine clinical procedures diminishes the weight of clinical staff. For instance, summing up the substance of patients' clinical records [34] is a tedious, however significant, work. For instance, while clinical staff are uncertain about status of the patient's malady, it may force them to pursue an irresistible illness discussion wherein an authority fastidiously looks into all the accessible patient information, and physically sums up divergent causes to suggest treatments and tests [35]. Specialists can make use of work arising from characteristic language age progressing in the direction of creating outlines from organized information, sparing genuinely necessary time.

6.14.4 CLINICAL SUPPORT AND AUGMENTATION

ML is helpful for supporting and expanding care. It opens doors for helping stresses on work that arises because of requirements of time and assets. It frequently prompts data misfortune and blunders (e.g., mixed up understanding ID, defective translations or erroneous recall). For this situation, it is proper to assess how models develop downstream results associate with clinical information instead of straight on correlations with clinical staff.

6.14.5 EXPANDING CLINICAL CAPACITIES

The ML can investigate a new skyline in screening, analysis and treatment by involving the clinical people. With the digitized human services records, physicians are confronted with an increasing measure of new information regarding patients and populaces. It brings about opening a chance to give the medicinal services framework another arrangement of abilities to convey social insurance in better and more astute ways. It is essential to make new limits that need the most contribution to clinical partners, and effect could be estimated regarding development and clinical worth.

6.14.6 Precision Medicine for Early Individualized Treatment

Accuracy medication looks for individualizing the treatment of every patient. This is specifically important for disorder conditions characterized by an assortment of manifestations the causes of which are not known. For example, Acute kidney injury (AKI) is characterized by an assortment of side effects describing kidney disappointment, not a fundamental cause. Two people may have created AKI for various reasons on the grounds that there are numerous reasons that kidneys can come up short. More estimation of the two people could uncover different causes, which gives rise to elective treatment strategies. By customizing, one can ascertain singular explicit treatment impacts to address the reason associated with the particular disease [36] in a specific person.

6.14.7 Open Doors for Innovative Research

Chain of command of chances in human services open doors for advancement. Significantly, clinical staff and AI specialists frequently have integral abilities. Various high-sway issues must be handled by community-oriented endeavours. We note a few promising bearings of exploration, explicitly featuring those that deal with issues such as information non-stationarity, model interpretability and finding proper portrayals.

6.14.8 Adding Communication to AI and Assessment

AI work in social insurance is offered with a chance to make frameworks that associate and team up with human specialists. Clinical staff contribute more than their expertise [17]. They additionally go about as parental figures, and compassion is perceived as a significant component of clinical practice. Building collective frameworks can use the integral qualities of doctors and learning frameworks. There are numerous strings of examination in the AI writing that can fill in as an establishment for such frameworks.

6.14.9 Distinguishing Representations in a Large and Multi-source Network

Portrayal learning is responsible for incredible advances in AI. The lower dimensional, subjectively important portrayals of imaging datasets learnt by convolutional neural systems can be considered as an example. Human services information needs such normal structures, and examinations concerning suitable portrayals ought to incorporate multi-source joining and learning space proper portrayals.

6.15 COMMON MACHINE LEARNING APPLICATIONS IN HEALTHCARE

There are multiple and endless ML application in healthcare industry. Some of the most common applications are cited in this section. ML helps streamlining the administrative processes in the hospitals. It also helps mapping and treating the infectious diseases for the personalized medical treatment. ML will affect physician and hospitals by playing a very dominant role in the clinical decision support. For example, it will help earlier identification of the diseases and customize treatment plan that will ensure an optimal outcome. ML can be used to educate patients on several potential disease and their outcomes with different treatment option. As a result, it can improve the efficiency hospital and health systems by reducing the cost of the healthcare. ML in healthcare can be used to enhance health information management and the exchange of the health information with the aim of improving and thus, modernizing the workflows, facilitating access to clinical data and improving the accuracy of the health information. Above all it brings efficiency and transparency to information process.

6.15.1   MACHINE LEARNING APPLICATION IN DRUG DISCOVERY

ML approaches have played key role in the process of drug discovery in the recent times. It has helped minimize the high failure rate in drug development by leveraging the availability of huge high-quality data. There are multiple challenges in ML for drug development. One of the important challenges is to ensure drug safety. One of the challenging and complex tasks in the process of drug discovery is to analyze and interpret the available information of the known effects of the drugs and prediction of their side effects. Researchers from various reputed universities/institutions and of course, many pharmaceutical companies have been continuously using ML to obtain relevant information from clinical data used in clinical trials. Analyzing and interpreting these data using ML in the context of drug safety is an active area of research in recent times. Above all, the computational solution in drug discovery has helped significantly reduce the cost of introducing drugs to the market.

6.15.2   NEUROSCIENCE AND IMAGE COMPUTING

Neuroscience Image Computing (NIC) pays particular attention for the development of advanced imaging approaches, and its interpretation into clinical studies. NIC studies attempt to discover the aetiology of brain disorders, including psychiatric disorders, neuro degenerative disorders and traumatic brain injuries by using advanced technologies.

6.15.3   CLOUD COMPUTING FRAMEWORKS IN BUILDING MACHINE LEARNING-BASED HEALTHCARE

AI in general and ML in particular have seen tremendous growth in the recent times because of its ability to use huge volumes of data and produce accurate and deep understanding about the issues at hand. Cloud computing has made it possible that are more cost effective and its ability to handle increasing market demand. Models using ML are seen to be more robust that are using cloud computing resources. The cloud computing resources can track data from device wearable devices and health trackers. Then they can stream and aggregate it cost effectively in cloud-based storage. The large volume of data can be analyzed efficiently using cloud-based compute infrastructure. This allows the ML models to be more accurate and robust.

6.15.4 MACHINE LEARNING IN PERSONALIZED HEALTHCARE

Internet of Things (IoT) in healthcare has made it increasingly possible to connect a large number of people, things with smart sensors such as wearable and medical devices and environments. Patient vitals and various types of real-time data are captured by sensors and smart assets in IoT devices. Data analytics technologies, such as ML, can be used to deliver value-based care to the people. For instance, operational improvements enhance efficiencies that provide quality care at reduced costs. Similarly, clinical improvements ensure quicker and relatively accurate diagnoses. It also ensures more patient-centric, scientific determination of the best therapeutic approach to support better health outcomes. ML uses collected dataset to improve illness movement method and sickness forecast. Explanatory models by using ML are incorporated into various human services applications. These models typically break down the collected information from sensor gadgets and different sources to recognize personal conduct standards and clinical states of the patient.

6.15.5 MACHINE LEARNING IN OUTBREAK PREDICTION

Multiple outbreak prediction models are widely used by researchers in the recent times to make most appropriate decisions and implement relevant measures to control the outbreak. For example, researchers are using some of the standard models such as epidemiological and statistical models for prediction of COVID-19. Prediction emerging from these models proved to be less robust and less accurate as it involves huge uncertainty and paucity of relevant data. Recently, many researchers are using ML models to make long term prediction of this outbreak. Researchers have shown that ML-based models proved to be more robust compared to the alternative models for this this outbreak.

6.15.6 MACHINE LEARNING IN PATIENT RISK STRATIFICATION

In healthcare, risk stratification is understood as the process of classifying patients into types of risks. This status depends on data obtained from various sources such as medical history, health indicators and the lifestyle of a population. The goal of stratifying risks includes addressing population management challenges, individualizing treatment plans to lower risks, matching risk with levels of care, and aligning the practice with value-based care approaches. Traditional models for predicting risk mostly hinges on the expertise and experience of the practitioner. ML does not demand human inputs—to analyze clinical and financial data for patient risk stratification. By using the availability of volumes of data such as medical reports, patients' records, and insurance records and apply ML to provide the best outcomes.

6.15.7 MACHINE LEARNING IN TELEMEDICINE

Tele-health in healthcare is an important industry. It makes the patient care process easier for both providers and patients. This industry is growing at a faster pace worldwide. The advancement of new technology such as ML in the healthcare has provided medical professionals with truly genuine tools and resources to manage the daily influx of patients. ML can help these professionals with a new way to analyze and interpret volumes of raw patient data and offer interesting insights and directions towards achieving better health outcomes.

6.15.8 MULTIMODAL MACHINE LEARNING FOR DATA FUSION IN MEDICAL IMAGING

Multimodal medical image fusion technique is a useful and significant technique to investigate diseases by deriving the complementary information from different multimodality medical images. These strategies have been consistently and progressively applied in clinical practice. Multimodal picture investigation and troupe learning strategies are developing fast and carrying remarkable incentive to clinical applications. Driven by the ongoing achievement of applying these learning strategies to clinical picture handling, researchers have proposed algorithmic design to administer multimodal picture investigation with cross-methodology combination at the component learning level, classifier level and at the dynamic level as well. At that point, a picture division framework dependent on profound convolutional neural systems is executed to shape the injuries of delicate tissue sarcomas utilizing multimodal pictures, including those from attractive reverberation imaging, registered tomography and positron discharge tomography. The system prepared with multimodal pictures shows better execution contrasted to systems prepared with single-modular pictures.

6.16 INCORPORATING EXPECTATIONS AND LEARNING SIGNIFICANT PORTRAYALS FOR THE SPACE

Singular patient information has expanded to incorporate numerous sources and modalities, making mix additionally testing in frameworks as of now battling with overload. New memory frameworks are required for succession forecast undertakings, in light of the fact that so many records are not equally dispersed, can cover extreme lengths and early occasions can influence understanding over many years.

Learning significant state portrayals that give great prescient execution on various errands and record for contingent connections of premium is a significant advance. Managing portrayals unequivocally might be beneficial in light of the fact that they can helpfully communicate pandemic anterior that are not explicit to a solitary prescient job. There are a few potency chances to speech for portrayals for a medical institution scope. Initial, a solitary persevering information (for example, physiologic information) can compare to numerous conceivable right yields (for example, demonstrative codification), and this must be conceivable in the portrayals we investigate. There has likewise been some underlying investigation into education portrayals of other information types that all the while catches chain of importance and similarity.

6.17 CONCLUSION

ML is known as the most important applications of AI technology. It unfolds numerous ways to support the healthcare policy. It takes care of a large number of people by adopting preventive strategies. It revolves round the patient-centred approach that covers patient advocacy and effective management of workforce and resources. The growing use of ML would offer tremendous possibilities for India to provide appropriate healthcare system to a large section of population. It would inspire the government in meeting the needs of common people in healthcare sector. In fact, ML is expected serves as a launching pad for making healthcare services more proactive – a welcome move from "sick" care to "health" care.

REFERENCES

1. Chen IY, Szolovits P, Ghassemi M. Can AI help reduce disparities in general medical and mental healthcare? *AMA J Ethics* 21(2), 167–179, 2019.
2. Du J, Xu J, Song HY, Tao C. Leveraging machine learning-based approaches to assess human papillomavirus vaccination sentiment trends with Twitter data. *BMC Med Inform Decis Mak* 17(Suppl 2), 69 2017 Jul 5. doi:10.1186/s12911-017-0469-6PMID: 28699569. Pubmed Central PMCID: 5506590.
3. Mackey TK, Kalyanam J, Katsuki T, Lanckriet G. Twitter-based detection of illegal online sale of prescription opioid. *Am J Public Health* 107(12), 1910–1915, 2017 Dec. doi:10.2105/AJPH. 2017.303994 PMID: 29048960.
4. Jones N. How machine learning could help to improve climate forecasts. *Nature* 548(7668), 379–380, 2017 Aug 23. doi:10.1038/548379a PMID: 28836613.
5. Khishdari A, Fallah Tafti M. Development of crash frequency models for safety promotion of urban collector streets. *Int J Inj Contr Saf Promot* 24(4), 519–533, 2017 Dec. doi: 10.1080/17457300.2016.1278237 PMID: 28118766.
6. Sadasivam RS, Cutrona SL, Kinney RL, Marlin BM, Mazor KM, Lemon SC, et al. Collective-intelligence recommender systems: Advancing computer tailoring for health behavior change into the 21st century. *J Med Internet Res* 18(3), e42, 2016 Mar 7. doi:10.2196/jmir.4448 PMID: 26952574. Pubmed Central PMCID: 4802103.
7. Goshen R, Choman E, Ran A, Muller E, Kariv R, Chodick G, et al. Computer-assisted flagging of individuals at high risk of colorectal cancer in a large health maintenance organization using the colonflag test. *JCO Clin Cancer Inform* (2), 1–8, 2018.
8. d'Alessandro B, O'Neil C, LaGatta T. Conscientious classification: A data scientist's guide to discrimination-aware classification. *Big Data* 5(2), 120–134, 2017 Jun. doi:10.1089/big.2016.0048 PMID: 28632437.
9. Darzi A *Better Health and Care for All: A 10-point plan for the 2020s*. IPPR. 2018 Availablefrom: https://www.ippr.org/files/2018-06/better-health-and-care-for-all-june2018.pdf
10. Ashrafian H, Darzi A, Athanasiou T. A novel modification of the Turing test for artificial intelligence and robotics in healthcare. *Int J Med Robot* 11(1), 38–43, 2015 Mar. doi: 10.1002/rcs.1570 PMID: 24442995.
11. Phillips SP, Hamberg K, Doubly blind: A systematic review of gender in randomised controlled trials. *Global Health Action* 9(1), 29597, 2016.
12. Subbaswamy A, Saria S, Counterfactual normalization: Proactively addressing dataset shift using causal mechanisms. In: *Uncertainty in Artificial Intelligence (UAI)*, Eds. Ricardo Silva, Amir Globerson, Amir Globerson, 947–957, Monterey, United States, 2018.

13. Gong JJ, Naumann T, Szolovits P, Guttag JV, *Predicting clinical outcomes across changing electronic health record systems*. In: *International Conference on Knowledge Discovery and Data Mining (KDD)*. ACM, 1497–1505, 2017.

14. Obermeyer Z, Lee TH, Lost in thought—the limits of the human mind and the future of medicine. *New England J Med* 377 (13), 1209–1211, 2017.

15. Manrai AK, Bhatia G, Strymish J, Kohane IS, Jain SH, Medicine's uncomfortable relationship with math: Calculating positive predictive value. *JAMA Int Med* 174(6), 991–993, 2014.

16. Letham B, Rudin C, McCormick TH, Madigan D, et al. Interpretable classifiers using rules and bayesian analysis: Building a better stroke prediction model. *The Ann Appl Statis* 9(3), 1350–1371, 2015.

17. Beam AL, Kohane IS, Big data and machine learning in healthcare. *JAMA*, Available from: +doi: 10.1001/jama.2017.18391, 2018.

18. Zhu J, Krähenbühl P, Shechtman E, Efros AA, *Generative visual manipulation on the natural image manifold*. In: *European Conference on Computer Vision*. Springer. 597–613, 2016.

19. Ranganath R, Perotte A, Elhadad N, Blei D, *Deep survival analysis*. In: *Machine Learning for Healthcare Conference*. 101–114, 2016.

20. Dressel J, Farid H, The accuracy, fairness, and limits of predicting recidivism. *Sci Adv* 4(1), eaao5580, 2018.

21. Che Z, Purushotham S, Cho K, Sontag D, Liu Y, Recurrent neural networks for multivariate time series with missing values. *Sci Rep* 8(1), 6085, 2018.

22. Lin C, Jain S, Kim H, Bar-Joseph Z, Using neural networks for reducing the dimensions of single-cell RNA-Seq data. *Nucl Acids Res.* 45(17), e156–e156, 2017.

23. Shah NH, Arnold M, Steven CB, Making machine learning models clinically useful. *JAMA* 322(14), 1351–1352, 2019.

24. Rajkomar A, Hardt M, Howell MD, Corrado G, Chin MH. Ensuring fairness in machine learning to advance health equity. *Ann Int Med* 169(12), 866–872, 2018.

25. Miscouridou X, Perotte A, Elhadad N, Ranganath R. *Deep survival analysis: Nonparametrics and missingness*. In: *Machine Learning for Healthcare Conference*, pp. 244–256, 2018.

26. Robins JM. Robust estimation in sequentially ignorable missing data and causal inference models. *Proc Am Statis Assoc* 1999, 6–10, 2000.

27. Ding P, Li F, Casual inference: A missing data perspective. *Statis Sci* 33(2), 214–237, 2018.

28. Ghassemi M, Wu M, Feng M, Celi LA, Szolovits P, Doshi-Velez F. Understanding vasopressor intervention and weaning: Risk prediction in a public heterogeneous clinical time series database. *J Am Med Inform Assoc* 24(3), ocw138, 2016.

29. Rajkomar A, Oren E, Chen K, Dai AM, Hajaj N, Liu PJ, et al. Scalable and accurate deep learning for electronic health records. arXiv preprint arXiv: 180107860., 2018.

30. Casey BM, McIntire DD, Leveno KJ. The continuing value of the Apgar score for the assessment of newborn infants. *N Engl J Med* 344, 467–471, 2001.

31. Wei W-Q, Teixeira PL, Mo H, Cronin RM, Warner JL, Denny JC. Combining billing codes, clinical notes, and medications from electronic health records provides superior phenotyping performance. *J Am Med Inform Assoc* 23, e20–e27, 2016.

32. McCoy TH, Yu S, Hart KL, Castro VM, Brown HE, Rosenquist JN, et al. High throughput phenotyping for dimensional psychopathology in electronic health records. *Biol Psychiatry* 83(12), 997–1004, 2018.

33. Shneiderman B, Plaisant C, Hesse BW. Improving healthcare with interactive visualization. *Computer* 46(5), 58–66, 2013.

34. Pivovarov R, Coppleson YJ, Gorman SL, Vawdrey DK, Elhadad N. *Can Patient Record Summarization Support Quality Metric Abstraction? AMIA Annual Symposium Proceedings. American Medical Informatics Association* 2016, 1020, 2016.
35. Fishbane S, Niederman MS, Daly C, Magin A, Kawabata M, de Corla-Souza A, et al. The impact of standardized order sets and intensive clinical case management on outcomes in community-acquired pneumonia. *Arch Int Med* 167(15), 1664–1669, 2007.
36. Bates DW, Gawande AA. Improving safety with information technology. *New England J Med*, 348(25), 2526–2534, 2003.

7 Demystifying the Capabilities of Machine Learning and Artificial Intelligence for Personalized Care

Vaidik Bhatt and P. Sashikala
Department of Operations & IT, ICFAI Business School (IBS), Hyderabad

CONTENTS

7.1 INTRODUCTION

Personalized care is a modern model of the health system where treatments are based not on 'one-size-fits-all' recommendations but specific patient characteristics ([1]). As epidemiological data systems continue to flourish in size and sophistication, it becomes important to analyze and create pronouncements from underlying data with influential methodologies such as statistical learning and Artificial Intelligence [2]. Machine Learning (ML) can be used via such research to promote personalized medicine through its precise predictions. Other Artificial Intelligence (AI) technologies will also lead to the personalization of treatment for patients' lifestyle diseases, such as diabetes and cardiac disorders. So, we can understand, how these innovations will encourage an extended task for more personalized medicine and hence, change the healthcare setting.

With the introduction of modernized, state-of-the-art technologies in healthcare, the standard of living and life expectancy of the population has been increased drastically ([3,4]). Today, with the help of modernized healthcare technologies it is possible to provide personalized care to almost every person in society ([5]), in the pandemic era created due to SARS-COV-19 virus, our healthcare system realized importance of modern technology adoption [6]. With the remarkable gains in life expectancy, the current society is becoming a society of geriatric patients of an ageing population. Adults and the geriatric population need constant care and support as most of them are suffering from lifestyle disorders like high blood pressure, cardiac arrhythmia, diabetes, etc. The geriatric patient needs more personalized care as they are unable to control their physical symptoms and constantly seeking support from family and medical practitioners [7].

Personalized medicine is defined as to adapt to the healthcare of individuals to the possible extent at all the phases starting from prevention, diagnosis and treatment, to post-treatment and further follow up. Some more concepts which are used mostly along with personalized medicine are genomic medicine, stratified medicine and precision medicine. A clear understanding of these terms helps in any miscommunication.

The main motivation for the evolution of personalized medicine is due to the generation of data coming from genome sequencing. The potential of personalized medicine is the forecasting of the disease risk, treatment response and care built on genomic sequence data. The variety of data that can be used to adapt to healthcare is far away from the genome sequence data. Moreover, the acceptability of participants in the expansion and execution of personalized medicine might be inclined with the discernment that genomics has not survived to the required level of hope and may lead to vulnerability to a whole mass of diseases. Hence it is necessary to answer the disapprovals that personalized medicine is grounded on the misapprehension that it denotes genomic prediction only [8].

The usage of information systems by the clinical laboratories helps in the consolidation of the reports and warnings and the outcomes to be applied with the help of electronic health records (EHR) and related systems. The gateways or the infrastructure facilitates accessing the genetic data and decides how they can be used. Currently, the development of the required infrastructure is in the nascent stage and the basic infrastructure for precision medicine is evolving.

The role of the patient is crucial for supporting precision medicine. The customized precision medicine can be provided to every patient whose genetic sequencing is unique by collecting as much information as possible [9]. EHRs are positioned to support the genetic information with the help of technology. They should facilitate the clinicians by providing complete information about the patient along with the genetic data. The information which is obtained should be systematized and demonstrated in such a way that it enables smooth diagnostics and the decisions related to treatment [10].

This biggest challenge of 21st-century medicine is to provide an effective treatment that is customized based on the precise biological condition of the patient to facilitate personalized healthcare solutions. Generally, an assessing scheme of the patient should evolve before the treatment starts to help the healthcare practitioners can provide exact medicine, dose or intervention. This led to the categorization of patients based on some genetic characteristics which provide an efficient model for providing balanced nutrition and lifestyle [11].

Apple in early 2015 announced the introduction of a ResearchKit which is a mobile platform that captures the iPhones of 700 million global users to identify the individuals who would be interested in human research studies. These apps comprised of a kit that will help the individuals to register themselves in the observational studies on Parkinson's (mPower app), cardiovascular health (MyHeart Counts), breast cancer (Share the Journey), asthma (Asthma Mobile Health), and diabetes (GlucoSuccess). These studies were conducted in collaboration with 17 various research institutions mostly in the US. Research Kit is striving creativity that pursues to connect along with mobile technology, wearable sensors for determining phenotypic indicators, and extremely penetrating machinery for determining genomic, epigenetic, proteomic and metabolic markers in blood, stool and tissue. This advent of technology along with the computational facilities to store, share, filter and analyze the data will lead to collect health and disease data for complete human inhabitants, which provide huge opportunities for biomedical research [12].

Another strong point of this mobile technology is that it provides the capability to monitor phenotypes in long run. With the usage of the mPower app, respondents could track how the disease affects gait, tremors, mood, cognition, fatigue, speech and sleep on a day-to-day basis. This allows understanding new patterns which may be the indicators for which reveal the development and severity of the disease. This enables to obtain statistical analysis with an adequate sample which helps in the stratification of diseases into precisely defined groups. This helps in faster diagnosis of the faster and effectively [12].

With the advent of these technologies and huge data is generated Data-driven and networks-driven rational and approaches become crucial in the development of personalized healthcare. Several diseases have avoidable risk features or at least are the predictors of risk. Proper clarification of these features would be beneficial for personalized healthcare and reduces the risk of diseases. Since the possible risk factors are complex it would be difficult to analyze the real-time data individually by a physician while interacting with the patient. In general, the healthcare providers look at the previous history of the patient and do the physical check-up and diagnosis to determine the health of the patient and predict the risk of the disease. This has a limitation to certain diseases and the ability and expertise of the practitioner and the challenging urgencies of the people. In this scenario, an analytics framework is required to combine and assimilate big data to obtain in-depth knowledge obtained from electronic medical records of the patient and comparing patients' information and influences with other patients and offer personalized disease risk profiles for every patient. This allows proactive medicine, aggressively dealing with the disease, and authorizing the patients.

Big data will have a high influence in healthcare particularly in personalized medicine. According to the report provided by The Institute for Health Technology Transformation, US healthcare organizations have generated enormous healthcare data [13], and this data will continuously increase shortly. If this extraordinary volume of data, is implicitly used, it can offer substantial acumens to circumvent redundant treatments, curtails drug misfortunes, maximizes complete wellbeing, and ultimately leads an effective and competent healthcare system, and achieves the goal of personalized medicine.

A broad variety of data is accessible during the patients' normal activities, which can be collected, processed and evaluated. The integration of mobile cloud platforms and Sensor-based IoT devices that share the data to cloud-based mHealth initiatives enables real-time patient health monitoring ([14]), Which helps patients in informed decision making. AI and ML are part of smart agents that are commonly used in medical systems and integrated via big data cloud in a triad of mHealth cloud, WHDs and big data. These smart agents work with a range of medical agents and deals with fitness-related issues. Together the system provides access to transparent information [15].

7.2 TEMPORAL DISPLACEMENT OF CARE

Healthcare providers can build value for themselves and individual patients who have autoimmune disease through IT and analytics and practicing the replacement of time where patients and physicians make interventions. Then health benefits are assessed with improved clinical outcomes. [16] suggests healthcare from foundations of temporality that IT and analytics to be generated by healthcare provider organizations for identification, tracking and analyzing of health situations at appropriate points of time as timeliness is an essential factor in monitoring and managing services and activities of chronic diseases.

The theory deals with where and when tasks and services are consumed by a group in the treatment system of chronic care, which also includes how an individual is being treated. The assumptions made by [16] are restricted to lifestyle chronic disorders and do not include infectious illness treatment or protocols to be followed in the treatment of acute diseases. However, there are some cases available in the present situation, where the theory stands true for acute and infectious disease conditions also. Patients with lifestyle disorders will be happy to engage and collaborate during their treatment period prescribed by the provider. However, [17]) identified non-compliance in diabetic type-2 patients and concluded that they remain an escape from the project.

For the implementation of better displacement of the intervention of time between care, a provider must be provided with IT and analytics, with the capabilities of codifying the time factor, treatment class, cost and consequences. Assimilation of information into IT systems enables knowledge to be accessible, captures and transmitted directions and details distributed, which expands the collaboration between stakeholders [18].

7.3 AI/ML USE IN HEALTHCARE

When a patient has been to a hospital, the practitioner cannot ensure that a specific procedure performs safely on the patient. For about half of the drugs and procedures being used, there is no data of either their efficacy or effectiveness for patients, as this evidence was focused on extremely limited sample samples, which cannot be replicated because the findings of the research are only considered by averages. This simply means that physicians do not have ample details in their hands to recommend an exact recovery plan for the patient. However, healthcare can be improved with the futuristic aim of including AI and our doctors can be much intellectual. AI will serve our physicians as the second set of trustworthy eyes.

AI has many implications where it comes to healthcare. AI is support for radiologists in analyzing medical images (C. W. L. [19]). Recently, the IDx-DR AI-enabled device, licensed by the United States Food and Drug Administration (US-FDA), which does not need clinician intervention to interpret the outcome of milder diabetic retinopathy in diabetes diagnosed adults [20]. This AI-enabled system allows the patient to be tested and if the findings are not favourable then the patient is referred to an ophthalmologist. Patient can be visited only within 12 months, with the unfavourable effects. With the help of AI and ML, development and evaluation of adaptive technologies for personal preventive healthcare is evolving opportunity to exploit AI in advancing youth wellbeing. Customized technologies powered by AI have multiple prospective advantages. AI can be used to influence how teenagers, as well as adult and geriatric users, use adaptive technology to create traits and knowledge [21].

Nowadays many smartphone apps have been developed and are easily available for specialist care of the physiological position [22–24]. Though there is a move towards personalized medicine, these developments suffer from certain issues such as scalability, safety and confidentiality. Moreover, these apps provide a picture of the physiological conditions but not the overall health over a while.

AI has many implications where it comes to healthcare. Smartphone apps have been developed and are easily available for specialist care of the physiological position.

With the advent of more recent developments in sensor networks research, we can move towards the path of innovative low-cost healthcare monitoring systems implanted within the home and living environments [25]. This led to the evolution of Ambient Intelligent (AMI) systems from the advances in AI. This is more penetrating, receptive, adaptive and universal. AMI systems are more capable to boost the field of healthcare vividly. It not only can be used to monitor the health status of elder patients suffering from chronic diseases but also provides proper care for individuals mentally and physically [26] and share their results and behaviour. This can be used to develop influential services to encourage people to have a healthy life and enhance the wellbeing of the people. Finally, it also helps the healthcare professionals to offer pioneering tools in communicating and monitoring the health in a transparent modest way. It can be used as a consistent service combined with various situations and devices.

According to [27], various ML algorithms provide an appropriate estimate of the probability of achieving the objective of personalized medicine. This model is combined with a web application that helps healthcare professionals to forecast with certainty. The physical actions of young adults are monitored using wearables and mobile sensors that simplify societal assessment and offer personalized intelligent feedback [28]. The wrist-worn heartrate device helps in monitoring the heart rate of the patient continuously. The recorded data is then demonstrated through fuzzy techniques to understand remote cardiac restoration sittings.

The acceptance of the IoT is leading to e-coaching through animated objects [29] by using these devices in day-to-day activities. For example, Patients with neurological complaints can frequently struggle with such activities, where they get confused about the order in which the responsibilities should be performed or may forget which action to be implemented for a given item. This work provides a set of samples that provides the usage of lights and audio on animated objects to impact movement by minimizing the uncertainty.

7.4   WEARABLE HEALTH DEVICES

Healthcare technologies such as the IoT, also known as the Internet of Medical Things (IoMT) and Wearable Health devices (WDs) plays a crucial role by their immense capability of generation and transmission of vital data ([4,30]). Today there are many WDs available in the market, which accurately measure heartrate, exercise tracking, body temperature, female health and other vitals [31]. Some of the advanced WDs notify the patient when they are suffering stress and provides its users with a guided breathing exercise to regain the SpO_2 – Oxygen level [32], where some other devices have the capabilities of generation and sharing of electrocardiogram also known as ECG [33–35]. Table 7.1 gives the details of wearable devices available for Indian users. Figure 7.1 shows the present practices in healthcare and how healthcare of the future can be. The present practices in healthcare and how healthcare of the future can be is shown in Figure 7.2.

TABLE 7.1
Various Wearable Health Device Available in India

Device	Health Functionality	Reference/Source
Samsung Active Watch	Sleep Cycle, Stress Level, Guided Breathing Exercise, Exercise Tracking, Blood Pressure, Female Health, Heart Rate, etc.	[32]
Fitbit Smart Watch	ECG, Heart Rate, Workout tracking, Workout Suggestions, Feale Health, Sleep Cycle Tracking, etc	[34]
Apple Smart Watch	Sleep cycle monitoring, Sleep Meditation, Workouts, ECG, Heart Rate, Temperature, Blood Pressure, etc.	([33]; [36])
MI Smart Band	Basic Functions of heart rate, step counts, aerobic and anaerobic activity tracker, etc.	[37]
Realme Smart Watch	Oxygen Level, Workout and exercise tracking, Sleep Cycle Monitoring, Steps to enhance sleep, Stress monitoring, Heart Rate, metabolism and calories burnt, etc.	[38]

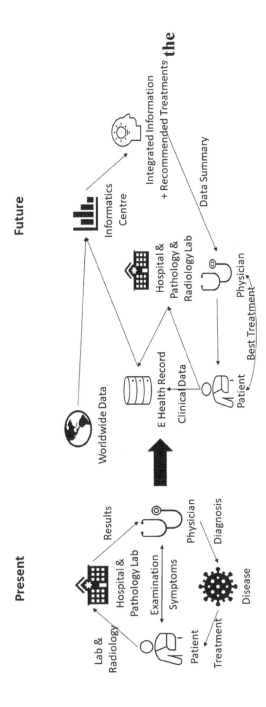

FIGURE 7.1 Shows the present practices in healthcare and how healthcare of the future can be. The present practices in healthcare and how healthcare of the future can be is shown in Figure 7.2.

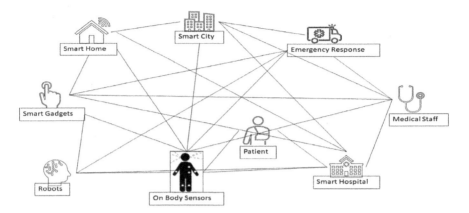

FIGURE 7.2   Indicates the futuristic healthcare in smart city scenario with smart devices.

7.5   CONCLUSION

To implement precision medicine, the role of the patient is crucial. It will help in providing customized precision medicine to every patient whose genetic sequencing is unique by collecting as much information as possible. Since EHRs are positioned to support the genetic information with the help of technology, they will ease the clinicians by providing complete information of the patient along with the genetic data. The information gained will be systematized and verified in such a way that it empowers smooth diagnostics and the decisions related to the treatment assessing scheme of the patient. It will help the healthcare professionals to evolve to provide the exact dose of the medicine or intervention before the treatment starts. This leads to the categorization of patients based on some genetic characteristics which provide an efficient model for providing balanced nutrition and lifestyle. It can be concluded that with the advent of AI this precision medicine would have a huge impact on healthcare. Usage of wearables and use of smartphones helps in the professional care of the physiological position.

With the advent of more recent developments in sensor networks, research in the healthcare sector moves towards innovative low-cost healthcare monitoring systems implanted within the home and living environments.

REFERENCES

1. Ho, D., Quake, S. R., McCabe, E. R. B., Chng, W. J., Chow, E. K., Ding, X., Gelb, B. D., Ginsburg, G. S., Hassenstab, J., Ho, C. M., Mobley, W. C., Nolan, G. P., Rosen, S. T., Tan, P., Yen, Y., & Zarrinpar, A. (2020). Enabling technologies for personalized and precision medicine. *Trends in Biotechnology*. doi:10.1016/j.tibtech.2019.12.021
2. Khan, O., Badhiwala, J. H., Grasso, G., & Fehlings, M. G. (2020). Use of machine learning and artificial intelligence to drive personalized medicine approaches for spine care. *World Neurosurgery*. doi:10.1016/j.wneu.2020.04.022

3. Chakraborty, S., Bhatt, V., & Chakravorty, T. (2019). Impact of iot adoption on agility and flexibility of healthcare organization. *International Journal of Innovative Technology and Exploring Engineering, 8*(11), 2673–2681. doi:10.35940/ijitee.K2119.0981119

4. Chakraborty, S., & Bhatt, V. (2019). Mobile IoT adoption as antecedent to Care-Service Efficiency and Improvement: Empirical study in Healthcare-context. *Journal of International Technology and Information Management, 28*(3), 101.

5. Chakraborty, S., & Bhatt, V. (2020). Interactional Resource Adoption. *Handbook of Research on Engineering Innovations and Technology Management in Organizations,* 253–268. doi:10.4018/978-1-7998-2772-6.ch014

6. Bhatt, V., Chakraborty, S., Chakravorty, T. (2020). Importance of digitech adoption for providing efficient healthcare services during COVID-19. *International Journal on Emerging Technologies, 11*(3), 1–13.

7. Li, J., Zhang, C., Li, X., & Zhang, C. (2020). Patients' emotional bonding with MHealth apps: An attachment perspective on patients' use of MHealth applications. *International Journal of Information Management, 51*(December), 102054. doi:10.1016/j.ijinfomgt.2019.102054

8. Simmons, L. A., Dinan, M. A., Robinson, T. J., & Snyderman, R. (2012). Personalized medicine is more than genomic medicine: confusion over terminology impedes progress towards personalized healthcare. *Personalized Medicine.* doi:10.2217/pme.11.86

9. Aronson, S. J., & Rehm, H. L. (2015). Building the foundation for genomics in precision medicine. *Nature.* doi:10.1038/nature15816

10. Hoffman, M. A., & Williams, M. S. (2011). Electronic medical records and personalized medicine. *Human Genetics.* doi:10.1007/s00439-011-0992-y

11. Nicholson, J. K. (2006). Global systems biology, personalized medicine and molecular epidemiology. *Molecular Systems Biology.* doi:10.1038/msb4100095

12. The coming era of human phenotyping. (2015). *Nature Biotechnology.* doi: 10.1038/nbt.3266

13. Terry, S. F. (2015). Obama's precision medicine initiative. *In Genetic Testing and Molecular Biomarkers.* doi:10.1089/gtmb.2015.1563

14. Chakraborty, S., Bhatt, V., & Chakravorty, T. (2020). Big-data, IoT wearable and mHealth cloud platform integration triads: A logical way to patient-health monitoring. *International Journal of Engineering and Advanced Technology, 9*(3), 388–394. doi: 10.35940/ijeat.c5241.029320

15. Bhatt, V., Sashikala, P., & Chakraborty, S. (2019). The impact of information technology and analytics on the performance of a hospital: Scale development in Indian context. *International Journal of Recent Technology and Engineering, 8*(3), 2861–2869. https://doi.org/10.35940/ijrte.C5229.098319

16. Thompson, S., Whitaker, J., Kohli, R., & Jones, C. (2020). Chronic disease management: How it and analytics create healthcare value through the temporal displacement of care. *MIS Quarterly, 44*(1), 227–256. https://doi.org/10.25300/misq/2020/15085

17. Brundisini, F., Vanstone, M., Hulan, D., DeJean, D., & Giacomini, M. (2015). Type 2 diabetes patients' and providers' differing perspectives on medication nonadherence: A qualitative meta-synthesis. *BMC Health Services Research.* doi:10.1186/s12913-015-1174-8

18. Kotlarsky, J., Scarbrough, H., & Oshri, I. (2014). Coordinating expertise across knowledge boundaries in offshore-outsourcing projects: The role of codification. *MIS Quarterly: Management Information Systems.* doi: 10.25300/MISQ/2014/38.2.13

19. Ho, C. W. L., Soon, D., Caals, K., & Kapur, J. (2019). Governance of automated image analysis and arti fi cial intelligence analytics in healthcare. *Clinical Radiology, 74,* 329–337. doi:10.1016/j.crad.2019.02.005

20. *FDA permits marketing of artificial intelligence-based device to detect certain diabetes-related eye problems | FDA*. (n.d.). Retrieved November 25, 2020, from https://www.fda.gov/news-events/press-announcements/fda-permits-marketing-artificial-intelligence-based-device-detect-certain-diabetes-related-eye

21. Pelánek, R. (2018). The details matter: methodological nuances in the evaluation of student models. *User Modeling and User-Adapted Interaction.* doi:10.1007/s11257-018-9204-y

22. Gregoski, M. J., Mueller, M., Vertegel, A., Shaporev, A., Jackson, B. B., Frenzel, R. M., Sprehn, S. M., & Treiber, F. A. (2012). Development and validation of a smartphone heart rate acquisition application for health promotion and wellness telehealth applications. *International Journal of Telemedicine and Applications* doi:10.1155/2012/696324

23. Milošević, M., Shrove, M. T., & Jovanov, E. (2011). Applications of smartphones for ubiquitous health monitoring and wellbeing management. *JITA - Journal of Information Technology and Applications (Banja Luka) - APEIRON.* doi: 10.7251/jit1101007m

24. Scully, C. G., Lee, J., Meyer, J., Gorbach, A. M., Granquist-Fraser, D., Mendelson, Y., & Chon, K. H. (2012). Physiological parameter monitoring from optical recordings with a mobile phone. *IEEE Transactions on Biomedical Engineering.* doi:10.1109/TBME.2011.2163157

25. Black, J., Segmuller, W., Cohen, N., Leiba, B., Misra, A., Ebling, M., & Stern, E. (2004). *Pervasive computing in healthcare: Smart spaces and enterprise information systems. MobiSys Workshop on Context Awareness*, USA.

26. Cook, D. J., Augusto, J. C., & Jakkula, V. R. (2009). Ambient intelligence: Technologies, applications, and opportunities. *Pervasive and Mobile Computing.* doi:10.1016/j.pmcj.2009.04.001

27. Dijkhuis, T. B., Blaauw, F. J., van Ittersum, M. W., Velthuijsen, H., & Aiello, M. (2018). Personalized physical activity coaching: A machine learning approach. *Sensors (Switzerland)* doi:10.3390/s18020623

28. Klein, M. C. A., Manzoor, A., & Mollee, J. S. (2017). Active2Gether: A personalized m-health intervention to encourage physical activity. *Sensors (Switzerland).* doi:10.3390/s17061436

29. Baber, C., Khattab, A., Russell, M., Hermsdörfer, J., & Wing, A. (2017). Creating affording situations: Coaching through animate objects. *Sensors (Switzerland)* doi:10.3390/s17102308

30. Bhatt, V., & Chakraborty, S. (2020). *Importance of Trust in IoT based Wearable Device Adoption by Patient: An Empirical Investigation. Proceddings, Fourth International Conference on I-SMAC (IoT in Social, Mobile, Analytics and Cloud)*, 1226–1231. doi:10.1109/I-SMAC49090.2020.9243533

31. Deshkar, S., Thanseeh, R.A., & Menon, V. G. (2017). A review on IoT based m-Health systems for diabetes. In *International Journal of Computer Science and Telecommunications* (Vol. 8, Issue 1). www.ijcst.org

32. *Samsung Galaxy Watch Active 2 – Specs & Features | Samsung India.* (n.d.). Retrieved April 19, 2020, from https://www.samsung.com/in/microsite/galaxy-watch-active2/

33. *ECG app and irregular heart rhythm notification available today on Apple Watch – Apple (IN).* (n.d.). Retrieved September 21, 2020, from https://www.apple.com/in/newsroom/2019/09/ecg-app-and-irregular-heart-rhythm-notification-available-today-on-apple-watch/

34. *Fitbit's atrial fibrillation app gets FDA approval.* (n.d.). Retrieved September 16, 2020, from https://www.modernhealthcare.com/patients/fitbits-atrial-fibrillation-app-gets-fda-approval

35. *Fitbit Versa 2 | Health & Fitness Smartwatch.* (n.d.). Retrieved April 19, 2020, from https://www.fitbit.com/in/versa

36. *Healthcare – Apple Watch – Apple (IN).* (n.d.). Retrieved September 21, 2020, from https://www.apple.com/in/healthcare/apple-watch/

37. *Mi Smart Band 4 @ ₹2,299 | Live More – Mi India.* (n.d.). Retrieved April 19, 2020, from https://www.mi.com/in/mi-smart-band-4/

38. *Realme Watch – realme (India).* (n.d.). Retrieved November 24, 2020, from https://www.realme.com/in/realme-watch

8 Artificial Intelligence and the 4th Industrial Revolution

Alok Kumar Sahai and Namita Rath
Faculty of Management Studies, Sri Sri University, Cuttack

CONTENTS

DOI: 10.1201/9781003125129-8

8.1   INTRODUCTION

Technological progression throughout the historical timeline is punctuated by radical changes predating the current digital era of computerization. These technological epochs brought about broad changes in social and political beliefs and material wealth in society.

The term technology is derived from two Greek words meaning systematic treatment of art and craft. It defines how scientific knowledge is employed for achieving required outcomes [1]. Technological changes improved human skills and application of deploying natural resources and gain competitive advantages. Requirements of the increased population, environmental and competitive challenges led to the development of tools to maximize and optimize the human efforts [2]. Machines were designed and developed to reduce or replace human efforts and converted electrical and mechanical energy to convert material and form from one to another. This led to a change in the economy from hunter–gatherer to agrarian to an industrial economy. The noun "industry" signifies the production of goods and services using technology and machines. Industrialization means the development of industries on a larger scale. The industrial revolution started in the latter part of the 18th century. The industrial revolution of the 1770s marks the shift from an agrarian society to an industrial society centred around the proliferation of industries [3]. The population and the wealth of nations have exploded ten-fold from the period of the first phase of industrialization of the 1770s [4]. This led to the 2nd and 3rd Industrial Revolutions necessitated by the surge in demand for goods and services for the teeming millions of consumers.

8.2   THE INDUSTRIAL REVOLUTIONS

The industrialization of the west followed by that of east took different paths marked by the differences in the geography and technological advances. The industrial revolution is taken as the period from the 1770s to 1870s when technological leaps enabled us to harness electrical and mechanical energy for social betterment. This led to several changes in the way manufacturing and production were practised. Newer forms of transport were discovered and developed which led to the creation of infrastructure for much of the society and in turn, this led to the expansion of populations geographically. Great Britain became the epicentre of the industrial and spread the technological waves to its very wide colonial footprint [5].

At the beginning of the 20th century, the world population crossed 1.6 billion with a corresponding increase in the world GDP, rapid advancements in generation and distribution of electricity, mass production of goods and the onset of globalization with faster modes of transportation appearing on the scene. By the middle of the 20th century, the world had witnessed two world wars which resulted in rapid industrialization. The war efforts necessitated changes in the way machinery and equipment were produced efficiently. New global power balances emerged, and nuclear power and advances in consumer electronics were witnessed. Gradually, the electronic gadgets became parts of everyday life culminating in the rise of mainframe computers. This was the dawn of the third wave of industrialization with the rise of information systems and automation of manufacturing systems. Advances in telecommunications shrunk the global dimensions and collapse of time zones. Newer frontiers in biological sciences, transportation, media, engineering, communication technologies, miniaturization and commercialization marked the last quarter of the 20th century. While the first wave of industrialization originated in Europe, second was focused on Europe and the USA. Asian countries emerged at the forefront of electronics with China, Japan and Korea Taiwan dominated the manufacture and engineering of consumer electronics and electronic parts. The rise of BRICS nations comprising of Brazil, Russia, India, China and South Africa emerged as a formidable block in the world economic scene. The colonization of India by the British for sourcing indigo and cotton fuelled the funds and consequently the industrial revolution in Britain [6]. The Asian giants India and China became the source of qualified and yet cheap information technology (IT) experts for the US IT market. Large scale industrialization was witnessed both in India and China which led to the emergence of these two countries as a major trading partner for providing the feedstock for the much-industrialized western countries.

The Space Race was another major facet of the third wave of industrialization. The first orbiting satellite, Sputnik, by USSR, started a race to put the first man in space. This race was dominated by the US and USSR. The Second World War produced the first rockets, which later helped in the Space Race. The rockets and the propulsion vehicles later gave a much-needed fillip to the communications satellites which were the steppingstones for the IT revolution due to appear in the next four decades. The personal computers appeared in the 1980s, and changed the acceleration of the 3rd Industrial Revolution.

With the maturity of the third wave of industrialization, the onset of the fourth wave was signalled by the emergence of a knowledge-based economy at the core of social change and economic growth [7]. The focus moved from energy transformation from one form to another as seen in the first and second waves of industrialization. The dawn of the 21st century gave way to a knowledge-based digital revolution from matured IT-based systems (Table 8.1).

Before modernization, manual labour by man and animals dominated work and travel. Mechanical energy from wind, water and fire was used for ages, such as sailing boats and water wheels. The steam engine was invented by Thomas Savery in 1698 to lift water in coal mines. Thomas Newcomen in 1712 modified the design of steam engines making them more versatile for a variety of uses. James Watt is credited with the steam engines as his design was a breakthrough in the conversion of thermal energy to mechanical energy which marked the dawn of an industrial revolution in Europe. By 1886, steam engines could generate 10,000 horsepower and were used to propel large steamships and long-haul steam locomotives [3]. By the turn of the century, gasoline engines had appeared, and the first automobile was built by Daimler [8].

The 3rd Industrial Revolution was marked by the digital revolution or the developments in microelectronics and semiconductor developments namely VLSI and IC which could place increasing numbers of transistors into a single chip [9].

TABLE 8.1
The Four Industrial Revolutions

Time Period	1780–1870	1880–1930	1950–1990	2000–2030
Stage/Phase	1st Industrial Revolution	2nd Industrial Revolution	3rd Industrial Revolution	4th Industrial Revolution
Characterized by	Mechanical Production	Mass Production	Internet and Information Technology-Enabled Services (ITeS)	Mobile Computing, Social Media & Governance, Blockchain, eCommerce Explosion, eCRM
Key technologies	Mechanical energy transformation	Electrical and fossil fuel energy transformation	Analogue to digital transformation, Information Technology	Bio Physical transformation, Internet of things (IoT), Nanotechnology, Biotechnology and Smart Networking systems
Thrust areas	Transportation	Electrification	Electronics and Information Technology, Flexible manufacturing, Lean Manufacturing, TQM, JIT, Six Sigma	Cyber-Physical Technology, Additive Manufacturing, Nanotechnology, Biotechnology and Artificial Intelligence

Digital electronics expedited the journey from analogue technology to digital technology which covered a large gamut of industries from media to communication to manufacturing and computing. Enterprise-wide computing was dominated by US-based companies namely IMB, HP and Microsoft among other Japanese and Korean companies like NTT Sony, Fujitsu and Samsung to name a few. The Arpanet was the precursor of the internet of connected computer systems which changed the technological landscape forever. The growth of the internet in the last decade of the 20th century laid the framework for data handling and storage, search engines, online trade mobile computing and even the social media revolution. Google, Apple, Facebook, Twitter and a host of others were at the forefront of digital and social revolution. The 3rd Industrial Revolution was marked by the connected workspaces on a very large scale. The technology-enabled the devices to be connected seamlessly using the telecommunication backbone and supercomputing servers to support the transfer of petabytes of information across the globe. The data exchange transactions happened at both mainframe server stage as well as the miniaturized and mobile data computing. From mainframe to personal to mobile data computing the third wave of industrialization put the command in the hands of the individual on the go. The marvel of the internet-enabled machines across the globe to communicate with each other. 4G telecommunications enable not just analogue voice but also file exchange and video messaging to video calling with data trunk lines carrying gigabytes per second. The availability of spectrum and mobile telecom opened newer vistas of business entities in the transportation, energy and utility infrastructures. Digital selling platforms and marketplaces abounded and flourished. The flipside of all this was the digital divide or the unequal internet access for all. In a country like India post COVID-19 it was revealed that internet and optic fibre network is not available throughout the country and there are several dark spots or data holes which need to be filled before online access could be made available for all.

Technological advances in biological science, space science spinoffs and material science, and healthcare and medical such as Machine Learning and Artificial Intelligence have the potential to cause a sea change in the quality of life and ease of doing work intelligently and have in turn indicated the onset of what is known as the 4th Industrial Revolution.

8.3 THE TECHNOLOGIES OF THE 4TH INDUSTRIAL REVOLUTION

Klaus Schwab, founder and executive chairman of the World Economic Forum, coined the term "4th Industrial Revolution" in 2016 [10]. to describe the hitherto unknown fusion of emerging technologies into the biological and physical worlds. Interestingly the German Government called for "Industrie 4.0" (or Industrial 4.0) developed earlier in 2010 [11]. In 2006 Helen Gill coined the term Cyber-Physical Systems to describe the machine-to-machine automation which formed the core of the Smart factory. All this is now encompassed by the term 4th Industrial Revolution and the attendant changes brought about in the economic, social and technological change.

8.3.1 INTERNET OF THINGS

The early computers of the 1970s found their way into the manufacturing systems, and the factories adopted Computer Integrated Manufacturing (CIM), Just in Time (JIT) and Theory of Constraints (ToC). Soon, this developed into deeper usage of computers in Computer-Aided Design (CAD) and Computer-Aided Manufacturing (CAM). Mark Weiser at Palo Alto Research Center originated the concept of the Internet of Things (IoT) [12]. Kevin Ashton [13]. coined the term IoT to describe the RFID enabled paging for Supply Chain Optimization. These ideas allowed users to manage their assets spread across their factory to warehouse to design, manufacturing to delivery. IoT evolved rapidly, and soon included a wide range of pressure sensors, solar panels, thermoelectric and a plethora of home appliance and other devices connected through the voice-activated internet. This customer-focused IoT was challenged by General Electric which came up with the Industrial IoT (IIoT) where the focus is on lifecycle approach covering design, development and manufacturing to the end customer logistics.

Micro and nanoscale technologies in physical materials have led to miniaturization. 3D printing of additive manufacturing [14]. is a digital technology for creating digitally controlled composites. Nanotechnology operates at the molecular level and has led to breakthroughs such as semiconductor designs, carbon nanotubes and molecular engineering in medical science applications. Nanotechnology deals largely with genetic engineering and molecular biologies [15,16]. such as gene therapy, gene splicing, gene grafting and genetically modified crops. The IoT will encompass smart grids, intelligent and adaptive supply chain, open banking systems, next-generation defence systems, intelligent highways and highway systems, robotic manufacturing and many more areas of development.

The building blocks of the 4th Industrial Revolution are the technologies that integrate materials, locations and machines with biological processes. The coalescing of the physical, biological and digital domains with these new technologies in an integrated manner gives rise to Artificial Intelligence and Machine Learning.

The game of chess is long recognized as a test of human intelligence, and the 20th century saw the first public test for Artificial Intelligence versus human. In 1996, Deep Blue, a supercomputer developed by IBM was tested to play a chess game against the world champion, Kasparov. Kasparov lost and called for a rematch the following year, but Deep Blue won the six-game challenge again in May 1997 [17]. Successive advancements in computing have resulted in computers up to 100 times faster, which consume a fraction of the power that Deep Blue did. It is interesting to know that an Apple iPhone 8 is 7 times more powerful than Deep Blue, yet fits snugly in the palm. Computing power has increased exponentially with simultaneous miniaturization coupled with reduced demands of power.

8.3.2   4TH INDUSTRIAL REVOLUTION: NEW TECHNOLOGIES

The 4th Industrial Revolution showcased breakthrough technologies in engineering, science and medicine and the pervasive effects of these technologies. Surprisingly, many of these breakthrough technologies of the 4th Industrial Revolution had their roots in the middle of the 20th century. The basic substrates for the IoT, virtual reality, augmented reality and Artificial Intelligence, nanotechnology, robotics and wearable technologies were discovered or perfected by the middle of the previous century.

8.3.3   MACHINE LEARNING AND ARTIFICIAL INTELLIGENCE

Artificial Intelligence was first used at the Dartmouth Conference in 1956 [18]. The AI concepts developed side by side with graphical user interface (GUI), advances in hardware technologies, programming languages and the development of VLSI and semiconductor technologies in the 1970s. The next decade saw the development of neural networks and intelligent agents. Deep neural networks developed a decade later with the emergence of supercomputing facilities.

The size of the ML and AI markets can be estimated by the size of the market of chipsets used in machine automation. The market for these chipsets is likely to touch $16 billion in volume and achieve a CAGR of 63% from 2016 to 2022 [19].

AI and ML cover the domains of predictive marketing, risk analytics, business analytics, fraud detection, predictive breakdown maintenance and business and network analytics. Artificial Intelligence applications are found in more and more industries now, notable among them are marketing, media, advertising, manufacturing, banking and transportation and automobile.

8.3.4 INTERNET OF THINGS, MICROELECTRO-SENSORS AND BIOSENSOR TECH

IoT started around the RFID technology but has come far in the intervening years. Today, IoT employs various sensors and telemetry. In its physical fusion, IoT is present in Jet propulsion engine turbines to automotive condition monitors and nuclear power plants, supply chain automation and robotics to meteorological measurement and optimization. Unmanned drones work through sensors to read accurate information and ground swath information and then using the onboard computer descend on their planned locations. Microscopic IoT sensors can be inserted in the skin, ingested or injected to monitor the biological health indicators of the host. These microscopic sensors are useful in mobile monitoring of health using platforms such as mobile and internet-based platforms such as mHealth and eHealth, and also in remote healthcare and diagnostics. Wearable technologies are now available which measure psychological and physiological stress levels that can be used with analytics for better monitoring and integration.

The size of the IoT market has been expanding exponentially. Gartner estimates 8.5 billion connected objects in 2017, while Cisco estimated to 50 billion objects by 2020 [20]. IDC estimated a market of $8.6 trillion and 212 billion connected things by 2020 [21]. BCG forecasted market size of $276 billion. Gartner forecasted that by 2020 more than 50% of all major businesses would incorporate some element of IoT and that IoT security would be the next big thing [22].

8.3.5 ROBOTICS

The software side of the AI is only half the story, and is completed by the hardware part of machine intelligence. IoT sensors in robotics lead to intelligent automation. Intelligent and multifunctional robotics is a breakthrough of the 4th Industrial Revolution, involving manufacturing, hazardous material handling and hazardous biological experiments. Starting from the unmanned aerial vehicles to unmanned guided vehicles, automatic flying robots the robotics field covers context-specific computing, distributed intelligence to the industrial robots. The Asian markets (especially China) employ industrial robots in automobile and heavy industries. Europe spearheaded robotic applications in electronics, metal processing, welding, rubber and automobiles.

8.3.6 VIRTUAL REALITY, AUGMENTED REALITY AND MIXED REALITY

Ivan Sutherland, in 1968, created the first virtual reality (VR) display system [23]. The VR models in three dimensions represent the real physical environment or imaginary environment which give an immersive experience to the users. By the

1990s, commercial, VR headsets were commercially available, manufactured by Sega and Nintendo in video game markets [24,25]. VR gaming gave way to industrial usage in the next two decades such as medical imaging, architecture and GIS systems for land use applications. Notable VR products in consumer products include Google Glass and Microsoft HoloLens. Augmented reality adds digital objects to real objects using a digital capture device such as a camera or a mobile phone. Mixed reality blends digital objects with physical objects in real-time. This is achieved by a concept called "digital twinning".

8.3.7   3D PRINTING AND ADDITIVE MANUFACTURING

The ever-increasing penetration of CAD and CAM has led to a new form of industrial design and manufacturing culminating into discrete manufacturing systems (DMS), Adjustable manufacturing systems (AMS) and flexible manufacturing systems (FMS) or reconfigurable manufacturing systems (RMS). All these manufacturing systems are helped by the use of Machine Learning and robotics.

Additive manufacturing or 3D printing is the latest development on stereolithography [26]. 3D printing is now more flexible and used in RMS for printing parts for jet engines by General Electric [27].

8.3.8   NEUROMORPHIC COMPUTING

Neuromorphic computing attempts to replicate the computational properties of biological elements; namely, their ability to store information and modify, update and adapt to environmental triggers. The current trend utilizes the mixed-signal techniques to imitate the organic carbon-based material using the alternative silicon-based material. The European Brain Project is a collaborative effort to emulate brain functions and accelerate learning and processing over and above the speed possible in biological systems.

The much-touted Moore's law in computing is no longer relevant as the focus of the latest research has shifted to large scale computing modelled on the way nature and biological systems work. The main advantage of this approach is significantly lower consumption of power. Artificial Intelligence, in general, requires huge power resources but a neomorphic chip consumes only 70 milliwatts power which is one-thousandth of the power consumed by an equally powerful Intel chip.

8.3.9   BIOCHIPS

Biologic computing involves nanomorphic cells that combine the biology and nature to use DNA as the medium of storage. The juxtaposition of nanoengineering and biotechnology is a great example of the 4th Industrial Revolution. The fusion of biological and technological systems will have a significant bearing for energy systems and computing speed. The devices such as biological and magneto-resistive sensors, hybrid car batteries and onboard networked devices represent the unfolding of the 4th Industrial Revolution [28].

8.4   AI APPLICATIONS IN THE 4TH INDUSTRIAL REVOLUTION

Artificial Intelligence has already reached the threshold where it touches human lives in many ways, analyzing to predict data in various industrial applications. The inclusion of AI has not only increased the operational efficiency of infrastructure, but also brought costs down. Some industrial applications of AI, characteristic of the 4th Industrial Revolution are described in this section.

8.4.1   GAMING INDUSTRY

The global gaming market was worth $152 billion in 2015 and is likely to reach $257 billion by 2025, registering a CAGR of 17%. From the board games to interactive strategy games, AI is in use everywhere. Carnegie Mellon University developed a neural net called Libratus. This deep learning algorithm makes statistical predictions, and also has a behavioural element to bluff as a strategy in poker. The AI is not designed to learn strategies like chess games, but to play by the rules and the information provided to it by the other player. Libratus has been effective where responses are required based on imperfect information. The deep learning schedule for Libratus included the equivalent of 15 million hours of training to polish its strategies. Libratus went on to win a 20-day poker tournament [29].

8.4.2   SURVEILLANCE AND HUMAN BEHAVIOURAL MARKETING

Surveillance and human behaviour tracking are key areas where Artificial Intelligence has created a useful niche. Machine Learning is used to detect anomalous behaviour of employees. Countries use the surveillance to flag security risks arising out of the employees breaking their normal routine behavioural patterns.

Here the Machine Learning captures the data such as the files that are routinely picked and whether any file picked up is outside the domain of that particular employee. This way, snooping employees or employee espionage in various industries or even governments can be detected early. This results in a reduction of security threats and increases communication.

For example, if an employee starts making unauthorized copies of files that they chance upon all of a sudden. Or employees stealing information which might be of interest to competitors. The surveillance also checks employees responding to a phishing attack or opening any malware in their emails [30].

8.4.3   IDENTITY MANAGEMENT

With the increased access of banks and other security information and security of digital wallets using voice-activated authentication uses AI to match the vibrations of the owner's voice with the known patterns. The digital assistant responds based on whether the audio match is established else the digital assistant stops.

IoT coupled with Machine Learning can be used to compare the voice and speech modulations of the owner to protect the identity theft by mimicry con artists. Voice

ID combined with biometrics is a very efficient way to ensure security for wireless devices. Mobile phones and Google assistant use speech training and then recognition to accept user commands [31].

8.4.4 CHATBOTS

Websites with high customer traffic and queries are employing AI-assisted chatbots which handle customer queries. Amazon uses chatbots to handle customers' queries regarding sales or deliver issues. University websites can handle 24×7 queries related to their courses and DTH operator TataSky uses chatbots to handle and resolve most customer problems. Deep neural training involves using up to 200,000 questions and their 800,000 answers and the result is a chatbot which detects the question type and its context and offers answers in a sympathetic tone to the user resulting in significant cost reductions and increased efficiency [32].

8.4.5 HEALTHCARE

AI was used in the UK to combat the problem of early detection of skin cancer. Early detection raises the five-year survival rate to 97% but can only be detected early by a trained dermatologist. Stanford University researchers applied Machine Learning using over 100,000 training images for image recognition of skin cancer patterns. After machine training, the software was tested vis-a-vis the expert dermatologists in three groups of carcinoma. Stanford University engineers and computer scientists trained the software to isolate the deadly and not so deadly skin cancers from the collection of images. The AI algorithm was able to match the pattern recognition ability when compared to 21 experienced clinicians [33].

8.4.6 WEARABLE WELLBEING MONITORS

Wearable technology is a recent phenomenon and new wearable gadgets are coming onto the market. Smartwatches and smart bands are now affordable and easily available in the consumer electronics market. These wearable gadgets collect data from the user to determine the baseline data which is then used to issue alerts when the readings hit the alarming levels. These wearable technologies can detect when a person is going to fall ill by monitoring the body temperature, pulse rates, blood oxygen levels etc. Wearable gadgets are, therefore having an important role in managing the health of users [34].

8.4.7 ASSET MONITORING AND MAINTENANCE

Heating and ventilation units in buildings are equipped with sensors. The elevators and motion sensors in key locations collect vital information about possible fire hazards by tracking temperature, humidity and power usage. Dams and power installations, as well as nuclear power generators, employ AI-based automatic asset monitoring systems to measure overloads to the pressure on the dam walls to indicate impending dangers or breakdowns. Machine Learning has enabled deep learning by impregnating with several years of data and then testing whether the system is successfully able to detect the next disaster [35].

8.4.8 Monitoring Fake News on Social Media

Social media usage is on a continuous uptrend, with the number of users of Facebook exceeding the inhabitants of the most populous country in the world. This poses a big threat of fake news, and the speed fake news spreads across the word on social media platforms such as Facebook, WhatsApp and Twitter. The misinformation fed in any social media platform can easily get traction and start trending. Here, AI enables flagging of the doubtful content and prevents the spread unabated. For example, WhatsApp detects the messages which have been forwarded in a chain of text messages and prohibits sending it to more than one individual. AI can enable fake news flagged by third parties and disseminate this information. Google, for example, flags possible spam messages depending on the header metadata. AI can also help in destroying the fake news economy by monitoring social media likes and patterns in share behaviour. Facebook started a campaign to identify and emasculate the spread of fake news. The campaign promoted in 14 countries simultaneously was designed to make people more discerning and aware readers [36,37].

8.4.9 Furniture Design

Autodesk Dreamcatcher, an engineering Machine Learning software package, was used to design a chair. The designer decided on the material and the fabric to be used and the software took over after that. The basic design such as the height and load-bearing capacity of the seat and a three-dimensional model of the chair was fed to the software and then the software went through several iterations to find the optimum furniture. Any excess metal or wood is shaved off. After several iterations the software removed the dead weight and optimized the joint placements for better load-bearing to create a streamlined final product [38].

8.4.10 Engineering Design in Aeronautics

The engineering design problem was to make lighter yet sturdy partitions separating the pilot area from the passenger area in an aircraft. The pilots sit on the fold-out seats which are supported by these partitions thereby requiring the partitions to be strong enough. Autodesk Dreamcatcher once again was used to design the partition using Machine Learning and 3D printing. The European passenger aircraft manufacturer Airbus partnered with Autodesk to design the partitions in the light of these requirements of lightweight and strength of the material. The final product was a 3D printed partition based on bone growth and was over 50% lighter than the original and exceeded the weight reduction target of 30% by a big margin [39].

8.4.11   SELF-DRIVING VEHICLES

A self-driving driverless car incorporates myriad technologies such as Machine Learning, image recognition, sensors, actuators, robotics and neural nets all inside one box. Most modern cars have some degree of AI built into them, where an onboard computer collects data from various sensors mounted under the hood and based on the engine speed, temperature and airflow decides the combustion of fuel. The onboard computer, with the help of a multipoint fuel injection system, optimizes engine performance in terms of power and economy.

The next step in AI application in passenger vehicles was assisted parking, where with the help of various cameras the onboard computer executes the manoeuvring of the car into a parking space. Self-driving driverless cars call for a lot more data to be captured and analyzed with on-road objects moving at various speeds. AI-enabled cars are equipped to respond quickly even to a surprise such as an accident, sudden braking in a car ahead or a pedestrian coming in front of the car. This will require a lot more processing power onboard to run a complex neural net of interacting AI subsystems. Driverless cars are already in the prototype stage, and Tesla and Ford have already started autonomous car projects of their own. Ford has invested $1 billion in "Argo AI" project for developing the technology for autonomous vehicles [40].

8.4.12   AI-ENABLED SMART GRIDS

Electricity demand is constantly on the rise year on year. As a commodity which cannot be stored, managing the demand and supply at various nodes in the power grid becomes important. With the focus shifting away from fossil fuel-based generators to cleaner sources of energy such as wind, solar and geothermal energy, power utilities need to think of ways to counter the widely fluctuating generating capacities of the alternate sources. National grids worldwide are switching to AI-enabled smart grids to manage the power demand at the nodes in the grid. Google DeepMind is using Machine Learning and provides more solutions than a human grid operator. The AI-based system will use Machine Learning to better predict demand and supply and save around 10% of the annual demand without needing any additional infrastructure investment [41,42].

8.5   CONCLUSION

AI has had a chequered history from the 1940s with lots of promises and fantastic predictions which overstated the then available capabilities and technologies to solve the problems on hand. The present-day multi-layered neural networks have come very far from the traditionally known computer technologies. They derive motivation and inspiration from the neural and cognitive sciences. Instead of programming the machines, the approach is to teach the machines to learn to find solutions as humans do. The thinking machines are made possible by the confluence of Machine Learning, big data and computing power. Machine intelligence is being built into everyday devices such as the humble automatic washing machine working with its fuzzy logic. Machine Learning and Artificial Intelligence are at the core of the 4th Industrial Revolution as computers and microprocessors were in the 3rd Industrial Revolution, electrical power in the 2nd Industrial Revolution and steam power in the 1st Industrial Revolution before that.

The new generation AI is like nothing we have seen before. In our quest to build and continuously improve our machine which can think for solutions with their context, we need to shift from the algorithm of instruction sets to the realm of neuroscience and cognitive sciences. In using Google Speech, we are using 10–12-layer deep neural network technology.

It may be recalled that the 4th Industrial Revolution is not driven by individual technologies, but by a combination of technologies which attempt a novel and evolving solution for complex problems. Machine Learning enables the generative design to generate novel designs which are otherwise too difficult to create using conventional manufacturing.

AI techniques are increasingly used to solve complex business problems endemic to their business sector from healthcare to education to manufacturing to surveillance, security and leisure. AI-enabled or AI centred technologies are providing a competitive edge to businesses. We are living in the era characterized by the fastest pace in technology and the business opportunities in the 4th Industrial Revolution are limited only by the imagination and are underway in some R&D lab somewhere in the world. The perpetual problem of how to do things better and more efficiently is at the forefront of all innovative AI technologies. The World Economic Forum's Global Agenda Council surveyed 800 top executives to gauge how these business leaders evaluated the penetration of the game-changing technologies of the 4th Industrial Revolution into the realm of the public domain [43].. The survey report listed 21 major shifts in applications of AI in industry and their trigger points, some of which are, reproduced in Table 8.2.

We may not be fully able to comprehend the speed and swath of the 4th Industrial Revolution. The possibility of billions of people interconnected by the internet and mobile telephony giving rise to gigantic scale processing power, cloud storage and unprecedented access to knowledge. The technical breakthrough at the confluence of Machine Learning, Artificial Intelligence, neural networks, IoT, additive manufacturing, nanotechnology, energy storage and advances in material sciences. Some of these innovations are in the nascent stage but hold immense promise to form the core of the revolution. Having already reached the critical mass these technologies are going to shape and accelerate the 4th Industrial Revolution. The newly evolved business models are changing the complexion of industries and businesses across the board. Governments and institutions alike are witnessing the paradigm shift in the way the pillars of healthcare, communication and transportation have undergone a sea change. We do not know for certain how the technology bundle of the 4th Industrial Revolution will unfold from here. We must develop a globally accepted shared view of how the new technologies are changing our lives in the social, economic and cultural contexts.

TABLE 8.2

Deep Shifts in Industrial Applications of AI and Their Trigger Points

Paradigm Shift	Trigger Point	Additional Information
Implantable technologies	The first implantable mobile commercially available	People are getting more closely connected with their devices and the devices are not only just worn but also implanted into bodies, enabling communications, location and vital health sign monitoring. Cochlear implants, tooth implants and pacemakers are some examples. A biodegradable pill developed by Novartis has a biodegradable device which communicates with the user mobile phone to inform on the drug kinetics.
The new Interface of Vision	10% of reading classes connected to the Internet	Google Glass is an example of how eyeglasses, eyewear/headsets can become intelligent and connect to the internet. These glasses allow the user to fluidly manipulate an object in three dimensions.
Wearable Internet	10% of people will wear clothes connected to the Internet	The mobile telephony is going to come closer than a mobile phone by embedding a chip to connect to the articles and the owner. Useful for monitoring of infants by hospitals or individual.
IoT	1 trillion sensors will be connected to the Internet	With a drop in hardware prices, it is economical to connect anything to the Internet. Intelligent sensors are available at competitive prices. The devices commented to the internet, will be able to communicate with one other too.
Smart Cities	The first city with at least 50,000 people and no traffic lights	The smart cities connect the services, roads or utilities to the internet. The smart cities manage their energy consumption, the flow of materials, logistics and project traffic. Singapore and Barcelona have already begun rolling out data-driven services, smart and intelligent parking system and also the automatic trash collection.
Paradigm Shift	Trigger Point	Additional Information
Big Data and Decision making	The first government to replace census by big data sources	Governments may start to turn to big data technologies for automating their populist programmes to deliver innovative services. Big data analysis will enable better and faster decision making.
AI and Decision Making	AI decision making at the corporate board level	AI can be used to analyze past data and situations to automate the complex decision-making process based on contextual inputs. Rational, data-based decisions.
Robotics in Services	Robotic pharmacist	Robotics is already present in agriculture to manufacturing. 75% of modern automobile manufacturing to packaging are done by robots. Robots in the service industry would be the next wave.
3D Printing and Manufacturing	First 3D printed car in production	Additive manufacturing or 3D printing can create complex objects without complex equipment. The printer would be able to print multiple objects from various input materials such as plastic, aluminium, steel, ceramic or some alloys. This would replace a host of equipment in factories making them smaller.
Neurotechnologies	Artificial memory chip implant in the human brain	Two of the largest funded research programmes in the world namely Human Brain Project by EC and Brain Research through Advancing Innovative Neurotechnologies (BRAIN) by the USA are focusing on scientific and medical research.

(Continued)

TABLE 8.2 (*Continued*)

Paradigm Shift	Trigger Point	Additional Information
3D printing in Healthcare	The first transplant of a human liver	Bioprinting might someday print human organs using material as diverse as titanium for bones, or ceramic for customized parts such as a tooth. Hospitals could choose prosthetic printing of body parts, splints, implants etc. customized for each patient.
Driverless Car	One tenth of all cars on the road to be driverless cars	Driverless cars, already in the trial stage are potentially safer and could achieve lower emissions and congestion on the road and improve logistics.

REFERENCES

1. Oxford English Dictionary, Technology, https://en.oxforddictionaries.com/definition/technology.
2. Age of Enlightenment, Age of Reason, Zafirovski, Milan, *The Enlightenment and Its Effects on Modern Society*, Springer 2010.
3. Baten, Jörg (2016). *A History of the Global Economy: From 1500 to the Present.* Cambridge University Press. p. 13–16. ISBN 9781107507180.
4. By El T – originally uploaded to en.wikipedia as Population curve.svg. The data is from the "lower" estimates at census.gov (archive.org mirror)., Public Domain, https://commons.wikimedia.org/w/index.php?curid=1355720.
5. Share of Global GDP, 1000 years, Data table in Maddison A (2007), *Contours of the World Economy I-2030AD*, Oxford University Press, ISBN 978-0199227204. By M Tracy Hunter – Own work, CC BY-SA 4.0, https://commons. wikimedia.org/w/index.php?curid=34088589.
6. Economic History: Why did Asia miss the Industrial Revolution that began in the 18th century?https://www.quora.com/Economic-History-Why-did-Asiamiss-the-Industrial-Revolution-that-began-in-the-18th-century.
7. Crouzet, François (1996). "France". In Teich, Mikuláš, Porter, Roy. *The Industrial Revolution in National Context: Europe and the USA.* Cambridge University Press. p. 45. ISBN 978-0-521-40940-7. LCCN 95025377.
8. Gottlieb Daimler's First Automobile (March 8, 1886), http://germanhistorydocs. ghi-dc.org/sub_image.cfm?image_id=1261.
9. The History of Integrated Circuits (2016), Nobleprize.org http://www.nobelprize.org/educational/physics/integrated_circuit/history/.
10. Klaus Schwab, *The 4th Industrial Revolution.* January 2016, World Economic Forum. ISBN 1944835008.
11. Jürgen, Jasperneite: Was hinter Begriffen wie Industrie 4.0 steckt in Computer & Automation. http://www.computer-automation.de/steuerungsebene/steuernregeln/artikel/93559/0/.
12. "Computer for the 21st Century, Mark Weiser, PARC, ACM SIGMOBILE Mobile Computing and Communications Review Vol 3 Issue 3, July 1999, 3–11 http://dl.acm.org/citation.cfm?id=329126.
13. Harnessing the power of feedback loops, Wired June 2011 https://www.wired.com/2011/06/ff_feedbackloop/all/1.

14. The rise of additive manufacturing, The Engineer, 2010, May 24 https://www.theengineer.co.uk/issues/24-may-2010/the-rise-of-additive-manufacturing/

15. Definition of Bioengineering, University of California, Berkley. http://bioeng.berkeley.edu/about-us/what-is-bioengineering.

16. Definition of Genetic Engineering, United States Environmental Protection Agency, EPA https://iaspub.epa.gov/sor_internet/registry/termreg/searchandretrieve/termsandacronyms/search.do?search=&term=genetic%20engineering&matchCriteria=Contains&checkedAcronym=true&checkedTerm=true&hasDefinitions=false

17. Endgame, *Defeating the World Chess champion*, http://www.computerhistory.org/chess/main.php?sec=thm-42f15cec6680f&sel=thm-42f15d3399c41.

18. A proposal for the Dartmouth Summer Research Project on Artificial Intelligence, August 31, 1955, Hannover, New Hampshire, http://www-formal.stanford.edu/jmc/history/dartmouth/dartmouth.html.

19. Artificial Intelligence (Chipsets) Market worth 16.06 Billion USD by 2022, n.d. maeketsandmarkets.com, http://www.marketsandmarkets.com/PressReleases/artificial-intelligence.asp%20.asp.

20. Gartner Says 8.4 Billion Connected "Things" Will Be in Use in 2017, Up 31 Percent From 2016, Gartner, February 7, 2017, http://www.gartner.com/newsroom/id/3598917.

21. The Internet of Things Is Poised to Change Everything, Says IDC, *Business Wire*, October 3, 2013 http://www.businesswire.com/news/home/20131003005687/en/Internet-Poised-Change-IDC.

22. Gartner Says By 2020, More Than Half of Major New Business Processes and Systems Will Incorporate Some Element of the Internet of Things, *Gartner Newsroom*, Jan 14, 2016. http://www.gartner.com/newsroom/id/3185623.

23. Ivan Sutherland A.M.*Turing Award* 1988, http://amturing.acm.org/award_winners/sutherland_3467412.cfm.

24. Sega-VR headset 1991, http://segaretro.org/Sega_VR.

25. Virtual Boy Nintendo 1995, http://nintendo.wikia.com/wiki/Virtual_Boy.

26. Erik Puik, Daniel Telgen Leo van MoergestelDarek Ceglarek Assessment of reconfiguration schemes for Reconfigurable Manufacturing Systems based on resources and lead time, *Robotics and Computer-Integrated Manufacturing* 43 (2017) 30–38.

27. Additive Manufacturing, GE, the world's largest manufacturer, is on the verge of using 3-D printing to make jet parts. *MIT Technology Review Martin LaMonica*, https://www.technologyreview.com/s/513716/additive-manufacturing/.

28. John Schmitz Reliability in the more than moor Landscape, Keynote, IEEE International Integrated Reliability Workshop, October 18, 2009, http://www.iirw.org/past_workshops/09/IIRW_keynote_final_posting.pdf.

29. AI just won a poker tournament against professional players, 31 Jan 2017, New Scientist https://www.newscientist.com/article/2119815-ai-just-won-a-poker-tournament-againstprofessional-players/.

30. AI tracks your every move and tells your boss if you're slacking 30 Jan 2017, New Scientist https://www.newscientist.com/article/2119734-ai-tracks-yourevery-move-and-tells-your-boss-if-youre-slacking/.

31. Voice-checking device stops hackers hijacking your Siri or Alexa, 30 Jan 2017, New Scientist https://www.newscientist.com/article/2119766-voice-checkingdevice-stops-hackers-hijacking-your-siri-or-alexa/.

32. AI agony aunt gives love advise online, 26 Jan 2017, New Scientist https://www.newscientist.com/article/2119347-ai-agony-aunt-learns-to-dole-out-relationship-advice-online/.

33. Stanford's new AI can recognize the warning signs of skin cancer as effectively as human dermatologists http://www.alphr.com/science/1005233/stanford-snew-ai-can-recognise-the-warning-signs-of-skin-cancer-as-effectively-as.

34. Digital Health: Tracking Physiomes and Activity Using Wearable Biosensors Reveals Useful Health-Related Information, *PLOS Biology Journal Li et al.* Jan 12 2017.

35. Smart buildings predict when critical systems are about to fail, 21 Jan 2017 New Scientist https://www.newscientist.com/article/2118499-smart-buildingspredict-when-critical-systems-are-about-to-fail/.

36. Managing Fake News on social media, Mark Zuckerberg, *Facebook founder*, 19 Nov 2016 https://www.facebook.com/zuck/posts/10103269806149061.

37. Facebook to tackle fake news with educational campaign, April, 2017 *BBC* http://www.bbc.co.uk/news/technology-39517033.

38. So. Algorithms Are Designing Chairs Now, n.d. https://www.wired.com/2016/10/elbo-chair-autodesk-algorithm/.

39. Airbus' Newest Design Is Based on Bones and Slime Mold n.d. https://www.wired.com/2015/12/airbuss-newest-design-is-based-on-slime-mold-and-bones/.

40. OEMs and connected-cars: Time to seize the connected future. *BearingPoint* 2017 https://www.bearingpoint.com/en-gb/our-success/thought-leadership/oems-and-connected-cars-time-to-seize-the-connected-future/.

41. Anthony, S., *"DeepMind in Talks with National Grid to reduce UK energy use by 10%,"* Ars Technica UK, 14 March 2017. [Online]. Available: https://arstechnica.co.uk/information-technology/2017/03/deepmind-national-gridmachine-learning/?comments=1. [Accessed 11 November 2020].

42. Mark, Skilton, Felix Hovsepian, *"Google's Deepmind Wants to cut 10% off the entire UK's energy bill"*, Business Insider UK, 13 March 2017. [Online]. Available: http://uk.businessinsider.com/google-deepmind-wants-to-cut-ten-percent-off-entireuk-energy-bill-using-artificial-intelligence-2017-3. [Accessed November 14 2020].

43. World Economic Forum- Deep Shift-Technology Tipping Points and Societal Impact Survey Report, *Global Agenda Council on the Future of Software and Society*, November 2015.

9 AI-Based Evaluation to Assist Students Studying through Online Systems

Nidhi Shukla
Associate Professor in Institute of Management Commerce
and Economics Department of Shri Ramswaroop Memorial
University in Lucknow, India

K. S. Perianayagam
Chief Technology Officer at Sahara Net Corp Ltd. India

Anand Sinha
Head of Operations at Sahara Net Corp Ltd., Lucknow (India)

CONTENTS

DOI: 10.1201/9781003125129-9

Currently there are different online methods for learning and evaluation which include virtual classrooms, video/audio tutorials, eBooks etc. There is very little evidence on the application of AI as an online teaching tool. We would like to present AI techniques to evaluate the effectiveness of online learning methods. The techniques presented here is independent of the current evaluation methods described. The most commonly accepted system to test a student is through the question-and-answer method which relies upon a sample-based questionnaire from a subject and collecting the responses from the student/examinee. The assessment is performed at the end of the course. An evaluation by this method is limited to the correctness of the answers and forms the basis on which we infer the student's knowledge on the subject. In this paper we propose that the student should be assessed on a continuous basis. This type of assessment is based on testing the student on a graded scale which is different from testing a student to qualify as 'Pass' or 'Fail'. We aim to focus on the AI techniques to assist grading the performance of a student in an online learning environment and provide a feedback to improve the learning process. A simple implementation based on Markov Decision Process is demonstrated to understand this approach.

9.1 PROBLEM DESCRIPTION

An online learning environment consists of learning material (lessons and associated questions), a lesson delivery mechanism and an evaluation process. All the three entities play a very important role in making the learning process very effective. It is important to note that each of these entities are related and share feedback to improve the effectiveness of the learning process. The student assessment is done through an evaluation process on a continuous basis till the student completes the online course. The evaluation is based on the question and answer Model. The questions are focused to test the student on the subject that he learned recently.

In this paper we will be focusing on the Evaluation Process driven by AI techniques. The evaluation is performed at regular intervals. It is an accepted fact that the effectiveness of the Learning Systems can be measured from the knowledge or skills acquired by the student. Hence the performance evaluation should be done as accurate as possible to provide a feedback to the learning environment to improve the learning process.

1 SaharaNext, Lucknow, India. 2 Shri Ramswaroop Memorial University, Lucknow, India

Hence the problem folds into:

To improve the performance of the learning process, to provide a good feedback to the learning environment, by evaluating the students learning through online methods.

9.2 THE ONLINE LEARNING ENVIRONMENT

Content Delivery and Evaluation Process are the key components of the online learning environment. The main objective is to provide an environment for the student to acquire the desired knowledge/skills. The content delivery is mainly responsible for

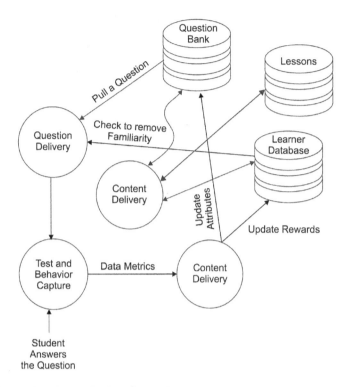

FIGURE 9.1   A typical online learning environment.

navigating the lessons. The evaluation process is responsible for performing periodic assessment and provides the feedback. The popular methods to evaluate the student are giving assignments (homework), question-and-answer sessions, conducting a quiz, etc. The most popular and suitable feedback mechanism is question-and-answer method. However, the analysis by Ann Polus, et al., demonstrated that effectiveness of feedback extends beyond mode of delivery and timeliness to include the credibility of the lecturer giving the feedback [1]. In a teacherless environment an automated feedback mechanism should take this credibility. A typical online learning environment is given in below in Figure 9.1

9.2.1   Content Delivery Process

The main task of content delivery is to present the learning material (text/audio/video) to the student, emulating a classroom environment. An experienced teacher in a classroom delivers the lessons in a face-to-face environment and he/she understands how well a student understands the subject being taught by analyzing the response of the student while answering questions. Then the teacher can enhance and explain the subject to assist the students. If we can simulate this model, then we could achieve an effective online learning environment. While in a classroom, the teacher faces a group of students with various capacities to learn, in an online there will be individual students and the content delivery should tailor the contents to each student. Hence it is necessary to assess each student separately.

A typical online learning environment is shown in Figure 9.1

The algorithms used may differ with various implementations.

9.2.2 EVALUATION PROCESS

The evaluation process provides feedback about the student to the content delivery process after evaluating the performance of the student. This process heavily depends upon the quality of questions, strategy to select the questions, capturing the behaviour of the student while answering. To enhance the generation of questions, automatic question generation was proposed in 2014 [2]. A review paper published in 'The *International Journal of Artificial Intelligence in Education* (IJAIED)', suggests the need to further improve experimental reporting, harmonize evaluation metrics and investigate other evaluation methods that are more feasible [3]. The evaluation process consists of question delivery, test and behaviour capture, evaluate and provide feedback.

The question delivery mechanism in an online learning environment should have consistent knowledge about the student to avoid repetition of the question. This differs from online tests aimed to test the subject knowledge in a broader sense at the end of the course. The application of Markov chain to assess the reliability of question classification and to classify the performance of the students based on the attainment of handling difficulty levels over a period of time was presented by Nandakumar et al [4].

9.3 QUESTION AND ANSWER MODEL

Typically, questions are randomly selected and presented to the students. The student's knowledge is judged from the answers. The questions are framed to judge the knowledge on a particular subject (topic or concept). If the answer is right, we infer that the student knows the subject, otherwise he/she does not know the subject.

Even though the question-and-answer method is widely accepted, it may not accurately find out whether the student has acquired the required knowledge. The main reason is the probabilistic nature of answering. To understand this, we shall first discuss the type of questions and classify them.

9.3.1 MOST WIDELY-USED QUESTION TYPES

The easiest and most widely used question is of YES (True) or NO (False) type. The answer is of Binary nature. This includes 'This or That', 'True or False' type questions also. Few examples are:

Example 1:

- *Python is a snake*
  - *YES*
  - *NO*

The student who does not have any knowledge about snakes can answer 'YES'. But if someone says 'NO', then we can infer with high probability that he/she does not know the species of snakes.

Example 2:

- *Python is a programming language*
  - *TRUE*
  - *FALSE*

The student who does not have any knowledge on programming languages can answer 'YES'. But if someone says 'NO', then we can infer with high probability that he/she does not know Python Programming Language.

Example 3:

- *Which is the heavier metal?*
  - *Aluminium*
  - *Copper*

The student who answers copper, may not know the density of copper (8,940 Kg per m^3) and that of aluminium (2,710 Kg per m^3).

In summary, it is difficult to infer the knowledge of a student from these types of questions.

The second type of question widely used is MCQ (Multiple Choice Question). The question presents a few choices and asks for an answer from these. The right answer could be one or more from the list of choices given.

Example 4:

- *For a given area, which shape has the smallest circumference?*
  - *Square*
  - *Triangle*
  - *Pentagon*
  - *Circle*
  - *Do not know*

If the student selects 'Circle', can we infer that he/she has knowledge on calculating area and circumference of various shapes and optimization techniques? No, since if the student has prior knowledge or familiarity with this question, and then he/she can select the right answer. However, if the student selects any answer other than Circle, then we can infer that he/she does not know how to use optimization techniques. Can we assume that this student knows how to calculate the area and circumference of different shapes? The intention of the question should always be to find one and only one aspect of knowledge. Hence if the intention of the question is to test the knowledge on area or circumference of various shapes, then we should reframe the question.

Example 5:

- *Which are the mutable objects in Python?*
  - *Int*
  - *String*
  - *List*
  - *Dictionary*
  - *Tuple*
  - *Do not know*

Let us analyze possible answers and their corresponding inferences on the knowledge of the student:

- *List and Dictionary – Correct. Knows Mutable and immutable objects in the given list. The person may or may not the complete list of mutable and immutable objects in Python.*
  - *List, Dictionary and String – Wrong. Does not know String is immutable.*
  - *List and String – Wrong. Does not know Dictionary is mutable and String is immutable.*
  - *String and Tuple – Wrong. Does not know mutable and immutable objects.*
  - *None of the above – Wrong. Does not know mutable and immutable objects.*

In summary, these types are limited with number of choices. They are also not immune to familiarity or prior incidences to the person answering.

We have other type of questions, which seek minimum input from the user. Questions like 'Correct the Sentence', 'Fill in the missing fields', 'Give alternate solution' etc.

We will look at the example given below:

Example 6:

- *Place parentheses so that the following expression is valid.*
  - $7^2 + 6^2 - 5^2 - 4^2 * 3^2 - 2^2 * 1 = 0$

This question aims to test the knowledge of the student about the order in which the expressions are evaluated. If a student answers it correctly, then we can infer that they have the required knowledge. The answer evaluation requires simple comparison with the correct known result. Since the answer is entered, rather than selected, the quality of inference will be more accurate.

In summary, as we involve the student more and more to work out a solution rather selecting or guessing an answer, the inference about the knowledge of the learner will be more accurate.

There are more type of questions and we will not be detailing each one of them. The approach given in this paper is applicable to all types of questions, provided they comply with a set of rules:

Rule 1: The intent of a question should be focused to test the knowledge of the student in one logically independent topic. It is not recommended to make a compound question to test in more than one related or unrelated topic. In such cases, the questions need to be hierarchically broken to form a group of logically connected questions, rather than a single question.

Rule 2: There should be a pool of large number of questions to address the same intent. This will help randomness in delivery. For example, it is possible to generate one million questions on expression evaluation.

   The above rules are the responsibility of the author/teacher who is expecting feedback on the performance of the learner.

Rule 3: In MCQ, option to select 'None of the above' shall not be used. Instead, the option 'Do Not Know' shall be used.

Rule 4: Each question should have a "life". After its life, it conducts a dormant period, and may be reborn again. This helps us to take care of familiarity or anticipation by the learner.

Rule 5: Each question should have a cooling period to avoid repetition.

Rule 6: Question should not be repeated, if already attempted successfully by the same person. If the question was not answered correctly, then it can be presented again with low priority (when no new questions can be selected from the pool).

Rule 7: In case of MCQs, the phrases/sequence of the answers can be modified to avoid familiarity.

Rule 8: If the student does not answer a question, it is treated as 'Do Not Know'.

The implementation of question generation is not in the present scope of this paper. We shall be focusing on using AI techniques for the evaluation process.

9.4   A SHORT INTRODUCTION TO AI AND MACHINE LEARNING

In 1950, Alan M Turing, in his paper titled 'Computing Machinery and Intelligence', mentions that "An important feature of a learning machine is that its teacher will often be very largely ignorant of quite what is going on inside, although he may still be able to some extent to predict his pupil's behaviour." This is in clear contrast with normal procedure when using a machine to do computations one's object is then to have a clear mental picture of the state of the machine at each moment in the computation' [5]. The term "teacher" used by him implied the computer and the algorithm used for learning. It is important to note that he has used three important entities: learning machine, teacher and pupil. He also mentioned the pupil's behaviour is predicable to some extent. The goal of the Machine Learning Algorithms is to make a prediction as accurate as possible.

   The term Artificial Intelligence was first introduced (coined) in 1956, by a group of scientists at a computer science conference in Dartmouth [6]. Their objective was to lay out a framework to better understand human intelligence. Based on their work, they identified the key factor for a machine to model human factors is Machine Learning.

   Machine Learning (ML) is a set of algorithms, data structures and models used to solve specific real-world problems. It is a subset of AI, used to understand and improve its performance, without any change in implementation (programming). Machines can learn to perform specific tasks. Examples of common tasks for ML is recognizing objects from digital pictures or predicting behaviour of a buyer doing an online purchase. ML techniques have contributed largely to applications that are commonly associated with Artificial Intelligence (AI).

9.5   SELECTION OF MACHINE LEARNING ALGORITHMS TO ADDRESS OUR PROBLEM

For every learning paradigm, there is a problem and a solution method. Usually, a learning paradigm uses the input data and produces an output to address the solution. We shall consider the widely used three major ML Paradigms viz supervised learning, Unsupervised Learning and Reinforced Learning.

Supervised learning refers to working with a set of known labelled training data. For every training data set, there exists an output object. The objective of supervised learning is to map the unseen samples that are not included in the sample dataset and produce an acceptable result. Supervised learning minimizes the error of the predicted output of the model with respect to a target specified in the training set. This learning paradigm is most suitable for classification, identification, prediction type of problems.

Unsupervised learning, where we liberate the machine to find a hidden pattern in a data set. We do not provide any known output against a data set. Hence, in unsupervised learning, hidden pattern in a dataset is identified and given as an output. unsupervised learning algorithms include clustering and Principal Component Analysis (PCA) and used for data mining type of applications to find a pattern or behaviour. PCA is an unsupervised algorithm used for dimensionality reduction of the input data and feature extraction. PCA tries to gather information matches in the data and derive a conclusion by grouping them.

Reinforced Learning (RL) uses a set of control actions in a sequential decision-making problem. Unlike the supervised and unsupervised learning algorithms, where the known data set is fixed, RL uses a continuously varying data set. RL is based on a feedback mechanism, which is the environment's feedback evaluating the behaviour of the agent. It is precisely the presence of feedback that also makes RL different from unsupervised learning. Also, if we want to use supervised learning or unsupervised learning algorithms, then we need to try every question with large number of students and collect their response to create a fixed set of known data. It is not an easy task to accomplish. In this paper, we use RL techniques to solve our problem.

9.5.1   REINFORCED LEARNING (RL)

There are four main elements in RL framework, viz Agent, Actions, Environment and Policy.

- Agent:
  This is the main element. It performs actions based on the current situation.
- Actions:
  The various actions that can be performed by the Agent.

- Environment:
  It is the context in which the agent performs. It consists of State, Dynamics and Rewards.
  State represents all possible existence of the environment. The Agent steps the environment through the states as per the current situation.
  Dynamics describe how actions influence the state of the environment.
  Rewards describe the agents' goal or environmental feedback.
- Policy describes the behaviour of the agent. Agent selects by following the policies.

We shall now map these elements to our problem.

The Agent we will detail is the Evaluation Mechanism. In the online learning environment, we have more agents like content delivery, question Generation etc. Actions for the Evaluation Process are:

- Selecting a question
- Performing the test
- Collect metrics
- Analyse the metrics
- Update the student level
- Update the question attributes

For the implementation, we shall focus on Analyzing the Metrics, Updating the student level and Updating the question Attributes.

Environment consists of

- Question and its attributes
- Student Levels (Grades)
  - Poor or Cannot Grade (Level 0)
  - Beginner (Level 1)
  - Average (Level 2)
  - Good (Level 3)
  - Excellent (Level 4)
- Environment State (Beginning, Basic, Average, Good and Poor)
- Rewards for the question (derived from the feedback by the evaluation process)
- Rewards for the content delivery (derived from the feedback by the evaluation process)

Policy:
The logic used by the agent to perform. The logic is built from the attributes of the question, student response metrics and Current Level of the Student. The policies are required:

- To select the question
- To measure the student level
- To update the attributes of the question

9.6   EVALUATION PROCESS

As stated above, the learning environment has two related entities: content delivery and evaluation process. Content delivery is not within our present scope. However, we will discuss the necessary feedback elements required to bind it with the evaluation process. We shall proceed to build a template implementation of Evaluation Process to demonstrate the use of RL techniques.

The main tasks to be performed by the Evaluation Process are:

1. Question delivery
2. Performing the test
3. Metrics collection
4. Assessment
5. Feedback to other agents

9.6.1   QUESTION DELIVERY

Question delivery comprises of question selection based on the current state of the evaluation, student level and the attributes of the question. Once the question is selected, it is presented to the student to answer. This is not our main scope, and hence we shall force a question to the student. However, the feedback from the evaluation process is important to ensure the questions are managed to follow the rules mentioned in Table 9.1. This is achieved by binding attributes to the questions.

9.6.2   QUESTION ATTRIBUTES

The attributes of the question required is classified as static and dynamic. The static attributes, given in Table 9.2, are only referred by the Evaluation Process. They do not change during the life of the question and assigned while the creation of a new question. The dynamic attributes are updated mainly by the evaluation process to provide a feedback to the learning environment.

TABLE 9.1
Rules and Its Relationship with Evaluation Process

Rule to be Associated	Question delivery	Presentation	Evaluation Feedback
Rule 4	Uses to prevent the question for presenting	None	Updates the data to maintain the life count
Rule 5	Uses to prevent the question for presenting	None	Updates the data to maintain the appearance
Rule 6	Uses to prevent the question for presenting	None	Updates the data accordingly
Rule 7		Uses to present the question	
Rule 8	None		Feedback Generated

TABLE 9.2
Static Attributes of a Question

Attribute Name	Description
Identifier	To identify the question in a Programming Environment.
Content	Statement of the question (text, audio, video)
Type	Question type such as MCQ, Yes or No, etc.
List of Answer(s) Choices	Each element in the list has a set of choices to select the correct answer(s). If None, then the student needs to enter the answer. The list is provided to reframe the choices to follow Rule 7.
List of Correct Answer(s)	List of Correct Answer(s) corresponding to the List of Choices.
Maximum Number of Appearances	Maximum number of times a question can be presented
Expected Answer Time	Time required to answer by a subject knowledgeable person
Interval Between Appearances	The number of other questions in the pool to be presented before this question can appear.
Visibility Time	The question will disappear at the end of this time.

The dynamic attributes, given in Table 9.3, are updated after the student completes answering the question.

The static attributes are referred (used) to select a question to be presented. Since we are not implementing the question delivery process, we shall force a question with minimal attributes to test our implementation.

9.7   EVALUATOR STATES AND ACTIONS

The Evaluator is implemented using a simple Markov Decision Process (MDP). The MDP States and the Actions are shown in Figure 9.2. It has five states: Beginning, Basic, Average, Good and Poor. The evaluator changes its state using present state, metrics collected from the student response to the question, and the student level.

Markov Decision Process Evaluator States and the Actions are shown in Figure 9.2.

The initial state of the Evaluator is S1 (Beginning). This state is assigned when the Evaluator is created to test a student on a new subject. The behaviour of the student, while answering the question, is observed and collected as metrics. They are listed below:

1. Answered
   a. Correct answer with first attempt
   b. Correct answer with iteration
   c. Partially correct answer
   d. Wrong answer
2. Not Answered

The logic used and the actions performed to implement the MDP uses these metrics. The State Transition Logic and the action taken is given below:

TABLE 9.3
Dynamic Attributes of a Question

Name	Description	Remarks	Inference
Answer Time	Time taken to answer the question correctly	Stored as a List. This is a subset of list of response Time	The maximum time, minimum time (best answer time) and average time taken shall be calculated
Response Time	Total Time spent by the person	Stored as a List	It is possible to derive whether the visibility time is
Part Answer Time	Time taken to answer partly correct	Stored as a List. This is a subset of list of response Time	
Number of correct answers	Number of persons answered correctly		Larger number indicates that the question is easy
Number of wrong Answers	Number of persons answered wrongly		Larger number indicates that the question is hard to solve or unclear
Number of partly correct answers	Number of persons answered partly correctly	Example: In MCQ, the correct answer could be more than one choice and the Person has selected a few and not a complete set. Not relevant for certain type of questions	Person lacks knowledge or insufficient time
Number of partly correct and partly wrong answers	Number of persons answered part correctly and part wrongly	Example: In MCQ, the correct answer could be more than one choice and the Person has selected a few correctly and few wrongly. Not relevant for certain type of questions.	The person has not understood the subject completely.
Number of First Attempt of correct answer	Number of persons answered in first attempt, without correcting the answer before submitting the answer	This value will be less or equal to Number of Persons correctly. This count excludes partly correct answers	The person is sure of the answer
Not Answered	Number of Persons not answered (may be due to timed out)		Larger this number indicates that the question is not clear and needs reframing
Current Appearance Number	A sequence number which gets incremented after every appearance		Indicated the maturity level of the question and the evaluation outcome

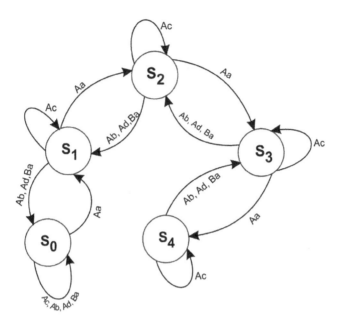

FIGURE 9.2   The MDP evaluator states and the actions.

A. Answered
- a) If the question is answered correctly in the first attempt, then both the State and student Level are incremented.
- b) If the question is answered correctly, but with iteration and if the Current State is not equal to the student level, then the State and student Level are decremented, else no change.
- c) If the question is answered part correctly, then the student Level is decremented.
- d) If the question is answered wrongly, then the both the State and student Level are decremented.

B. Not Answered
- a) If the question is not answered, then the State is decremented.

The state transition matrix is given in Table 9.4.

We assign Level 1 to a student when he/she starts to learn a particular subject. The progress of the student is measured periodically by conducting the evaluation process. The Student Level and the Evaluator State gets modified as per the metrics collected while answering the question. In addition to this, the evaluation process provides a feedback on the quality of the question itself. Since designing the questionnaire is important, this feedback on the question helps to achieve an effective learning environment. Also, this will help to implement Rules 1 and 2, to maintain the question bank.

The evaluation process relies on the behaviour of the person answering the question. The metrics collected is used to update the dynamic attributes of the question. The MDP described above uses only few attributes (Answered/Not Answered, Full

TABLE 9.4
Evaluator State Transition Matrix

Behaviour	Current State	Next State	Student Level – Current	Student Level – Next
Correct Answer with first attempt	S_i	S_{i+1}	L_i	L_{i+1}
Correct Answer with iteration	S_i	If CurrrentState is NotEqual to Student Level then S_i, else S_{i-1}	L_i	If CurrrentState is NotEqual to Student Level then L_i else L_{i-1}
Partly Correct answer	S_i	S_i	L_i	L_{i-1}
Wrong Answer	S_i	S_{i-1}	L_i	L_{i-1}
Not Answered	S_i	S_{i-1}	L_i	L_i

Correct/Partly Correct, FirstAttempt/Iterated). We have few more attributes, like Answer Time, Ratio of Correct and Wrong Answers, that could be used to improve the ML Process.

9.8   IMPLEMENTATION

A sample evaluator process is written in Python 3.8x. Listing 1 has all the necessary Classes needed and Listing 2 is a test program to test the implementation.

9.8.1   LISTING 1

```
# evaluator.py
"""

"""

class Student:
    """

    """

    def __init__(self, name):
        """
        Initializer
        Args:
            name : Name of the Student
        """
        self.level = 1
        self.name = name
        self.top_level = 4
        self.bottom_level = 0

    def reset(self, subject):
        """
```

```
    Resets the Evaluator state to the Beginning
    Args:
      subject(str): Subject Name
    """

    self._level = 1
    self._subject = subject

def begin_course(self, subject):
    """

    Creates an Evaluator for the course
    Args:
      subject = Name of the Subject
    """

    self.subject = subject
    self.evaluator = Evaluator()

def answer_correctly_firstattempt(self, question):
    """

    Simulates the behaviour of the student responding with correct answer
    in first attempt.
    Args:
      question: Question for which the behaviour is observed and metrics
    collected
    Returns:
      metrics object of type Answer.
    """

    metrics = Answer()
    metrics.sample_answer_metrics(question, True, 1, True, 70.9)
    return metrics

def answer_correctly_with_iteration(self, question):
    """

    Simulates the behaviour of the student responding with correct answer
    with iteration.
    Args:
      question: Question for which the behaviour is observed and metrics
    collected
    Returns:
      metrics object of type Answer.
    """

    metrics = Answer()
    metrics.sample_answer_metrics(question, True, 1, False, 100)
    return metrics

def answer_partly(self, question):
    """
```

Simulates the behaviour of the student responding with partly correct answer.
Args:
   question: Question for which the behaviour is observed and metrics collected
Returns:
   metrics object of type Answer.
   """

```
metrics = Answer()
metrics.sample_answer_metrics(question, True, 2, False, 200)
return metrics
```

```
def answer_wrongly(self, question):
```
   """

Simulates the behaviour of the student responding with wrong answer.
Args:
   question: Question for which the behaviour is observed and metrics collected
Returns:
   metrics object of type Answer.
   """

```
metrics = Answer()
metrics.sample_answer_metrics(question, True, 0, False, 100)
return metrics
```

```
def did_not_answer(self, question):
```
   """

Simulates the behaviour of the student did not answer.
Args:
   question: Question for which the behaviour is observed and metrics collected
Returns:
   metrics object of type Answer.
   """

```
metrics = Answer()
metrics.sample_answer_metrics(question, False, 0, False, 100)
return metrics
```

```
class Question:
```
   """

This class is created to test the Evaluator Class
   """

```
def __init__(self, expected_answer_time, max_no_appearances,
          interval_between_appearances, visibility_time):
```
   """

Initializer to intialize attributes of the question
   """

```python
# The following attributes are initialized while the question object is created
        self._expected_answer_time = expected_answer_time
        self._max_no_appearances = max_no_appearances
        self._interval_between_appearances = interval_between_appearances
        self._visibility_time = visibility_time

# The following attributes are updated everytime after the question is answered
        self.no_of_appearances = 0;
        self.no_correctly_answered = 0
        self.no_of_first_attempted_correct_answers = 0
        self.no_of_partly_answered = 0
        self.no_of_wrongly_answered = 0
        self.no_of_unattempted = 0
        self.visibility_time = visibility_time
        self.list_of_answer_times = [expected_answer_time]# time taken to answer
    correctly by students
    def present_question(self):
        """

        Presents the question and collect answer
        """

        #Presenting the question is out of our scope

class Answer:
    """

    This class is created to test the logic used in
    the Evaluator Class
    """


    def __init__(self):
        """

        Initialize to set default values for an answer.
        """

        self.answered = False
        self.correct_answer = 0
        self.first_attempt = False
        self.answer_time = 0

    def sample_answer_metrics(self, question, answered, correct_answer,
    first_attempt,
                        answer_time):
        """

        To create a metrics based on the response from the student given as
        arguements
        and update the dynamic attributes of the question
        Args:
            question;  The question being answered
            answered: True if answered or False
```

Correct_answer: 0 for wrong answer, 1 for correct answer, 2 for part correct answer
first_attempt: True if first ateempt, False for Iterated
answer_time: time taken to answer
"""

```
self._question_answered = question
self.answered = answered
self.correct_answer = correct_answer
self.first_attempt = first_attempt
self.answer_time = answer_time
question.no_of_appearances +=1
question.list_of_answer_times.append(answer_time)
if answered:
  if correct_answer == 1:
    if first_attempt:
      question.no_of_first_attempted_correct_answers += 1
    elif correct_answer == 2:
      question.no_of_partly_answered += 1
    elif correct_answer == 0:
      question.no_of_wrongly_answered = +1
else:
  question.no_of_unattempted +=1
```

class Evaluator:
"""

A simple evalautor to implement the MDP
"""

def __init__(self):
"""

Constructor for the Evaluator Class
"""

```
self._state = 1
self._lower_state = 0
self._upper_state = 4
```

def evaluate(self, student, metrics):
"""

This function evaluate and update of the state of the Evaluator.
Also updates the level of the student as a feedabck to the content
delivery
Args:
  answered: Boolean. TRUE if answered or FALSE
  correct_answer: Integer 0 for Not Correct, 1 for all correct,
  2 for partial correctness

first_attempt: Boolean. True for answered without iteration or False
answer_time: in Seconds
Returns:
Return the Performance score after evalauting the student
based on the input arguments.
"""

```
if metrics.answered:
    if metrics.correct_answer == 1 and metrics.first_attempt:
        if self._state != self._upper_state:
            self._state += 1
        if student.level != student.top_level:
            student.level +=1
    elif metrics.correct_answer == 1 and metrics.first_attempt== False:
        if student.level == self._state:
            if self._state != self._lower_state:
                self._state -= 1
            if student.level != student.bottom_level:
                student.level -=1
    elif metrics.correct_answer == 2:
        if student.level != student.bottom_level:
            student.level -= 1
    elif metrics.correct_answer == 0:
        if self._state != self._lower_state:
            self._state -= 1
        if student.level != student.bottom_level:
            student.level -=1
else:
    if self._state != self._lower_state:
        self._state -= 1

# print("The Evaluator State is {} and the Student {} Level is {} ".
#       format(self._state, student.name, student.level))
return (self._state + student.level)
```

#End of Listing 1

9.8.2 Listing 2

#testcases.py

```
from evaluator import *
```

#Create Seven Students and Register them for Algebra Class

```
studentA = Student('Anand')
studentA.begin_course('Algebra')
```

```
studentB = Student('Bob')
studentB.begin_course('Algebra')
studentC = Student('Charlie')
studentC.begin_course('Algebra')
studentD = Student('Dravid')
studentD.begin_course('Algebra')
studentE = Student('Eshwar')
studentE.begin_course('Algebra')
studentF = Student('Fred')
studentF.begin_course('Algebra')
studentG = Student('Glen')
studentG.begin_course('Algebra')


#Create Sample Question Templates
#Question(ExpectedAnswerTime, MaximumNumberOfAppearances,
    IntervalBetweenAppearances, VisibilityTime)
question1= Question(120.0, 100, 20, 360)
question2= Question(100.0, 100, 20, 400)
question3= Question(200.0, 100, 20, 500)
question4= Question(100.0, 100, 20, 360)
question5= Question(150.0, 100, 20, 300)
question6= Question(100.0, 100, 20, 300)
question7= Question(200.0, 100, 20, 400)
question8= Question(200.0, 100, 20, 400)


#Evaluate the students as per the Table 9.4
#Evaluate StudentA
print("Evaluating {} (StudentA)".format(studentA.name))
metricsA = studentA.answer_correctly_firstattempt(question1)
studentA.evaluator.evaluate(studentA,metricsA)
metricsA = studentA.answer_correctly_firstattempt(question2)
studentA.evaluator.evaluate(studentA,metricsA)
metricsA = studentA.answer_correctly_firstattempt(question3)
studentA.evaluator.evaluate(studentA,metricsA)
metricsA = studentA.answer_correctly_firstattempt(question4)
studentA.evaluator.evaluate(studentA,metricsA)
metricsA = studentA.answer_correctly_firstattempt(question5)
studentA.evaluator.evaluate(studentA,metricsA)
metricsA = studentA.answer_correctly_firstattempt(question6)
studentA.evaluator.evaluate(studentA,metricsA)
metricsA = studentA.answer_correctly_firstattempt(question7)
studentA.evaluator.evaluate(studentA,metricsA)
metricsA = studentA.answer_correctly_firstattempt(question8)
performance_scoreA = studentA.evaluator.evaluate(studentA,metricsA)
```

#Evaluate StudentB
print("Evaluating {} (StudentB)".format(studentB.name))
metricsB = studentB.answer_correctly_firstattempt(question1)
studentB.evaluator.evaluate(studentB,metricsB)
metricsB = studentB.answer_correctly_firstattempt(question2)
studentB.evaluator.evaluate(studentB,metricsB)
metricsB = studentB.answer_correctly_firstattempt(question3)
studentB.evaluator.evaluate(studentB,metricsB)
metricsB = studentB.answer_correctly_firstattempt(question4)
studentB.evaluator.evaluate(studentB,metricsB)
metricsB = studentB.answer_correctly_with_iteration(question5)
studentB.evaluator.evaluate(studentB,metricsB)
metricsB = studentB.answer_correctly_with_iteration(question6)
studentB.evaluator.evaluate(studentB,metricsB)
metricsB = studentB.answer_correctly_with_iteration(question7)
studentB.evaluator.evaluate(studentB,metricsB)
metricsB = studentB.answer_correctly_with_iteration(question8)
performance_scoreB = studentB.evaluator.evaluate(studentB,metricsB)

#Evaluate StudentC
print("Evaluating {} (StudentB)".format(studentC.name))
metricsC = studentC.answer_correctly_firstattempt(question1)
studentC.evaluator.evaluate(studentC,metricsC)
metricsC = studentC.answer_correctly_with_iteration(question2)
studentC.evaluator.evaluate(studentC,metricsC)
metricsC = studentC.answer_correctly_firstattempt(question3)
studentC.evaluator.evaluate(studentC,metricsC)
metricsC = studentC.answer_correctly_with_iteration(question4)
studentC.evaluator.evaluate(studentC,metricsC)
metricsC = studentC.answer_correctly_firstattempt(question5)
studentC.evaluator.evaluate(studentC,metricsC)
metricsC = studentC.answer_correctly_with_iteration(question6)
studentC.evaluator.evaluate(studentC,metricsC)
metricsC = studentC.answer_correctly_firstattempt(question7)
studentC.evaluator.evaluate(studentC,metricsC)
metricsC = studentC.answer_correctly_with_iteration(question8)
performance_scoreC = studentC.evaluator.evaluate(studentC,metricsC)

#Evaluate StudentD
print("Evaluating {} (StudentD)".format(studentD.name))
metricsD = studentD.answer_correctly_with_iteration(question1)
studentD.evaluator.evaluate(studentD,metricsD)
metricsD = studentD.answer_correctly_firstattempt(question2)
studentD.evaluator.evaluate(studentD,metricsD)
metricsD = studentD.answer_correctly_with_iteration(question3)

```
studentD.evaluator.evaluate(studentD,metricsD)
metricsD = studentD.answer_correctly_firstattempt(question4)
studentD.evaluator.evaluate(studentD,metricsD)
metricsD = studentD.answer_correctly_with_iteration(question5)
studentD.evaluator.evaluate(studentD,metricsD)
metricsD = studentD.answer_correctly_firstattempt(question6)
studentD.evaluator.evaluate(studentC,metricsC)
metricsD = studentD.answer_correctly_with_iteration(question7)
performance_scoreD = studentD.evaluator.evaluate(studentD,metricsD)


#Evaluate StudentE
print("Evaluating {} (StudentE)".format(studentE.name))
metricsE = studentE.did_not_answer(question1)
studentE.evaluator.evaluate(studentE,metricsE)
metricsE = studentE.did_not_answer(question2)
studentE.evaluator.evaluate(studentE,metricsE)
metricsE = studentE.did_not_answer(question3)
studentE.evaluator.evaluate(studentE,metricsE)
metricsE = studentE.did_not_answer(question4)
studentE.evaluator.evaluate(studentE,metricsE)
metricsE = studentE.did_not_answer(question5)
studentE.evaluator.evaluate(studentE,metricsE)
metricsE = studentE.answer_correctly_with_iteration(question6)
studentE.evaluator.evaluate(studentE,metricsE)
metricsE = studentE.answer_correctly_firstattempt(question7)
studentE.evaluator.evaluate(studentE,metricsE)
metricsE = studentE.answer_correctly_with_iteration(question8)
performance_scoreE = studentE.evaluator.evaluate(studentE,metricsE)


#Evaluate StudentF
print("Evaluating {} (StudentF)".format(studentF.name))
metricsF = studentF.did_not_answer(question1)
studentF.evaluator.evaluate(studentF,metricsF)
metricsF = studentF.did_not_answer(question2)
studentF.evaluator.evaluate(studentF,metricsF)
metricsF = studentF.did_not_answer(question3)
studentF.evaluator.evaluate(studentF,metricsF)
metricsF = studentF.answer_correctly_with_iteration(question4)
studentF.evaluator.evaluate(studentF,metricsF)
metricsF = studentF.answer_correctly_with_iteration(question5)
studentF.evaluator.evaluate(studentF,metricsF)
metricsF = studentF.answer_correctly_firstattempt(question7)
studentF.evaluator.evaluate(studentF,metricsF)
metricsF = studentF.answer_correctly_firstattempt(question8)
performance_scoreF = studentF.evaluator.evaluate(studentF,metricsF)
```

#Evaluate StudentG
```
print("Evaluating {} (StudentG)".format(studentG.name))
metricsG = studentG.did_not_answer(question1)
studentG.evaluator.evaluate(studentG,metricsG)
metricsG = studentG.answer_correctly_firstattempt(question2)
studentG.evaluator.evaluate(studentG,metricsG)
metricsG = studentG.did_not_answer(question3)
studentG.evaluator.evaluate(studentG,metricsG)
metricsG = studentG.answer_correctly_firstattempt(question4)
studentG.evaluator.evaluate(studentG,metricsG)
metricsG = studentG.did_not_answer(question5)
studentG.evaluator.evaluate(studentG,metricsG)
metricsG = studentG.answer_correctly_firstattempt(question6)
studentG.evaluator.evaluate(studentG,metricsG)
metricsG = studentG.did_not_answer(question7)
studentG.evaluator.evaluate(studentG,metricsG)
metricsG = studentG.answer_correctly_firstattempt(question8)
performance_scoreG = studentG.evaluator.evaluate(studentG,metricsG)
```

#Print the summary of perfoamance score for each of the above students
```
print("Performance Score  of {} is {}".format(studentA.name,
    performance_scoreA))
print("Performance Score  of {} is {}".format(studentB.name,
    performance_scoreB))
print("Performance Score  of {} is {}".format(studentC.name,
    performance_scoreC))
print("Performance Score  of {} is {}".format(studentD.name,
    performance_scoreD))
print("Performance Score  of {} is {}".format(studentE.name,
    performance_scoreE))
print("Performance Score  of {} is {}".format(studentF.name,
    performance_scoreF))
print("Performance Score  of {} is {}".format(studentG.name,
    performance_scoreG))
```

End of Listing 2

Listing 1 and 2 are available in https://github.com/perianayagam/Evaluator

9.8.3   IMPLEMENTATION DETAILS

In evaluator.py we have created:

- Student class
- Question class
- Answer class
- Evaluator class

StudentClass has the following functions to:

- create new student
- begin a new course
- answering a question
  - Correct in first attempt
  - Correct with iteration
  - Partially correct
  - Wrong
- not answering a question

The answering functions use the answer object to collect the relevant metrics.

The Question class is written only to show the implementation of static and dynamic attributes.

The other functions like presentation etc. are not implemented, since there are not in our scope.

The Answer Class supports to collect metrics for the various answering scenarios and make it available for the Evaluator to make a decision to state change. It also updates the dynamic attributes of the question.

Evaluator Class evaluates the metrics and make a decision for the state transition. It also updates the student level and calculates performance of the student as a reward. It returns this performance as a feedback to the content delivery.

9.8.4 TESTING THE EVALUATOR

To test the evaluator, we have created the following:

- Seven students
- Eight questions
- Sample behaviour for each student while answering the questions

A Python Program given in Listing 2 is used to implement the above and collect the results.

We have shown in Table 9.5 the student behaviour and the Performance (Sum of Evaluator State + Student Level) of the students at the end of answering the questions is shown as progress. It is to be noted that the Performance is available after answering each question and not shown here.

9.8.5 TESTCASE OUTPUT

The output after executing the testcases coded in *testcases.py* is shown below:
Evaluating Anand (StudentA)
Evaluating Bob (StudentB)
Evaluating Charlie (StudentB)
Evaluating Dravid (StudentD)
Evaluating Eshwar (StudentE)

TABLE 9.5
Summary of the Results from the Evaluator

Student	Q1	Q2	Q3	Q4	Q5	Q6	Q7	Q8	Evaluator State(Final)	Student Level(Final)	Sum of State and Level (Performance P)
StudentA	1	1	1	1	1	1	1	1	4	4	8 Good
StudentB	1	1	1	1	2	2	2	2	0	0	0 Poor
StudentC	1	2	1	2	1	2	1	2	1	1	2 Poor
StudentD	2	1	2	1	2	1	2	1	0	0	0 Poor
StudentE	0	0	0	0	0	2	2	1	1	2	3 Bad
StudentF	0	0	0	2	2	2	1	1	2	3	5 Average
StudentG	0	1	0	1	0	1	0	1	1	4	5 Average

Evaluating Fred (StudentF)
Evaluating Glen (StudentG)
Performance Score of Anand is 8
Performance Score of Bob is 0
Performance Score of Charlie is 2
Performance Score of Dravid is 0
Performance Score of Eshwar is 3
Performance Score of Fred is 5
Performance Score of Glen is 5
    The above result can be classified as follows:

- P is 7 or 8 then Good
- P is 5 or 6 then Average
- P is 3 or 4 then Bad
- P is 0 or 1 or 2 then Poor

9.9   CONCLUSION

It is demonstrated that a simple MDP implementation of an evaluation process can help in assessing the progress of the student and provide feedback to the other processes. We can expand the policy of the evaluator to take into account of more behaviour attributes of the students. Selecting the right question is an important task of the evaluator, and we have not included in our scope. This small exercise reveals the power of AI techniques to enhance the online learning environment.

REFERENCES

1. https://www.researchgate.net/publication/232893466_Effectiveness_of_Feedback_ The_Students'_Perspective
2. Afzal, N., & Mitkov, R. (2014). Automatic generation of multiple choice questions using dependency-based semantic relations. *Soft Computing*, *18*(7), 1269–1281.

3. Ghader, K., Jared, L., Bijan, P., Uli, S., & Salam, Al.-E. (2019). A Systematic Review of Automatic Question Generation for Educational Purposes. *The International Journal of Artificial Intelligence in Education (IJAIED)*, *30*, 121–204, 2020.

4. https://www.academia.edu/11820245/APPLICATION_OF_HIDDEN_MARKOV_MODEL_IN_QUESTION_ANSWERING_SYSTEMS

5. https://www.csee.umbc.edu/courses/471/papers/turing.pdf

6. https://250.dartmouth.edu/highlights/artificial-intelligence-ai-coined-dartmouth

10 Investigating Artificial Intelligence Usage for Revolution in E-Learning during COVID-19

Pooja Rani
Research Scholar, Department of Management Studies,
J.C. Bose University of Science and Technology, YMCA,
Faridabad, Haryana

Rachna Agrawal
Associate Professor, Department of Management Studies,
J. C. Bose University of Science and Technology, YMCA,
Faridabad, Haryana

CONTENTS

10.1 INTRODUCTION

The first COVID-19 outbreaks were in China in late 2019 and early 2020, and Italy was the first country seriously affected by COVID-19. A full lockdown was declared in Italy on March 4 [1]. In India, on 30 January 2020, the first case of the virus was identified, and after that, it spread to the maximum number of districts in India. The Total number of confirmed observable cases reported in India was 5,734, with 166 deaths as of 9 April 2020, causing a lot of stress on the part of health officials and administration [2]. The only interventions to manage the infection were social distancing and lockdown [1]. The COVID-19 pandemic not only affects people's lives and health, but also has a detrimental effect on all industries in the region. Yet the

DOI: 10.1201/9781003125129-10

education sector is the sector most affected by this pandemic. The lockdown resulted in the closing of schools and universities due to the pandemic, which disrupted the academic calendar and also led to tension and anxiety among parents, teachers and students [3]. All colleges have begun online classes and have modified their academic calendar to cope with this pandemic situation. For both faculty and students, this system of online classes resulted in some tremendous improvements in the learning pattern. The evaluators found increased knowledge and awareness of AI, creates new and unique techniques and improvements in learning and teaching. There is a need for high-level authoring tools from which experienced teachers can develop teaching materials which include AI techniques. It is now realistic to expect cost-benefits of AI technology. One such benefit is that AI allows the building of better training and is no more expensive than conventional CBT and demonstrably more cost-effective than other means [4].

The main objective of this paper is to examine the portrayal of AI in E-learning during COVID-19, and the second objective of this study is to investigate the future of AI in e-learning in post COVID-19. The present study is diverse from previous studies in several aspects. Earlier one of the significant studies [5] has focused on the best practices for implementing E-learning during the pandemic. This research paper focuses on investing AI usage for revolution in E-learning during COVID-19 and data is analyzed with an objective to draw some of the innovative practical implications.

10.2   REVIEW OF EXISTING LITERATURE

India currently has a high number of cases confirmed in Asia. On March 24, 2020, India's Prime Minister announced a nationwide lockdown affecting 1.3 billion people in India (Source: CNBC World News). People are told to stay home and work from home because of this compulsory lockdown. Online classes in India have been started by both schools and universities. The use of AI for the revolution of E-learning during COVID-19 is experimental in this research paper. The analysis of current studies is intended to fill the research gaps for the same reason.

Favale et al. [1] & Jolivet et al. [6] explained that the only step to save the economy from the pandemic is social distancing and lockdown. People have to change their behaviours and follow online learning services due to lockdown, such as individuals using the Microsoft Teams collaboration network, VPM, zoom, WebEx, etc. In the midst of the COVID-19 outbreaks, Ramij and Sultana [7] & Jæger and Blaabæk [8] conduct a report on online class preparedness in developing countries. For this reason, the analysis is about an interview with 402 students from different universities and uses the binary logistic regression model to evaluate the findings. The results of the author's research suggest that all schools and colleges are closed, and online courses are mandatory to cover the student's losses and keep them psychologically healthy.

But this study doesn't apply in all cases, as developing countries face many difficulties such as internet speed, mobile data prices, the financial status of the family and the mental health of the students. The government of all developing countries needs to focus on the current constraints and help introduce online learning to a broader cluster of students (Dev & Sengupta [9]. AI is a branch of computer science that is capable to perform the task that typically requires human intelligence. AI techniques help to improve the efficiency and effectiveness of all the branches like marketing, advertising, hospitality sector, etc. Bounatirou and Lim [10] & Farré et al. [11] studied a case on the impact of the AI on a hospitality company. According to the researchers, AI techniques enabled businesses to have an accurate insight into buying patterns, helped to optimize real time data, helped the employees to be more efficient in their work, helped to exempt repetitive task, helped to forecast on decision making to achieve the desired result.

Phobun and Vicheanpanya [12] & Ferdig et al. [13] studied the adaptive intelligent tutoring systems for e-learning systems, predicting that AI acts as multi-agent system during e-learning. The trainer is able to detect learner emotion during distance learning with the help of AI. Bounatirou and Lim [10] & Kraemer et al. [14] concluded that the adoption of AI techniques helped in creating continuous financial benefit as well as a competitive advantage. AI is a technique that uses heuristic programming and natural language interfaces which improve the ease of use, organization of data in online services. Previously, keyword search methods made online searching more difficult, and the lack of integration in online database service directly affects the quality of service. Applications of AI technology in online database services further explain the importance of Artificial Intelligence. AI promises to improve the infrastructure and also improves the elements of CDROM software [15].

Because of online teaching, the need for AI technology brings many challenges to the economy. At the time of COVID-19, Scull et al. (2020), King et al. [16] & conducted a study of developments in teacher education, according to his study during COVID-19 all studies take place via online mode from an Australian perspective. The transition from a face-to-face environment to an entirely online environment has not been a simple task. The teachers at all universities need many creative practices in this duration. Online learning showed that people work remotely and hold their meetings electronically, which enabled people to use information technology more effectively [17–19]. Online inter-professional education allows both teachers and students to retain human interaction, group learning and transparency in the virtual world [20].

From the above review discussion, it can be concluded that the global lockdown emanated from the COVID-19 pandemic and brought a paradigm change in the education sector [21]. For students in all educational institutions, E-learning is the new platform [22,23]. AI is a scientific discipline that helps stimulate human intelligence extension and expansion. It is gradually discussed in this research paper how the use of AI technology brings about a shift in the education sector that was not explored before and after this pandemic.

10.3   OBJECTIVE OF THE STUDY

The goal of the research is to study the use of AI for the E-learning revolution and to explore the future of AI in post COVID-19. Consequently, the two basic objectives of the present study are consistent with the aforementioned fact

- Investigate the representation during COVID-19 of AI in E-learning. Investigate the future of AI in E-learning in post COVID-19.

10.4 RESEARCH METHODOLOGY

Focus is applied to the target groups, sampling techniques, data collection and data analysis techniques in research methodology. Data were obtained predominantly from primary sources. Faculties are considered from separate private and government institutions. The questionnaire is created with the help of the Online Google form to collect information on the decision to follow an online learning method during this outbreak from faculty of various private and government universities. A questionnaire was administered to the faculty that gathered primary data on several aspects directly related to the study. A conclusion will be drawn based on this data on the impact of AI on online learning and what will be the potential reach of AI after COVID-19. In this analysis, the 5-point Likert scale was used to test the views of the Faculty. In five sentences, which are strongly agreed (SA), agreed (A), neutral (N), disagree (DA) and strongly disagree (SD). Faculty were asked to provide their opinion on the usage of AI for revolution in online Education during this pandemic.

10.5 DATA ANALYSIS AND DISCUSSION

AI is considered as interdisciplinary science with multiple approaches and the advancement in AI techniques lead to the shift in the virtual industry into a tech-industry. The approaches of AI help in impersonating human speech, translating languages, diagnosing human cancer, drafting legal documents and playing games. The importance of artificial management has increased, and it attracts a great deal of attention because of this pandemic (Tables 10.1 and 10.2).

The Statistical Package for Social Science (SPSS) is used to analyze the data. The Maximum number of participants strongly agreed that AI brings a revolution in the education industry and in the future also AI techniques will effectively bring advancement in education industry.

Due to the lockdown all the digital transactions like digital payments, online training, online booking and all the digital activities like online learning and online seminar or conferences have been increased. Lots of studies have already been done on AI but still much more work is needed. An understanding of AI technique will benefit knowledge management and human resource management in many ways. Previous researches were conducted on the adaption of AI techniques in various industries like the tourism industry, healthcare industry, etc. Thus, we extended our literature to identify the potential of AI techniques for bringing a revolution in the education industry during COVID-19 and what will be the future of AI techniques after this pandemic.

10.6 IMPLICATIONS AND CONCLUSION

The findings of the study will be implemented to discover that the technological advancement in the education industry which will be helpful to the practitioner's decision makers, learners and the government too. The COVID-19 pandemic

TABLE 10.1

AI Usage for Revolution in E-Learning During COVID-19

	N	Minimum	Maximum	Mean	Std. Deviation
Do you think AI solution provide Real time solution to the problems during E-learning?	204	2.0	5.0	4.059	.8284
Do you think AI techniques helps to processing in human language?	204	1.0	5.0	3.966	.9064
Do you think AI techniques helps to provide personalized tutoring session?	204	1.0	5.0	3.245	1.0067
Do you think AI techniques helps to acquire new knowledge?	204	1.0	5.0	3.245	1.0165
Do you think AI technique helps to technologically upgrade during COVID-19?	204	1.0	5.0	3.270	1.0127
Do you think AI techniques helps to change in learning material during E-learning?	204	2.0	5.0	3.946	.8257
Do you think AI techniques helps to efficiently manage the data during E-learning?	204	2.0	5.0	3.912	.8076
Do you think the advanced AI technique helps to reduce human resources?	204	2.0	5.0	3.902	.8004
Do you think AI techniques helps to reduce error?	204	1.0	5.0	3.877	.8479

Source: Calculated and complied by the researchers

totally modified the education sector curriculum. It can be found that COVID-19 pandemic lockdown modifies people's behaviour and online services are followed by individuals. The transition from face-to-face to a fully online world was not an easy task. AI techniques helped to effectively implement online classes during COVID-19. With the help of the AI techniques, following revolution is made in the education industry.

- All the textbooks are digitalized with the help of AI.
- With the help of AI, data analysis is faster, and theories can be developed more easily.
- Human educators can be replaced with the help of AI techniques.

This study opens up the doors to future research because the scope of AI is not only limited to the education sector but also in various sectors of an economy. Its scope is unlimited. In the end, it can be concluded that the AI technique will serve as a support system to a human expert.

TABLE 10.2

The Future of AI in E-Learning in Posts COVID-19

	N	Minimum	Maximum	Mean	Std. Deviation
Do you think AI techniques will be able to provide tech tolls which are useful for research in future?	204	2.0	5.0	3.917	.8173
Do you think because of the advancement in AI people will have more carrier option available in future after COVID-19?	204	2.0	5.0	3.936	.7946
Do you think techniques of AI techniques effectively emphasizes in that areas of E-learning that need improvement in future after COVID-19?	204	2.0	5.0	3.897	.8270
Do you think AI techniques in future will help to create immersive experiences, not lessons in distance learning?	204	2.0	5.0	3.882	.8339
Do you think because of AI techniques big data analytics will be faster and simple?	204	1.0	5.0	3.892	.8411
Do you think AI techniques will help to make promising most of the elements of E-learning in future?	204	2.0	5.0	3.877	.8001
Do you think AI techniques will help students to explore in-depth in E-learning?	204	2.0	5.0	3.897	.8089
Do you think that in future AI instructors during E-learning will more dedicated, knowledgeable than human instructors?	205	2.0	5.0	3.941	.7961
Do you think that AI techniques will help to provide smart learning content in future?	205	2.0	5.0	4.063	.7988
Do you think AI techniques in E-learning will act as virtual facilitators?	205	2.0	5.0	4.107	.8033

Source: Calculated and complied by the researchers.

10.7   LIMITATION AND FUTURE SCOPE

The limitations of the study provide several opportunities for future research. Although the sample size for this study was limited for the analysis which restricts the generalization of the current findings it becomes clear path to go forward. This research paper is limited to the usage of AI for online service during COVID-19. Some sectors are at the start of the AI journey, such as media, customer service, healthcare, manufacturing and transportation. Therefore, there is a wide scope of research to be done in other sectors as well. AI is building a modern future age. There is far more space for future studies to understand what the future of online classes will be after the use of advanced AI technologies.

ACKNOWLEDGEMENT

This research paper has not received any grant from any of the funding agencies. The authors don't have any conflicts of interest.

REFERENCES

1. Favale, Thomas, Francesca Soro, Martino Trevisan, Idilio Drago, & Marco Mellia. 2020. "Campus Traffic and E-Learning During COVID-19 Pandemic." *Computer Networks* 176: 107290. doi:10.1016/j.comnet.2020.107290.

2. Tomar, Anuradha, & Neeraj Gupta. 2020. "Prediction for the spread of COVID-19 in India and effectiveness of preventive measures". *Science of the Total Environment* 728: 138762. doi:10.1016/j.scitotenv.2020.138762.

3. Izumi, Takako, Vibhas Sukhwani, Akhilesh Surjan, and Rajib Shaw. 2020. "Managing and Responding to Pandemics in Higher Educational Institutions: Initial Learning from COVID-19". *International Journal Of Disaster Resilience In The Built Environment* 12 (1): 51–66. doi:10.1108/ijdrbe-06-2020-0054.

4. Williams, Noel. 1992. *"The artificial intelligence applications to learning programme"*. *Computer Assisted Learning: Selected Contributions From The CAL '91 Symposium*, 101–107. doi:10.1016/b978-0-08-041395-2.50019-4.

5. Morgan, Hani. 2020. "Best practices for implementing remote learning during a pandemic". *The Clearing House: A Journal Of Educational Strategies, Issues And Ideas* 93 (3): 135–141. doi:10.1080/00098655.2020.1751480.

6. Jolivet, R. Rima, Charlotte E. Warren, Pooja, Sripad, Elena, Ateva, Jewel, Gausman, Kate, Mitchell, Hagar, Palgi Hacker, Emma, Sacks, & Ana, Langer. 2020. "Upholding rights under COVID-19: The respectful maternity care charter."

7. Ramij, Md. Golam, & Sultana, A.. 2020. "Preparedness of Online Classes in Developing Countries Amid COVID-19 Outbreak: A Perspective from Bangladesh". *SSRN Electronic Journal*. doi:10.2139/ssrn.3638718.

8. Jæger, Mads Meier, & Ea Hoppe Blaabæk. 2020. ""Inequality in Learning Opportunities During Covid-19: Evidence from Library Takeout". *Research in Social Stratification and Mobility* 68: 100524. doi:10.1016/j.rssm.2020.100524.

9. Dev, S. M., & R. Sengupta. 2020. *"COVID-19: Impact on the Indian Economy."* Indira Gandhi Institute of Development Research. 2020–13, Mumbai, India.

10. Bounatirou, M., & Lim, A. (2020). "A Case Study on the Impact of Artificial Intelligence on Hospitality Company." *Advanced Series in Management Sustainable Hospitality Management*, 179–187. doi:10.1108/s1877-636120200000024013

11. Farré, Lídia, Yarine Fawaz, Libertad González, & Jennifer Graves. 2020. "How the COVID-19 lockdown affected gender inequality in paid and unpaid work in Spain." 13434. SSRN: 3643198.

12. Phobun, Pipatsarun, & Jiracha Vicheanpanya. 2010. "Adaptive intelligent tutoring systems for E-learning systems". *Procedia - Social and Behavioral Sciences* 2 (2): 4064–4069. doi:10.1016/j.sbspro.2010.03.641.

13. Ferdig, Richard E., Emily Baumgartner, Richard Hartshorne, Regina Kaplan-Rakowski, & Chrystalla Mouza. 2020. *"Teaching, Technology, and Teacher Education During the Covid-19 Pandemic: Stories from the Field"*. AACE-Association for the Advancement of Computing in Education, Chesapeake, USA.

14. Kraemer, Moritz U. G., Chia-Hung, Yang, Bernardo, Gutierrez, Chieh-Hsi, Wu, Brennan, Klein, David M. Pigott, & Louis du Plessis et al. 2020. "The effect of human mobility and control measures on the COVID-19 epidemic in China". *Science* 368 (6490): 493–497. doi:10.1126/science.abb4218.

15. Gross, Daniel. 1988. "Applications of AI Technology in Online Database Services." *Online Review* 12(5): 283–289. doi:10.1108/eb024285.

16. King, Tania, Belinda Hewitt, Bradley Crammond, Georgina Sutherland, Humaira Maheen, & Anne Kavanagh. 2020. "Reordering gender systems: can COVID-19 lead to improved gender equality and health." *The Lancet* 396: 80–81.

17. Chiodini, Jane. 2020. "Online Learning in the Time of COVID-19." *Travel Medicine and Infectious Disease*, 34–101669. doi: 10.1016/j.tmaid.2020.101669

18. Baria, Bhagirath Prakash. 2020. "COVID-19 Pandemic As a Set of Economic Shocks in India: A Short Note". *Economic Affairs* 65 (3). doi:10.46852/0424-2513.3.2020.18.

19. Robinson, Maureen, & Lee Rusznyak. 2020. "Learning to Teach Without School-Based Experience: Conundrums and Possibilities in a South African Context". *Journal of Education for Teaching* 46 (4): 517–527. doi:10.1080/02607476.2020.1800408.

20. Khalili, H. (2020). "Online Interprofessional Education During and Post-COVID-19 Pandemic." *Journal of Interprofessional Care*. doi:10.1080/13561820.2020.1792424 [Taylor & Francis Online].

21. Kapilashrami, Anuj, & Kamaldeep Bhui. 2020. "Mental Health and COVID-19: Is the Virus Racist?". *The British Journal of Psychiatry* 217 (2): 405–407. doi:10.1192/bjp.2020.93.

22. Sohrabi, Catrin, Zaid Alsafi, Niamh O'Neill, Mehdi Khan, Ahmed Kerwan, Ahmed Al-Jabir, Christos Iosifidis, & Riaz Agha. 2020. "World Health Organization Declares Global Emergency: A Review of the 2019 Novel Coronavirus (COVID-19)." *International Journal of Surgery* 76: 71–76. doi:10.1016/j.ijsu.2020.02.034.

23. Zu, Zi Yue, Meng Di Jiang, Peng Peng Xu, Wen Chen, Qian Qian Ni, Guang Ming Lu, & Long Jiang Zhang. 2020. "Coronavirus Disease 2019 (COVID-19): A Perspective from China". *Radiology* 296 (2): E15–E25. doi:10.1148/radiol.2020200490.

24. Scull et al. (2020), *Journal of Education for Teaching: International Research and Pedagogy* 46 (5): 1–10. doi:10.1080/02607476.2020.1802701.

11 Employee Churn Management Using AI

Sujata Priyambada Dash
Department of Management, Birla Institute of Technology, Mesra, Ranchi, India

Pradosh Kumar Gantayat
Department of CSE, DRIEMS Autonomous Engineering College, Tangi, Cuttack, Odisha, India

Sambit Mohanty
Software Developer CTSC, Hydrabad, India

CONTENTS

11.1 INTRODUCTION

In this era of globalization and digitization, workforce is an important asset for every kind of business. Organizations are facing various issues in managing these workforces efficiently, and here the role of the human resource management department comes into play. Human resource management not only manages the employees, but also handles the employee lifecycle, from recruitment and the initial job advertisement, to giving clearance to an employee who leaves the organization. [1,2] They are also part of the training and development of the workforce, enabling the organization to perform to its best. In this journey human resource management department faces so many difficulties to manage these tasks, hence, AI can play a vital role to help them in managing these things in a smart and faster way.

DOI: 10.1201/9781003125129-11

In this chapter we are trying to develop a Machine Learning model which can help a typical human resource management department deal with employee churn. By using this model, we can predict which employee will leave the organization in the near future by analyzing the previous data set of the organization in a meaningful way. If the human resource management get this information early enough, they can take steps to manage those employees, and act for the benefit of organization [3]. As per various research, acquiring a skilled employee is more difficult than maintaining them. Hence, no organization will want to lose their workforce. To develop this model, factors such as salary, satisfaction level, performance evaluation and work accident rates are taken into consideration. We have implemented various Machine Learning algorithms, like random forest, XGBoost, KNN and tried to get more accurate model which can give better performance.

11.2 PROPOSED METHODOLOGY

To find the best classifier for predicting the employee churn, we are proposing a method, which will take the dataset and find the best classifier to work on this problem. Figure 11.1 indicates the classifier of employee churn.

Classifier for Employee Churn is shown in Figure 11.1.

11.2.1 DATASET REVIEW

We have collected this dataset from Kaggle platform, which is an open-source platform for data scientist and data enthusiastic and a repository of dataset which are used for analysis. The data set is present in CSV (Comma-Separated Values) format.

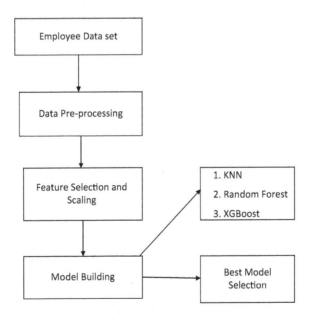

FIGURE 11.1 Classifier for Employee Churn.

TABLE 11.1
The Data Set Will Show Top 5 Rows Having These Columns

Satisfaction Level	Last Evaluation	Number Project	Average Monthly Hrs	Time Spent Company	Work Accident	Left	Promotio_ Last_5years	Departments	Salary
0.38	0.53	2	157	3	0	1	0	Sales	Low
0.80	0.86	5	262	6	0	1	0	Sales	Medium
0.11	0.88	7	272	4	0	1	0	Sales	Medium
0.72	0.87	5	223	5	0	1	0	Sales	Low
0.37	0.52	2	159	3	0	4	0	Sales	Low

```
data = pd.read_csv("HR_comma_sep.csv")
data.head()
```

FIGURE 11.2   Shows the function read_csv()

We are using Python as the programming language for analyzing the dataset as it is open source, freely available and has huge free libraries enabling analyses of the datasets. We are also using Jupyter notebook as the editor for this kind of work, as it is open source and has support for data analysis. Python has a library called Pandas which is mostly used to load and read the dataset and it also has so many functionalities which helps in further data analysis. To load and read the CSV file we will use the panda's in-built function read_csv() and to see the first 5 rows (Table 11.1) of the data set need to use head(). Figure 11.2 shows the function read_csv().

Shows the function read_csv() is shown in Figure 11.2.

The data set consists of 14,999 employee records, and each record consist of 10 attributes, including the target features. To know more about the dataset and its attributes, we can use info() of Pandas library.

The Dataset feature description is shown in Figure 11.3.

The data set consist of the following features like:

satisfaction level: It is employee satisfaction point, which ranges from 0 to 1 and its data type is Float.

last evaluation: It is evaluated performance by the employer, which also ranges from 0 to 1 and its data type is Float.

number project: How many numbers of projects assigned to an employee and its data type is integer.

average_montly_hours: How many average numbers of hours worked by an employee in a month and its data type is integer.

Time_spend_company: Time_spent_company means employee experience. The number of years spent by an employee in the company and its data type is integer.

```
data.info()

<class 'pandas.core.frame.DataFrame'>
RangeIndex: 14999 entries, 0 to 14998
Data columns (total 10 columns):
satisfaction_level        14999 non-null float64
last_evaluation           14999 non-null float64
number_project            14999 non-null int64
average_montly_hours      14999 non-null int64
time_spend_company        14999 non-null int64
Work_accident             14999 non-null int64
left                      14999 non-null int64
promotion_last_5years     14999 non-null int64
Departments               14999 non-null object
salary                    14999 non-null object
dtypes: float64(2), int64(6), object(2)
memory usage: 1.0+ MB
```

FIGURE 11.3   Dataset feature description.

Work accident: Whether an employee has had a work accident or not and its data type is integer.

promotion_last_5years: Whether an employee has had a promotion in the last 5 years or not and its data type is integer.

Departments: Employee's working department/division and its data type is String.

Salary: Salary level of the employee such as low, medium and high and its data type is string.

Left: Whether the employee has left the company or not and its data type is integer. It is the resultant or target variable which is the outcome. Here 0 means employee is currently working there, and 1 means employee has resigned from that company.

Exploratory data analysis: To know more about the data set we will do some more deeper data analysis, when we use describe() then it will give us some more interesting story about the data set.

The employee dataset currently working in organization is shown below in Figure 11.4.

Here, in this dataset, we have only two types of employee: those who are currently working in the organization and one are who left the company. Hence, if we compare both of these then will get some more information about the behaviour of employees. The above figure shows employee dataset currently working in organization.

The employee dataset left the company is shown in Figure 11.5.

This graph clearly shows that out of 14,999 employees, 11,428 employees are currently working and 3,571employees left the company. Thus, total around 23% of employee left the company (Figure 11.4)

Employee left VS Employee present is shown in Figure 11.6.

```
data.describe()
```

	satisfaction_level	last_evaluation	number_project	average_montly_hours	time_spend_company	Work_accident	left	promotion_last_5years
count	14999.000000	14999.000000	14999.000000	14999.000000	14999.000000	14999.000000	14999.000000	14999.000000
mean	0.612834	0.716102	3.803054	201.050337	3.498233	0.144610	0.238083	0.021268
std	0.248631	0.171169	1.232592	49.943099	1.460136	0.351719	0.425924	0.144281
min	0.090000	0.360000	2.000000	96.000000	2.000000	0.000000	0.000000	0.000000
25%	0.440000	0.560000	3.000000	156.000000	3.000000	0.000000	0.000000	0.000000
50%	0.640000	0.720000	4.000000	200.000000	3.000000	0.000000	0.000000	0.000000
75%	0.820000	0.870000	5.000000	245.000000	4.000000	0.000000	0.000000	0.000000
max	1.000000	1.000000	7.000000	310.000000	10.000000	1.000000	1.000000	1.000000

FIGURE 11.4   The employee dataset currently working in organization.

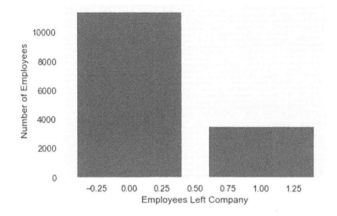

FIGURE 11.5   The employee dataset left the company.

left	satisfaction_level	last_evaluation	number_project	average_montly_hours	time_spend_company	Work_accident	promotion_last_5years	Departments	sala
0	0.666810	0.715473	3.786684	199.060203	3.380032	0.175009	0.026251	5.819041	1.3477
1	0.440098	0.718113	3.855503	207.419210	3.876505	0.047326	0.005321	6.035284	1.3458

FIGURE 11.6   Employee left VS Employee present.

From this graph we can conclude those employees who left the company has lower satisfaction level, lower promotion and less salary and worked more in comparison to those who present in company. So, we can say that these might be the driving factors for the employees who left the company. To understand these things more, we need to go deeper to analyze the data.

Let's analyze all the features of the dataset by plotting the graph using seaborn module of Python.

Features of data set is shown in Figure 11.7.

From this graph we can conclude some important points about the dataset like most of the employees are working on 3 to 5 projects, there were fewer promotions within 5 years, and most of the employees' salaries are in the range low to medium.

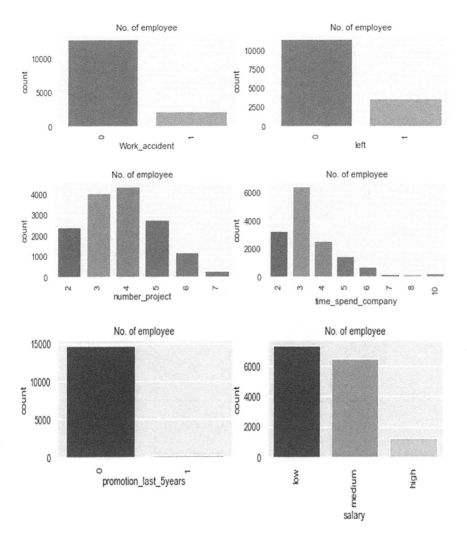

FIGURE 11.7   Features of data set.

To get more information about the employees who left and those present in the organization we have plotted the graph of all features in connection with employee left and current employee.

No. Employee vs all the features of dataset is in Figure 11.8.

From the above graphs we can say that employees who have more than 5 projects are leaving company. Those with 3–5 projects are not interested in leaving the company. Some employees having less project leave the company. Another important point is most of the employee crossing 3 year marked leaving the company. Person having 3–5 years' experience with the company are leaving, but those having more than 6 years with company are less interested to leave. Employees are leaving company if they don't receive promotion within these years. Another major point is employees having salary low or medium are leaving the company.

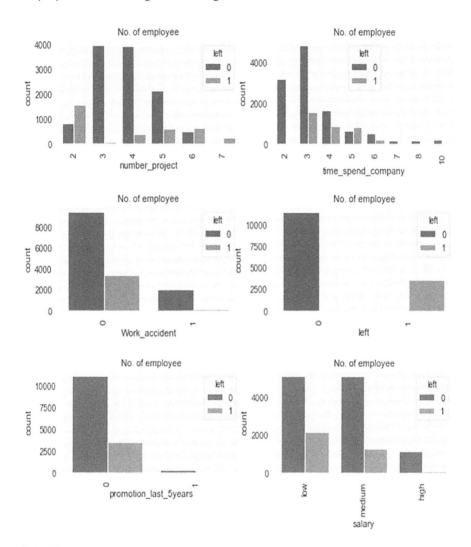

FIGURE 11.8   No. employees vs all the features of dataset.

11.3   MODEL BUILDING

Before building the model for the dataset, we need to ensure that the dataset is cleaned and structured. We checked the data set for null values and other issues, and found none to be present. This data set contains 9 features, out of which 2 are non-numeric. So, these two features need to be converted into numerical form. These two features are "Salary" and "Department". As salary and departments contains various categories or classes so "Label Encoder" is to be used to convert these categorical values into numerical forms. To do this we need to use sklearn library of Python.

```
scalar = StandardScaler()
X_scaled = scalar.fit_transform(X)
```

```
X_scaled
```

```
array([[-0.93649469, -1.08727529, -1.46286291, ..., -0.14741182,
         0.39372503, -0.55495458],
       [ 0.75281433,  0.84070693,  0.97111292, ..., -0.14741182,
         0.39372503,  1.04300352],
       [-2.02247906,  0.95755433,  2.59376348, ..., -0.14741182,
         0.39372503,  1.04300352],
       ...,
       [-0.97671633, -1.08727529, -1.46286291, ..., -0.14741182,
         0.74231612, -0.55495458],
       [-2.02247906,  1.42494396,  1.7824382 , ..., -0.14741182,
         0.74231612, -0.55495458],
       [-0.97671633, -1.14569899, -1.46286291, ..., -0.14741182,
         0.74231612, -0.55495458]]])
```

FIGURE 11.9   Scaled input features.

```
# Import LabelEncoder
from sklearn import preprocessing
#creating LabelEncoder
le = preprocessing.LabelEncoder()
# Converting string labels into numbers.
data['salary']=le.fit_transform(data['salary'])
data['Departments ']=le.fit_transform(data['Departments '])
```

After converting into numerical form, salary contains 3 classes low →1, medium→2, and high →3. Similarly, departments are divided into 7 classes based on the department names. For model building we need to divide the dataset into 2 parts, i.e., features or independent variable and labels or the dependent variable or result. Here the column named "Left" is the outcome or result or the dependent part and rest of the columns are independent part. Now we divided the dataset in to two parts X and Y, where X contains independent features and Y contains resultant.

If we notice the dataset, we can see that all the features are not in a single scale, which means all the column values have different ranges. So, to get a more accurate model, we need to bring down all the values onto the same scale. For this purpose, we need to use the "Standard scaler" class of sklearn module, which converts all the column values into the same scale. After scaling, values look like below image:

Scaled input features is shown below in Figure 11.9.

11.3.1   TRAIN TEST SPLIT

To develop the model, we need the data to feed so we divide the entire X dataset and Y into two parts, train and test datasets. Train dataset or X_train and Y_train is used for model building or learning for the model and the test or X_test is used for testing the performance of the model or X_test is the unseen data which helps us to know the accuracy and performance of the model.

There is no strict convention of how much data will go for training and how much will go for testing.

```
x_train, x_test, y_train, y_test = train_test_split(X_scaled, y, test_size=0.25, random_state=1)
```

In our case we have taken 75% of the data for training and 25% of data for testing. Now it's the time for model building using different Machine Learning algorithms.

11.3.2 MODEL BUILDING

K Nearest Neighbour

KNN is a nonparametric regulated learning calculation that makes the model structure from the given dataset. In KNN, k is a number that chooses the number of closest neighbours are utilized to give the best outcome to the dataset. Let 'a' is point whose mark is to be anticipated then first, we need to discover the K nearest point close to 'a'. At that point, it forms a specific class having closet information [4]. The different classes can be formed based on several available separation algorithms such as Euclidian separation, Hamming separation, Manhattan separation etc. Finding the best k esteem for the informational index is a difficult undertaking. For each informational collection k esteem is unique. In any case, some supposition says k esteem is an odd number that gives the best outcomes. We can say that the estimation of k is the controlling component for the issue. Examination shows that in the event that we take k esteem as a lesser number, at that point it might prompt overfitting issues; choosing proper k value is very important otherwise it will have a greater effect on real forecast [5]. In the event that we take a bigger estimation of k, at that point it prompts costly calculation. Along these lines, we have to locate an ideal estimation of k. We can locate the best k esteem by playing out our procedure on the informational collection by utilizing diverse k esteems. The k esteem which gives the best outcome will be taken for that specific informational collection.

After applying the KNN we tested the training data and achieved accuracy of 0.9688861232109521, but when we tested the model with the unseen data (the test data set which are already separated before the model creation), we got accuracy of 0.9562666666666667.

Next, we applied hyperparameter tunning techniques to improve the performance of the model. For that we used GridSearchCV which is present in Sklearn module. It gives us a set of better parameters which can give us better accuracy. After getting a best set of parameters we again trained the model with these best parameters and we tested it with trained dataset and got an accuracy of 0.9799093252733576 which is more than previous set of parameters which was used before. Now we tested the model again with unseen data which gives us an accuracy of 0.9586666666666667 which is also better than previous.

Hence, after hyperparameter tunning we got slightly high accuracy than without.

11.3.3 Random Forest Classifier

Random forest is a type of ensemble technique that is used for both regression and classification problems. It contains a large number of decision trees to find the output. Every decision tree uses its own things to find the better result. Then, after getting all the results from these decision trees, random forest polls to find which output is best. [6] The classification problems and the class which get maximum votes become the output of the random forest model. For regression task, the mean value of the score is the final output of the model. Random forest always looks for better features from the data, rather than just taking all the data. It starts from the root node and moves towards the leaf node, and the final output is always present in the leaf node [7]. For classification tasks, leaf node contains the predicting class. Whilst both decision tree and random forest work in a similar way, there exist differences in the operations. In deep decision tree there might be a chance of overfitting, but random forest handles the situation by taking the subset of the features and building smaller trees using those subset features. It then combines those smaller trees to arrive at the final outcome. Random forest provides better results in comparison to decision trees as decision tree suffers from low bias and high variance problem so it may not give accurate prediction values.[8] Therefore, to overcome such type of problem in random forest many numbers of decision trees are used so that the high variance problem can be reduced, and it will provide more accurate prediction. The main problem with random forest is it makes the process slower when number of decision tree increases.

We have applied the random forest algorithm to build the model as it handled the imbalanced dataset very well. After creating the model, we tested it with train dataset, which returned an accuracy of 0.9978664770201796. But when we tested the model with unseen data or test dataset, it gave us an accuracy of 0.9864, which is a good one.

11.3.4 XGBoost

XGBoost is a new kind of Machine Learning algorithm which is an implementation of gradient boosted decision trees designed for speed and performance. XGBoost is a perfect combination of hardware and software to solve Machine Learning problems. It takes very less time and provides better result in comparison to other algorithm. It is also called as "Extreme Gradient Boosting" [9]. Boosting is an ensemble technique where new models are added to correct the errors made by existing models.

XGBoost uses parallelized approach to build sequential decision trees which takes less time than other tree-based algorithm. This algorithm is designed to make efficient use of hardware resources like using the buffers properly which make it faster. XGBoost supports both regression and classification problems. Even in most of the problems, XGBoost does not require hyperparameter tunning; it naturally performs better. For this reason, XGBoost is the most prefered by modern day data scientists.

We have used XGBoost algorithm on our dataset to see its performance. When we tested the model with training data, we got an accuracy of 0.9959107476220108 but when we tested the model with the unseen data or test data then we got an accuracy of 0.9877333333333334 which is slightly lower than train data.

11.4 COMPARISON

To compare the performance of these algorithms we used various parameters like Confusion Matrix and F1 score (Table 11.2). Confusion matrix is 2-dimensional table having 4 distinct parameters like True positive, True Negative, False positive and False negative.

Confusion Matrix is shown in Figure 11.10.

TP: Model predicted Positive and its True

TN: Model predicted Negative and its True

FP: Model predicted Positive but its False

FN: Model predicted Negative but it False

TABLE 11.2
Model performance comparison

	Accuracy	Confusion Matrix	F1 Score
KNN	0.9586	[2766 88] [67 829]	0.9145
Random Forest	0.9864	[2846 8] [43 853]	0.9709
XGBoost	0.9877	[2863 8] [38 841]	0.9733

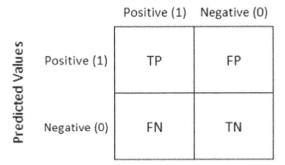

Figure 15.10. Confusion Matrix

FIGURE 11.10 Confusion Matrix.

$$F\text{-}measure = \frac{2*Recall*Precision}{Recall + Precision}$$

FIGURE 11.11   F1 Score.

F1 Score is a metric which gives us the accurate information about the model. It balances between recall and precision. F1 score helps to measure recall and precision same time by using harmonic mean.

F1 Score is shown below in Figure 11.11.

11.4.1   AUC–ROC CURVE

AUC is called as Area Under Curve of Receiver Characteristic Operator. It is mostly used to visualize how our model performing well. ROC or Receiver Characteristic Operator is used for classification problem which plots True positive vs False positive. [10] AUC or Area Under Curve is a measure to show how much portion is acquired by which model. When AUC value is 1 that means our model perfectly and correctly classifies the True positive and False negative. If AUC value is 0 then our model wrongly classifies all False negative as True positive and vice versa. When AUC value is 0.5 that means our model is not able to classify True positive and False negative. When AUC value falls between 0.5 and 1 then there is a good and high chance that our model is correctly classifying the True positive and False negative.

ROC Curve of KNN is shown below in Figure 11.12.

ROC Curve of random forest is shown below in Figure 11.13.

If we see the value of AUC Score of both KNN and random forest algorithm-based model, then we can see that random forest classifier model has slightly high score than KNN classifier.

ROC Score KNN and random forest is shown in Figure 11.14.

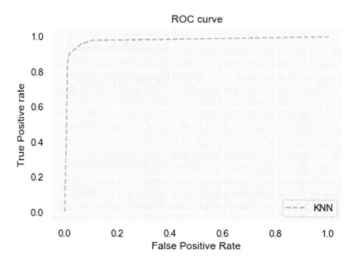

FIGURE 11.12   ROC Curve of KNN.

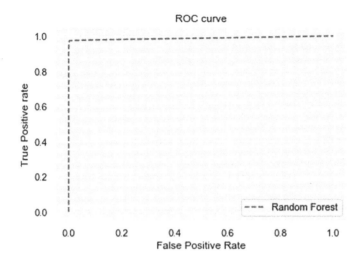

FIGURE 11.13 ROC Curve of Random Forest.

```
auc_score1 = roc_auc_score(y_test, pred_prob1[:,1])
auc_score2 = roc_auc_score(y_test, pred_prob2[:,1])
print(auc_score1,auc_score2)

0.9791176023517265 0.9877824238680089
```

FIGURE 11.14 ROC Score KNN and random forest.

We have also done the ROC-AUC analysis of XGBoost model to know the performance of the model and we got a relatively good score in comparison to both.

ROC Curve of XGBoost is shown in Figure 11.15.

ROC Score of XGBoost is shown in Figure 11.16.

For XGBoost the AUC score is 0.99403091 which is a good score. We have also plotted a single ROC–AUC graph for all the model to visualize the area under curve of different model.

ROC Curve of KNN Vs random forest vs XGBoost is shown in Figure 11.17.

11.5 CONCLUSION

In this chapter, we have used three different Machine Learning algorithms on the employee churn dataset, and observe that XGBoost has better performance in comparison to random forest and KNN. There exist other algorithms and deep learning techniques which can be applied to this dataset to check the performance. We can use different types of hyperparameter tuning methods to get more better results. By using this kind of model an organization can keep track of their human resources and which can also help them to plan better strategy to keep their assets and collect better performance from the employees. By using AI in HR, it will improve

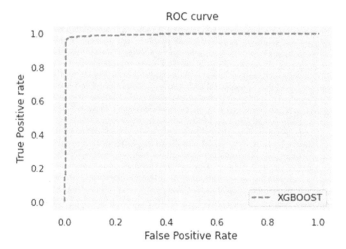

FIGURE 11.15 ROC Curve of XGBoost.

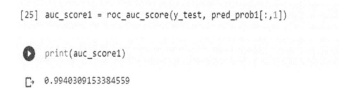

FIGURE 11.16 ROC Score of XGBoost.

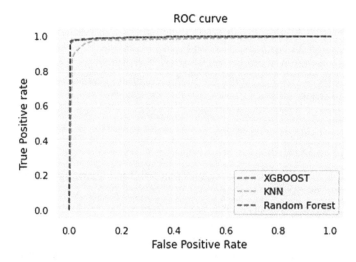

FIGURE 11.17 ROC Curve of KNN Vs random forest vs XGBoost.

the HRM system and will result in better performance to the organization in terms of managing their employees. For any organization, a skilled workforce can increase performance and reduce product or service delivery time. Hence, no organization would want to lose those employees, and this is why organizations try to find employee satisfaction and reduce the pressure on their employees. Some organizations create different types of interactive fun based on the work environment so that employees are not be under huge work pressure. At last, we can say that for any employee in any organization, salary, promotion, work pressure and work environment matters to decide whether to stay in that organization or leave. Therefore, to predict these types of behaviour of employees these models will help lot and organization will act accordingly to improve their work culture and other associated activities.

REFERENCES

1. Jauhari, A. "*How AI and Machine learning will impact HR practices*", News corp Vccirle limited partners summit, 2017.
2. Matsa, P. and Gullamajji, K. "To study the impact of Artificial Intelligence on Human Resource Management" *IRJET* 6(8), 2019.
3. Nunn, J. "Emerging impact of AI on HR" Forbes Technology Council, February 6, 2019.
4. Milani, L. et al. "*Exploring the Impact of AI on HRM*", London School of Economics, 2017.
5. Verma, R, Bandi, S. "*Artificial Intelligence & human resources management in Indian IT Sector, Proceeding of 10th International Conference on Digital Strategies for Organizational Success*, 2019.
6. Ahmed, O. (2018) Artificial intelligence in HR, *IJRAR* December 2018, 5(4) pp 971–978.
7. Capplli, P., Tambe, P. and Yakubovich, V. "Artificial Intellengence in Human Resource Management: Challenges and a path forward" *SSRN Electronics Journal*, 2018 doi:10.2.139/ssm.3263878
8. Saklani, P. Sometimes small data is enough to create small product" *Harvard Business Review*, 2019 available at https://hbr.org/2017/07/sometimes-small-data-is-enough-to-create-smart-products
9. Pfeffer, J. and Sutton, R. "*Evidence based Management*", 2019. Available at https://hbr.org/2006/01/evidence-based-management
10. Meskó, B., Hetényi, G., and Győrffy, Z. "Will Artificial Intellengence solve the Human Resource crisis in healthcare?" *BMC Health Services Research*, 18(1), 2018.

12 Machine Learning
Beginning of a New Era in the Dominance of Statistical Methods of Forecasting

Vijay Shankar Pandey
Assistant Professor, Institute of Management Sciences,
University of Lucknow, Lucknow, India

CONTENTS

12.1 INTRODUCTION

Robotics and robots have intelligence to sense like human beings. The algorithm-based AI in these machines begins a new era of scientific journey. From recognition of voice to sensing of human emotions and working somehow beyond systematic patterns has completely changed the outcomes predicted with the help of statistical modelling. AI techniques based on trial and error are consistently changing, with outcomes improved each time (HamzacEebi et al. [1], Deng [2], Zhang and Suganthan [3], Salaken et al. [4]).

In line with the above outcomes, the use of AI for the purpose of forecasting time series data became a peculiar subject attracting academics. The use of ML in form of neural network gained momentum. A number of research papers based on MLs suggested methodological advancement to improve accuracy in the forecasting of the future. In recent years, forecasting of stock prices gained momentum and dominated the field of forecasting. The forecasting of stock prices is classified into two branches: one called fundamental analysis, and the other technical analysis. The concept of fundamental analysis is based on a company's financial statement analysis, while technical analysis incorporates past historical data to find future trends. The accuracy of forecasted results depends on the modelling of data with appropriate models. In

DOI: 10.1201/9781003125129-12

line of this author analyzed some of the prominent studies published under the aegis of prominent publishers i.e., Science Direct, Elsevier, Francis & Taylor, Springer and JSTOR etc.

12.2 ANALYZING PROMINENT STUDIES

Hansen et al. [5] analyzed time series data with the help of exponential smoothening, auto regressive moving average (ARIMA), partial adaptive estimated ARIMA models and ML models to capture the characteristics of the trends, cycles, seasonal and random components. The results show that support vector ML weakly dominates over other models and achieved best results in eight of nine different data sets.

Carbonneau et al. [6] used advanced Machine Learning techniques including neural network, recurrent neural network and support vector machine for the purpose of forecasting supply chain demand distorted due to bullwhip effect. They made a comparison of results with traditional models, i.e., naive forecasting, trend and moving average and linear regression. Their findings suggest that Machine Learnings techniques are superior to the traditional techniques but the difference in forecasted results is statistically insignificant. This means they are not providing a drastic improvement over traditionally owned techniques.

Choudhary and Garg [7] used hybrid ML based on Genetic Algorithm (GA) and Support Vector Machine (SVM) to forecast stock market data. Their findings show that hybrid GA-SVM outperforms the standalone SVM system. The continuous success of technical analyst to gain from market strategies has raised the question against Efficient Market Hypothesis (EMH). In the current decade, there is increasing momentum of the use of AI techniques for the purpose of forecasting given successful results. By these consequences, in the present scenario, EMH is used by researchers as null hypothesis to forecast stock market data.

Tsai and Wang [8] tried to forecast stock prices of the Taiwan stock exchange listed companies using hybrid ML techniques. The use of decision tree (DT) and artificial neural network (ANN) had better predictive ability. The hybrid model (DT+ANN) gave 77% forecasting accuracy. Their findings to ANN suggest that it is based on biological nervous system as like human brain has good forecasting ability but lacking explanatory powers to outcomes. Their suggestion is to model stock prices using SVMs, GA can be used to obtain better prediction.

Ahmed et al. [9] tried to forecast M3 data consisting of 3,003 daily, quarterly and monthly time series data. The data set was generated to organize a competition by the International Journal of Forecasting [10]. The models used for comparison were multilayer perceptron, Bayesian neural network, Radial basis functions, generalized regression neural network (also called Kernel Regression), Classification and Regression Trees (CART) regression trees, support vector regression and Gaussian processes. These methods are used in conjunction with the ML forecasting models. The finding suggests that two models as multilayer perceptron (MLP) and Gaussian Propagation (GP) are better performer to others used models.

Cheggaga [11] tried to improve wind speed forecasting with the help of neural networks. The characteristic of this technique is that it is able to map random input vectors to corresponding output vectors without assuming any fixed relationship between them. An MLP with LM learning algorithm used to predict wind speed. The finding of the model shows promising results.

Chang et al. [12] developed a grey silhouette coefficient to create an applicable hybrid model to forecast small samples. Before using the grey silhouette coefficient model some of the single models are used to find the tendency of a real sequence. The findings shows that use of multimodal procedure reduce the predictive errors and improve forecasting results for small samples. Authors in this study claimed that popular forecasting techniques such as statistical methods, data mining and ANNs are incapable to accurately forecast the small samples.

Chen et al. [13] tried to predict movie goers based on microblogs and real time social media to better arrange income and expenditure. GA used for feature selection and five ML models, i.e., multiple linear regression (MLR), Decision tree regression (DTR), Random forecast regression (RFR), support vector regression (SVR), and neural network regression (NNR) to predict weekly movie goers. The findings suggest that the predictive ability of the ML models are high as compared to linear models used for predictive work.

Yilddiz et al. [14] did comparative analysis of regression and ML models to forecast electricity load of commercial building to minimize environmental hazards and enhance economic benefit. The ANN and Bayesian Regulation Backpropagation have lowest mean absolute percentage error in case of modelling campus load than single building load. While the regression model still performed better compared to advanced ML models.

Makridakis et al. [15] applied eight families of Machine Learning models called MLP, Bayesian Neural Network (BNN), Radial Basis Functions (RBF), Generalized Regression Neural Networks (GRNN), also called Kernel Regression, K-Nearest Neighbour Regression (KNN), CART Regression Trees (KART), SVR and Gaussian Processes (GP). The ranking of these models based on symmetric mean absolute percentage error (SMAPE), MLP was ranked one then BNN, GP, GRNN, KNN, SVR, CART and RBF ranked respectively. Along with this they used two more models called recurrent neural network (RNN) and Long Short-Term Memory Network (LSTM). The comparison of top M3 models with six statistical models called random walk model adjusted to seasonality, Simple Exponential Smoothing (SES), Holt and Damped exponential smoothing and the fifth is combination of all three exponential smoothing method, the sixth model used called Theta method. The Theta method achieved superior result compared to M3 models. These findings show though MLs have superiority over traditionally used models but not significant.

Moghadam et al. [16] used a ML approach to find flood susceptibility of Haraz watershed (Mazandaran province in Iran). The eight individual models used by them are ANN, CART, Flexible Discriminant Analysis (FDA), Generalized Linear Model (GLM), Generalized Additive Model (GAM), Boosted Regression Trees (BRT), Multivariate Adaptive Regression Splines (MARS), and Maximum Entropy (MaxEnt), and seven ensemble models such as Ensemble Model committee averaging (EMca), Ensebble Model confidence interval Inferior (EMcilnf), Ensemble Model confidence interval Superior (EMciSup), Ensemble Model to estimate the coefficient of variation(EMcv), Ensemble Model to estimate the mean (EMmean), Ensemble Model to estimate the median (EMmedian), Ensemble Model based on weighted mean (EMwmean). The model's performance is statistically shown by the statistics area under the receiver operating characteristics (AUROC). All the models used for forecasting are highly significant as per the statistics significant all models value is less than 0.05 (Sig = 0.000). Among individual models, BRT and GML are the best models among Ensemble Models EMmedian and EMmean are the best models can be used for the purpose of forecasting. Though there is no significant difference between ML models and Ensemble models still they favoured ensemble models more useful in point of view of generalization ability and sustainability in predictive accuracy.

Oh and Suh [17] examined the time lags of meteorological variables on a wave forecasting model. Use of ML such as ANN and a hybrid model was used to forecast significant wave heights and periods with the combination of empirical orthogonal function and wavelet analysis in short called EOFWNN model. The use of wavelet analysis empowered the ANN model to deal with non-stationary data. This study also analyzed time lag effect of methodological data. The findings show the highest level of accuracy subject to condition of used time lag.

Pathak et al. [18] used hybrid ML models to forecast chaotic process. ML techniques provide promising result as compared to the knowledge-based models used in the past. The combination of ML and knowledge-based technique fills the non-defined gap of old techniques.

Pechacek et al. [19] used Machine Learning algorithm to develop military reten-tion prediction model. The objective of this study was to predict when individual service members would leave the military. A high level of accuracy was acheived by the model as predictive accuracy of the model for up to one year was 88%, up to four years 80%, and for up to longer periods predictive accuracy was 78%.

Shi et al. [20] studied predictive accuracy of wind speed used for wind energy. The proposed forecasting models based on spatial temporal correlation (SC) theory and Wavelet Coherence Transformation Analysis (WCT). The result shows that there is strong correlation between adjacent wind turbine and targeted wind turbine. This study used deep neural network models and compared same with traditional methods used for wind speed forecasting. The findings shows that root mean square error (RMSE), mean absolute error (MAE), mean absolute percentage error (MAPE) are lowest for ML models. The overall findings concluded hybrid models used for wind prediction are better than those used in the future.

Sun et al. [21] used ML and Internet search index to forecast tourist arrivals in China, the same was compared with Google Index and Baidu Index. The Kernel Extreme Learning Machine (KELM) model with integrated tourist volume series of Baidu Index and Google Index gave a better forecasted result. The modelling of tourist data in the form of "tourist volume series + Baidu index + Google index" provided more accurate and robust results. This study complements the studies performed by [22,23]).

Feizabadi [24] used ML techniques to forecast demand and supply chain performance. ARIMAX and Neural Network in their hybrid form used to forecast variance amplification emanating of demand and supply chain information due to multi-stage supply chain distortion. The modelling with ML significantly improved the forecasted results.

12.3   TABULATION OF PROMINENT STUDIES FORECASTING TIME SERIES DATA USING MACHINE LEARNINGS TECHNIQUES

S. No.	Authors	Research Methodology	Outcomes
01	Hansen et al. [5]	The methods used include exponential smoothing, autoregressive integrated moving average (ARIMA), and partially adaptive estimated ARIMA models and improved Machine Learnings techniques called SVM learning.	The objective of this study is to compare efficiency of SVM learning models with three other proven models. The result shows that SVM learning weakly dominate over other models and achieved best results in eight of nine different data sets.
02	Carbonneau et al. [6]	This study has used the technique of neural network with advanced ML techniques, recurrent neural networks and SVM to forecast distorted demand (bullwhip effect).	They made a comparison of result with traditional models, i.e., naive forecasting, trend and moving average and linear regression. Their findings suggest that MLs techniques are superior to the traditional techniques.
03	Choudhary and Garg [7]	The techniques used to forecast the stock prices are hybrid Machine Learning system based on GA and SVM.	Their findings show that hybrid GA-SVM outperform the standalone SVM system. The continuous success of technical analyst to gain from market strategies has raised the question against EMH.
04	HamzacEebi et al. [1]	Iterative and direct method of ANN is used to forecast multi-period time series data. The comparison is made with ARIMA and partial adoptive estimation technique.	Directive method is based on one step ahead on observed data is better than iterative method. In the case of iterative method the forecasted date became input for next time period caused increases of the forecasted error. Overall, ANN method is better than other models used for comparison.
05	Tsai and Wang [8]	This study has used DT and ANN technique to forecast stock prices.	The DT + ANN and DT + DT models are used to forecast Taiwan stock market. The hybrid model (DT+ANN) give 77% forecasting accuracy is one of the best models in terms of forecasting accuracy.
06	Ahmed et al. [9]	This study made comparison of MLP, BNN, RBF, generalized regression neural network (also called Kernel Regression), CART regression trees, SVR and Gaussian processes. These methods are used in conjunction with the ML forecasting models.	The findings suggest that two models of MLP and GP are better performer to others used models.

(Continued)

S. No.	Authors	Research Methodology	Outcomes
07	Cheggaga [11]	The technique MLP with Levenberg-Marquardt learning algorithm is used for predicting wind speed. The model is developed to forecast t+1 day.	An MLP with LM learning algorithm used to predict wind speed. The finding of the model shows promising results.
08	Deng [2]	Deep learning or ML techniques which originated from ANN were used. Deep learning is broadly categorized into three parts, called generative deep architecture, discriminative deep architecture and hybrid deep architecture.	This paper presents brief history of deep learnings. Single Deep learning technique is capable of all type of classifications. AI, i.e., causality inference and decision making are the most important outcomes of deep learnings techniques. Speech recognition, machine translation and information retrieval are the effective task performed through Machine Learnings.
09	Chang et al. [12]	This study used two-stage procedure to forecast small samples in early hours of the business. The first stage is called grey incidence analysis and the second one is grey silhouette coefficient used to create hybrid forecasting model.	The created model is used for forecasting purpose show that results are improved significantly. The new developed model called MM's results are compared with popular forecasting models show significant improvements. The comparison of MM with LR, BPN, SVR and EGM show significant improvement in the forecasting.
10	Chen et al. [13]	GA used for feature selection and five ML models i.e., MLR, DTR, RFR, SVR and NNR to predict weekly movie goers.	The findings suggests that the predictive ability of the Machine Learning models is high as compared to linear models used for predictive work.
11	Zhang and Suganthan [3]	ANN techniques to analyze randomized data.	In this paper authors have reviewed the literatures which used ANN techniques as random method to learn forecasting ability. This paper discussed the technique of standard Feed-forward Neural Network with randomization, random vector functional link neural network, radial basis function network, recurrent neural networks, deep neural networks and conventional neural networks, kernel matrix methods. The randomized back propagations and approximation methods are the best methods can be used for future work.

(Continued)

S. No.	Authors	Research Methodology	Outcomes
12	Salaken et al. [4]	Extreme ML (EML) technique is used to find algorithm to transfer learning (TL) algorithm.	This study has discussed in-depth procedure of using ELM based transfer learning algorithm can be used in different fields' i.e., forecasting, classification and clustering. This study is helpful for the users of Machine Learning tools to analyze future data using ELM based TL techniques.
13	Yilddiz et al. [14]	Thermal model, Auto Regressive Models called ARIMA modelling, ML Models called ANNs, SVM Learning and Regression Tree used to forecast electricity consumption by commercial building using different independent variables.	The ANN and Bayesian Regulation Backpropagation have lowest MAPE in case of modelling campus load than single building load. While the complexity of the ML models still give chance to prefer regression models.
14	Makridakis et al. [15]	ML tools are used to forecasting. A comparison with traditional forecasting technique is done.	Eight families of Machine Learning models called MLP, BNN, RBF, GRNN, also called Kernel Regression, K-Nearest Neighbour Regression (KNN), CART Regression Trees (KART), SVR and Gaussian Processes (GP). The ranking of these models based on symmetric MAPE (SMAPE), MLP was ranked one then BNN, GP, GRNN, KNN, SVR, CART and RBF ranked respectively. Overall, the comparison with Box Jenkins series of models such as ARIMA and GARCH with Machine Learnings show that latter have better predictive power than the former one.
15	Moghadam et al. [16]	The eight individual models used by them are ANN, CART, FDA, GLM, GAM, BRT, MARS, and Maximum Entropy (MaxEnt), and seven ensemble models such as Ensemble Model committee averaging (EMca), Ensebble Model confidence interval Inferior (EMcilnf), Ensemble Model confidence interval Superior (EMciSup), Ensemble Model to estimate the coefficient of variation(EMcv), Ensemble Model to estimate the mean (EMmean), Ensemble Model to estimate the median (EMmedian), Ensemble Model based on weighted mean (EMwmean).	Relative Operating Characteristics (ROC) was used to evaluate the performance of individual and ensemble models. AUROC a quantitative metric used for evaluation of the models. The value of AUROC is 0.5 or more models are operating randomly. More the value of AUROC indicates higher performance of the model. Accordingly, among individual models BRT and GML are the best models. Among Ensemble Models EMmedian and EMmean are the best models can be used for the purpose of forecasting.

(Continued)

S. No.	Authors	Research Methodology	Outcomes
16	Oh and Suh [17]	This paper used a hybrid model by combining empirical orthogonal function (EOF) analysis and wavelet analysis with the neural network (EOFWNN) model. EOF is used to find the relationship between spatially distributed meteorological variable and waves to wave forecasting model and to forecast waves at multiple stations simultaneously.	The findings show the highest level of accuracy subject to conditions of used time lag. The value of NRMSE for 24-hour lead time lag is between 0.038 to 0.069.
17	Pathak et al. [18]	This study has combined knowledge-based approach and ML approach to build a hybrid model for weather forecasting.	ML techniques provide promising result as compared to the knowledge-based models used in the past. The combination of ML and knowledge-based technique fills the non-defined gap of old techniques.
18	Pechacek et al. [19]	ML algorithm used to develop military retention prediction model.	The objective of the study to predict individual service member will separate from military. A high level of accuracy performed by the model as predictive accuracy of the model for up to one year is 88%, up to four years it shows 80% and for up to longer periods predictive accuracy is 78%.
19	Shi et al. [20]	The proposed forecasting models used in the study based on SC theory and WCT. This study focused on LSTM a deep learning model is from the family of deep neural network.	The result shows that there is strong correlation between adjacent wind turbine and targeted wind turbine. This study used deep neural network models and compared same with traditional methods used for wind speed forecasting.
20	Sun et al. [21]	This study used ML technique and Internet search indexes to forecast tourist arrival in China and compared same with Google and Baidu search engine generated results.	The KELM model with integrated tourist volume series of Baidu Index and Google Index give better forecasted result.
21	Feizabadi [24]	This research work is based on hybrid method based on ML technique by blending ARIMAX and Neural Networks.	ARIMAX and Neural Network in their hybrid form used to forecast variance amplification emanating of demand and supply chain information due to multi-stage supply chain distortion. The modelling with ML has significantly improved the forecasted results.

12.4 CONCLUSION

The above literature review shows that ML methods play crucial roles in the domain of forecasting time series data. The use of eight individual models by Moghadam et al. [16] and eight families of Machine Learning models called MLP, BNN, RBF, GRNN, also called Kernel Regression, K-Nearest Neighbour Regression (KNN), CART Regression Trees (KART), SVR and Gaussian Processes (GP) by Makridakis et al. [15] show that Machine Learning has better prospects over traditional models. Chen et al. [13] and Chang et al. [12] also used GA and two-stage procedure to forecast small samples in early hours of the business show improved results over traditional models. The overall analysis of the models and techniques used for the purpose of forecasting time series data indicate that ML techniques will become the future learning tools in the field of forecasting.

REFERENCES

1. HamzacEebi, C. Akay, D. and Kutay, F. (2009). "Comparison of Direct and Iterative Artificial Neural Network Forecast Approaches in Multi-period Time Series Forecasting". *Expert System with Applications*, 39(2 Part2): 3839–3844. doi:10.1016/j. eswa.2008.02.042.

2. Deng, L. "A Tutorial Survey of Architectures, Algorithms, and Application for Deep Learning-ERRATUM". *APSIPA Transaction on Signal and Information Processing*, 3(2014): 1–29.doi:10.1017/atsip.2013.9.

3. Zhang, L. and Suganthan, P.N. "A Survey of Randomized Algorithms for Training Neurak Networks". *Information Sciences*, 364–365 (Supplement C) (2016): 146–155. doi:10.1016/j.ins.2016.01.039.

4. Salaken S. M. Khosravi, A. Nguyen, T. and Nahavandi, S. "Extreme Learning Machine Based Transfer Learning Algorithms": A Survey. *Neurocomputing*, 267(2017): 516–524. doi:10.1016/j.neucom.2016.06.

5. Hansen, J. V. McDonald, J. B. and Nelson, R. D. "Some Evidence on Forecasting Time-Series with Support Vector Machines". *The Journal of Operational Research Society*, 57(9) (2006): 1053–1063. http://www.jstor.com/stable/4102320.

6. Carbonneau, R. Laframboise, K. and Vahidov, R. "Application of Machine Learning Techniques for Supply Chain Demand Forecasting". *European Journal of Operational Research*, 184(2008): 1140–1154. doi:10.1016/j.ejor.2006.12.004.

7. Choudhary, R. and Garg, K. "A Hybrid Machine Learning System for Stock Market Forecasting". *Word Academy of Science, Engineering and Technology*, 39(2008): 315–318. http://www.researchgte.net/publication/238747905.

8. Tsai, C. F. and Wang, S. P. "Stock Price Forecasting by Hybrid Machine Learning Techniques". *Proceedings of the International Multiconference of Engineering and Computer Scientists*, 1(2009): 1–6. ISBN: 978-988-17012-2-0. Corpus ID: 14233594.

9. Ahmed, N. K. Atiya, A. F. El-Gayar, N. and EL-Shishiny, H. "An Empirical Comparison of Machine Learning Models for Time Series Forecasting". *Economic Review*, 29(5–6) (2010): 594–621. doi:10.1080/07474938.2010.481556.

10. Makridakis, S. and Hibon, M. "The M3-Competetion: Results, Conclusions and Implications". *International Journal of Forecasting*, 16(2000): 451–476. doi:10.1016/ S0169-2070(00)00057-1.

11. Cheggaga, N. "New Neural Networks Strategy Used to Improve Wind Speed Forecasting". *Wind Engineering*, 37 (4) (2013): 369–379. http://www.jstor.org/stable/43857250.

12. Chang, C. Dai, W. and Chen, C. "A Novel Procedure for Multimodel Development Using the Grey Silhouette Coefficient for Small Data –Set Forecasting". *The Journal of Operational Research Society*, 66(11, 2015): 1887–1894. http://www.jstor.org/stale/43830589.

13. Chen, R. Xu, W. and Zhang, Xi. "Dynamic Box Office Forecasting Based on Microblog Data". *Quantitative Economics and Its Development*, 30(15) (2016): 4111–4124. doi:10.2298/FIL1615111C.and http://www.jstor.org/stable/24899494.

14. Yilddiz, B. Bilbao, J. I. and Sproul, A. B. "A Review and Analysis of Regression and Machine Learning Models on Commercial Building Electricity Load Forecasting". *Renewable and Sustainable Energy Reviews*, 73 (2017): 1104–1122. doi:10.1016/j.rser.2017.02.023.

15. Makridakis, S. Spiliotis, E. and Assimakopoulos, V. "Statistical and Machine Learning Forecasting Methods: Concerns and Ways Forward". *PloS ONE* 13(3) (2018): 1–26. e0194889. doi:10.1371/journal.pone.0194889.

16. Moghadam, H. S. Valavi, R. Shahabi, H. Chapi, K. and Shirzadi, A. "Novel Forecasting Approaches Using Combination of Machine Learning and Statistical Models for Flood Susceptibility Mapping". *Journal of Environmental Management*, 217(2018): 1–11. doi:10.1016/j.jenvman2018.03.089.

17. Oh, J. and Suh, K. D. "Examining the Effect of Time Lags of Meteorological Variables on a Wave Forecasting Model". *Journal of Costal Research*, Special Issue 85, *Proceedings of the 15th International Costal Symposium*, Haeundae, Busan (2018): 1186–1190. http://jstoe.org/stable/26488405.

18. Pathak, J. Wikner, A. Fussell, R. Chandra, S. Hunt, B. R. Girvan, M. and Ott, E. "Hybrid Forecasting of Chaotic Processes: Using Machine Learning in Conjunction with a Knowledge-based Model". *CHAOS:A International Journal of Nonlinear Science*, 28(2018): 041101–041109. doi:10.1063/1.5028373.

19. Pechacek, J. Gelder, A. Roberts, C. King, J. Bishop, J. Guggisberg, M. and Kirpichevsky, Y. "A New Military Retention Prediction Model: Machine Learning for High-Fidelity Forecasting". *Institute of Defence Analysis*, (2019):1–18. http://www.jstor.com/stable/resrep22733.

20. Shi, X. Huang, S. Huang, Q. Lei, X. Li, J., Li, P. and Yang, M. "Deep-Learning based Wind Speed Forecasting Considering Spatial-temporal Correlation with Adjacent Wind Turbine". *Journal of Coastal Research*, Special Issue No. 93(2019): 623–632. http://www.jstor.org/stable/26853328.

21. Sun, S. Wei, Y. Tsui, K.-L., Wang, S. "Forecasting Tourist Arrivals with Machine Learning and Internet Search Index". *Tourism Management*, 70(2019): 1–10. doi:10.1016/j.tourman.2018.07.010.

22. Song, H. and Witt, S. F. "Tourism Demand Modeliing and Forecasting:Modern Econometric Approach". *Journal of Retailing and Consumer Services*, 9(1) (2000): 54–55. doi:10.1016/S0969-6989(01)00010-8.

23. Song, H. and Li, G. "Tourism Demand Modeling and Forecasting- A Review of Recent Research". *Tourism Management*, 29(2) (2008): 203–220. doi:10.1016/j.tourman.2007.07.016.

24. Feizabadi, J. "Machine Learning Demand Forecasting and Supply Chain Performance". *International Journal of Logistic Research and Applications*, 23(5) (2020): 1–24. doi:1 0.1080/13675567.2020.1803246.

13 Recurrent Neural Network-Based Long Short-Term Memory Deep Neural Network Model for Forex Prediction

Minakhi Rout, Dhiraj Bhattarai, and Ajay Kumar Jena

School of Computer Engineering, Kalinga Institute of Industrial Technology (Deemed to be) University, Bhubaneswar, Odisha

CONTENTS

13.1 INTRODUCTION

The prediction of forex data is a crucial and challenging task in short- and long-run financial decision making. The accurate prediction of foreign currency exchange rate can be beneficial to the financial institutions to deal with global import and export business as the risk associated with it minimized. Thereby, the investors and economists are always eager to anticipate the succeeding forex value to rely upon the business. To determine the future values of forex rate with cent percent accuracy is almost impossible due its dynamic nature. For decades, many linear statistical methods have been introduced and implemented. However, the introduction of artificial neural network (ANN) in this field has reduced the percentage of error by adjusting the model parameters in each iteration with calculated errors. Also, the complex architecture of neural network has minimized the error and risk associated with high-frequency financial time series. It can also handle the complex non-linear data and is able to predict the long-term exchange rate forecasting with better accuracy. Thus, in this study we have been motivated to use the advanced form of neural network; that is, deep learning neural network for the prediction of exchange rate.

The remaining parts of this chapter are organized as follows: section 13.3 describes related work done so far in the field of forex prediction, section 13.4 elaborate the working principle of the proposed deep learning-based model LSTM for exchange rate forecasting, simulation, result analysis and discussion carried out in section 13.5, and finally, section 13.6 describes the conclusion of the work.

13.2   RELATED WORK

Various Machine Learning-based prediction models have been implemented by many researchers in the field of forex prediction to enhance the accuracy of the model. The standard deviation of daily forex data in the logarithm rate over a statistical model [1], weighted average of daily high and low-price forecasts are empirically better than daily close price forecast. Forecasting of forex [2] rates using three ANN (i.e., Standard Back-propagation (SBP), Scaled Conjugate Gradient (SCG) and Back-propagation with Bayesian Regularization (BPR)) outperformed traditional ARIMA model. Five moving average technical indicators are used to develop and investigate estimation, where SCG gave the best output among three ANN. Technical analysis of financial markets [3] applying NN in USD vs GBP predicted with low values of MSE and conjunction with other forms of technical & fundamental analysis. Short-term exchange rate predictions are generally more accurate [4] than long-term. Use of weekly, monthly and quarterly datasets can increase the accuracy in long-term prediction. In comparison of different frequencies of input data [5], one week ahead prediction is better than one day & month ahead prediction because weekly data have appropriate fluctuation information of exchange rate. To improve overall performance of the model, many researchers [6,7] have developed hybrid model merging different individual methods. To increase accuracy of ensemble model, each individual performance must be good. A hybrid ANN applying genetic algorithm to integrate with local regressive models [8], genetically optimized adaptive ANN [9] combines genetic optimization learning algorithm and extended Kalman filter (EKF) to evolve the structure and train multilayer neural networks. The outcome of the proposed model succeeded in achieving significant improvement in accuracy for one week ahead prediction. Another hybrid structure [10] consisting of two parallel systems (Least Mean Square (LMS) and adaptive Functional Link Artificial Neural Network (FLANN)) provides more accurate and efficient result than individual LMS and FLANN. Recurrent Cartesian Genetic Programming [11] has ability to select the best possible feature, network architecture and connectivity pattern to decide whether to use a recurrent connection or a feed-forward connection. The accuracy of the model increased with number of feedback paths and improves the capabilities of the network. As exchange rate forecasting became popular, use of various ANN techniques increased. The newly developed Deep Belief technique [12,13] had some improvements and gave better results than typical forecasting methods (such as Feed-Forward Neural Network (FFNN)). This improved model using Continuous

Restricted Boltzman Machines has ability to model continuous data. Adaptive Smoothing Neural Network [14] uses adaptive smoothing techniques to adjust the ANN learning parameters automatically. This model tracks signals under dynamic varying environments, and speed up network training process and convergence, and make network's generalization stringer than the traditional Multilayer Feed-Forward Network (MLFFN). Similarly, regularized dynamic self-organized multilayer perceptron network [15], using immune algorithm improve the financial time series prediction. Multilayer Perceptron [16] uses the old statistical techniques such as Simple Moving Average (SMA) and Autoregressive Integrated Moving Average (ARIMA) as input and compared with Single Layer Perceptron (SLP), Multilayer Perceptron (MLP), Radial Basis Function (RBF) and Support Vector Machine (SVM). A paper on SVM [17] has demonstrated a better forecasting performance than ARIMA based model. Efficient prediction of forex rate,[18] single layer ANN based model with non-linear inputs is trained using past data, yields excellent prediction and can predict one month ahead. Bootstrap-based [19] multiple neural network (for both daily and weekly) time series prediction, use to contrast multiple learning model and combine each model output with the help of combination function. This model performs better than the traditional single model (Neural network, support vector machine, etc.). Two stage hybrid forecasting model [20] incorporates parametric (ARIMA and Vector Autoregressive) and non-parametric (MLP and SVR), which is able to estimate the parameters of the mathematical model by determine the number of previous values of dependent & independent variables. For quadratic convex programming problem, the Support Vector Regression (SVR) outperforms the MLP by achieving a global optimum solution. The simple ANN with single or multiple layer or hybrid neural network has been applied earlier with various learning algorithms. However, these models struggle with long term dependency problem. Thus, any neural architecture having memory unit to memorize by storing the previous data is able to handle long-term dependency problem there by the model can be useful to minimize the error as well as to enhance the performance of the model. Day by day, the deep learning based neural network models are gaining popularity due to their characteristics of processing long sequence of data accurately. The versatile features of these models make it successfully and widely applying to the various Machine Learning applications. One of these applications is speech recognition and a deep bidirectional LSTM is proposed by the authors in [21] for speech recognition and proved that a well-trained RNN is able to provide better results. One more research has reported for stack market prediction using RNN based forecasting model [22]. The accurate prediction of stock prices is difficult due to its volatility and non-linear features. With the advantage of LSTM memories of RNN architecture, it is possible to forecast the stock values with a greater precision. The application of Long Short-Term Memory Neural Network (LSTM)[23] has been also reported in the field of tourism flow and the experiments reveals that LSTM model performed well than the adaptive models (Auto Regressive Integrated Moving Average (ARIMA) model and Back Propagation Neural Network (BPNN). A stacked LSTM [24] model is used successfully for sentiment intensity prediction and outperforms lexicon-, regression- and conventional NN-based methods proposed in previous studies. Thus, we thought to use LSTM for exchange rate forecasting to achieve high precision of accuracy.

13.3 WORKING PRINCIPLE OF LSTM

The Long Short-Term Memory networks were first introduced by Hochreter and Schmidhuber in 1997 [25], and was modified and popularized by other researchers in a wide range of research fields. The feature of memorizing the information for long periods of time is able to overcome the problem of long-term dependency in RNN architecture. Due to this feature of RNN networks it can resembles the process of human understanding based on their experiences by having loop of similar networks to persist the information which required to predict the future values.

In this paper, the Long Short-Term Memory networks (LSTMs), a special type of RNN that has the capability to learn long-term dependencies, has been implemented to predict foreign currency exchange rates.

In this model, back-propagation algorithm is used to train LSTMs through time, and it solves the problem of vanishing gradient. Thus, sophisticated Recurrent Neural Network (RNN) can be developed to implement on different sequence problems. LSTMs model has memory blocks in the place of neurons. A block contains a gate that decides which cell state and output of the component should choose. The cell state (C_{t-1} or C_t), is the soul of LSTM, runs as a conveyor belt performing some simple linear calculation. The LSTM is capable to remove old information and add new information with the help of neural structures known as gates. Gates (Forget gate, Input gate and Output gate) are composition of an activated Sigmoid layer and point-wise multiplication. Sigmoid layer outputs value between 0 to 1 and decides how much & which one value let through.

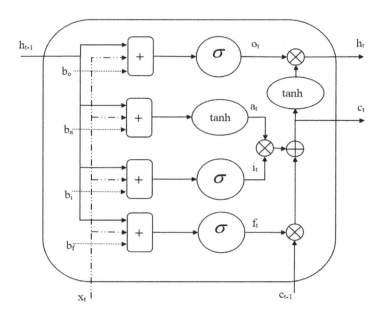

FIGURE 13.1   Long Short-Term Memory networks (LSTMs) cell.

Input variables are passed through the block (Figure 13.1) and activated using Sigmoid function. The forget gate (f_t) decides what information must discard from the state using Sigmoid activation function $\left(s = \dfrac{1}{1+e^{-x}} \right)$ over the inputs h_{t-1} and x_t, where h_{t-1} is the input from previous hidden layer and x_t is the input from outside the network.

$$f_t = \sigma\left(W_f \cdot x_t + U_f \cdot h_{t-1} + b_f\right) \tag{13.1}$$

Long Short-Term Memory networks (LSTMs) cell is shown below in Figure 13.1.

Next step decides which new information is going to store in the cell state. In this step, a Sigmoid layer (i.e., input layer, i_t) outputs the updating value and *tanh* layer $\left(\tan h = \dfrac{\left(e^x - e^{-x}\right)}{e^x + e^{-x}} \right)$ creates a vector value a_t.

$$i_i = \sigma\left(W_i \cdot x_t + U_i \cdot h_{t-1} + b_i\right)$$
$$a_t = \tanh\left(W_a \cdot x_t + U_a \cdot h_{t-1} + b_a\right) \tag{13.2}$$

Point-wise multiplication of these two layers is used while updating the cell state C_{t-1} into C_t. The update is carried out by adding the multiplication of f_t & old state C_{t-1} with $i_t * \tilde{c}$.

$$c_t = f_t \cdot c_{t-1} + i_t \cdot a_t \tag{13.3}$$

Finally, the output operation is to be performed. The filtered version of the cell state will be the output. First, output gate decides which value of the cell state going to output. We let cell state through *tanh* layer and multiply with result of output gate to get the final output.

$$o_t = \sigma\left(W_o \cdot x_t + U_o \cdot h_{t-1} + b_o\right)$$
$$h_t = o_t * \tanh(c_t) \tag{13.4}$$

For the simplicity of the calculation, we regroup the above parameters in a matrix form.

$$S_t = \begin{bmatrix} a_t \\ i_t \\ f_t \\ o_t \end{bmatrix}, W = \begin{bmatrix} W_a \\ W_i \\ W_f \\ W_o \end{bmatrix}, U = \begin{bmatrix} U_a \\ U_i \\ W_f \\ W_o \end{bmatrix}, b = \begin{bmatrix} b_a \\ b_i \\ b_f \\ b_o \end{bmatrix} \tag{13.5}$$

Before back-propagating the differences of the actual value and predicted value using LSTM approach, we have to calculate the loss function or error of the model.

$$e = \frac{\left(o - \hat{o}\right)^2}{2} \tag{13.6}$$

For the back-propagation, we have to calculate the derivatives of the loss function.

$$\delta e = \Delta t = o - \hat{o} \tag{13.7}$$

Now for the back-propagation of the LSTMs model.

$$\delta h_t = \Delta t + \Delta h_t \tag{13.8}$$

Δh_t Where Δt is the difference between the output of subsequent layers and is the output difference as computed by the next time-step LSTMs.

$$
\begin{aligned}
\delta c_t &= \delta h_t \cdot o_t \cdot \left(1 - \tan h^2\left(c_t\right)\right) + \delta c_{t+1} \cdot f_{t+1} \\
\delta a_t &= \delta c_t \cdot i_t \cdot \left(1 - a_t^2\right) \\
\delta i_t &= \delta c_t \cdot a_t \cdot i_t \cdot \left(1 - i_t\right) \\
\delta f_t &= \delta c_t \cdot c_{t-1} \cdot f_t \cdot \left(1 - f_t\right) \\
\delta o_t &= \delta h_t \cdot \tan h\left(c_t\right) \cdot o_t \cdot \left(1 - o_t\right) \\
\delta x_t &= W^t \cdot \delta s_t \\
\Delta h_{t-1} &= U^t \cdot \delta s_t
\end{aligned} \tag{13.9}
$$

The final updates to the internal parameters are computed as:

$$
\begin{aligned}
\delta W &= \sum_{t-0}^{T} \delta s_t \cdot x_t \\
\delta U &= \sum_{t-0}^{T-1} \delta s_{t+1} \cdot h_t \\
\delta b &= \sum_{t-0}^{T} \delta s_{t+1}
\end{aligned} \tag{13.10}
$$

To adjust the neural network model, previous weight values of the weight matrix must update by adding the multiplicative results of learning rate and changes in weight matrix.

$$
\begin{aligned}
W^{new} &= W^{old} - \lambda \cdot \delta W \\
U^{new} &= U^{old} - \lambda \cdot \delta U \\
b^{new} &= b^{old} - \lambda \cdot \delta b
\end{aligned} \tag{13.11}
$$

Where W^{new} and U^{new} and b^{new} are new weights and new bias value; W^{old} and U^{old} and b^{old} old values and the δW, δU and δb are the values change in weight and bias; and λ is the learning rate of the neural network.

13.4   RESULTS AND SIMULATIONS STUDY

In this study, we have implemented three neural network models, BPNN, FLANN and LSTM, for forecasting forex values. We have considered and compared five different currency exchange values for prediction using these three models. The historical exchange rate value couldn't be applied directly to the prediction models, so we need to go for extracting features from the historical data and details of the data preparation as explained in section 13.5.1, as well as to evaluate the prediction accuracy, we need to rely on some performance measures, as discussed in section 13.5.2.

13.4.1   DATA PREPARATION

The historical forex data sets were downloaded from the Financial Forecast Center (www.forecasts.org). Five different currencies (Indian Rupee (INR), Australian Dollar (ASD), Canadian Dollar (CAD), British Pound (GBP) and Japanese Yen (JPY) in terms of 1 US Dollar), are obtained over the period of January 2012 to April 2018. There are 1,570 daily exchange rate samples are obtained in each exchange rate datasets.

After downloading the data sets, these samples are initially normalized in the range of [0,1], max–min normalization techniques. Using the concept of sliding window, the input feature patterns are determined from the normalized samples. Similarly, the subsequent input feature patterns have been extracted by sliding the window size one step at a time and so on. From the samples of each sliding window three features are extracted, those are 12th value, mean and standard deviation. The data having N number of samples and W sliding window size, the total number of pattern generation will be (N–W+1). For this study we have taken window size is 12 as many researchers have reported the same window size for their analysis in this domain. The extracted feature patterns are further divided into two different sets by splitting 80% samples for the training purpose and 20% samples for the testing purpose.

13.4.2   PERFORMANCE MEASURE

To evaluate and validate the performance of the prediction models, we have used two widely accepted error measures, Mean Absolute Percentage Error (MAPE) and Root Mean Square Error (RMSE). The less MAPE and RMSE value we obtained during testing phase of the prediction the more accurate is the prediction model. These two error measures can be calculated as follows:

$$\text{MAPE} = \left(\frac{1}{n} \sum \frac{|d_a - d_f|}{d_a} \right) * 100\% \tag{13.12}$$

$$\text{RMSE} = \sqrt{\frac{1}{n} \sum (d_a - d_f)^2} \tag{13.13}$$

Where d_a is the actual forex value, d_f is the predicted forex value and n is the number of testing sample carried out for the prediction.

13.5 RESULTS AND DISCUSSION

All three prediction models are simulated and trained properly with the 80% of training data individually for each of the forex data set and results are obtained in terms of performance measures during testing phase of the model and tabulated. Tables (13.1–13.8) shows the prediction performance of three different models Backpropagation NN, Functional Link ANN and Long Short-Term Memory network for

TABLE 13.1

1 Day Ahead Prediction of 1 USD to Five Different Currencies Using Three Different Models

Currency	BPNN		FLANN		LSTM	
	MAPE	RMSE	MAPE	RMSE	MAPE	RMSE
AUD	0.4874	0.0047	0.5123	0.005	**0.3724**	**0.0036**
GBP	0.5836	0.0095	0.5209	0.0087	**0.4068**	**0.0068**
CAD	0.3477	**0.0058**	0.4215	0.0069	**0.3397**	**0.0058**
INR	0.6024	0.4288	0.575	0.4247	**0.188**	**0.1694**
JPY	0.7647	1.0177	0.6663	0.9135	**0.4112**	**0.6097**

TABLE 13.2

3 Days Ahead Prediction of 1 USD to Five Different Currencies Using Three Different Models

Currency	BPNN		FLANN		LSTM	
	MAPE	RMSE	MAPE	RMSE	MAPE	RMSE
AUD	0.8793	0.0085	0.8382	0.008	**0.7094**	**0.0068**
GBP	0.9599	0.0158	0.8319	0.0138	**0.7274**	**0.0122**
CAD	0.6774	0.0109	0.7148	0.0115	**0.6299**	**0.0103**
INR	0.7114	0.5222	0.6365	0.4791	**0.4202**	**0.3595**
JPY	1.0726	1.4522	0.9037	1.2279	**0.7265**	**1.007**

TABLE 13.3

5 Days Ahead Prediction of 1 USD to Five Different Currencies Using Three Different Models

Currency	BPNN		FLANN		LSTM	
	MAPE	RMSE	MAPE	RMSE	MAPE	RMSE
AUD	1.2024	0.0116	1.1013	0.0107	**0.8951**	**0.0087**
GBP	1.2385	0.0205	1.0651	0.0178	**0.9075**	**0.0149**
CAD	0.921	0.0147	0.9345	0.0149	**0.8952**	**0.0143**
INR	0.8108	0.6003	0.6896	0.5268	**0.4434**	**0.3612**
JPY	1.3582	1.803	1.1083	1.4746	**0.9516**	**1.3141**

TABLE 13.4

7 Days Ahead Prediction of 1 USD to Five Different Currencies Using Three Different Models

Currency	BPNN		FLANN		LSTM	
	MAPE	RMSE	MAPE	RMSE	MAPE	RMSE
AUD	1.4377	0.0139	1.3272	0.0129	**1.1948**	**0.0116**
GBP	1.4975	0.025	1.3105	0.0219	**1.2086**	**0.0204**
CAD	1.1022	0.0178	1.1028	0.0177	**1.0274**	**0.0164**
INR	0.911	0.6718	0.7463	0.5669	**0.5246**	**0.436**
JPY	1.6045	2.1194	1.2959	1.7111	**1.077**	**1.47**

TABLE 13.5

10 Days Ahead Prediction of 1 USD to Five Different Currencies Using Three Different Models

Currency	BPNN		FLANN		LSTM	
	MAPE	RMSE	MAPE	RMSE	MAPE	RMSE
AUD	1.7753	0.0173	1.6431	0.0162	**1.3444**	**0.0131**
GBP	1.8717	0.0308	1.6495	0.0274	**1.419**	**0.0243**
CAD	1.3582	0.0222	1.3355	0.0217	**1.2609**	**0.02**
INR	1.0476	0.7702	0.821	0.625	**0.5997**	**0.5001**
JPY	1.985	2.5702	1.5486	2.0214	**1.2943**	**1.7395**

TABLE 13.6

15 Days Ahead Prediction of 1 USD to Five Different Currencies Using Three Different Models

Currency	BPNN		FLANN		LSTM	
	MAPE	RMSE	MAPE	RMSE	MAPE	RMSE
AUD	2.1576	0.0213	2.0076	0.0203	**1.6717**	**0.0169**
GBP	2.373	0.0385	2.1214	0.035	**1.7597**	**0.0297**
CAD	1.7032	0.028	**1.6432**	**0.027**	1.7325	0.0279
INR	1.2217	0.8943	0.9331	0.7076	**0.7066**	**0.5929**
JPY	2.5606	3.2738	1.9034	2.5005	**1.7073**	**2.2659**

TABLE 13.7

20 Days Ahead Prediction of 1 USD to Five Different Currencies Using Three Different Models

Currency	BPNN		FLANN		LSTM	
	MAPE	RMSE	MAPE	RMSE	MAPE	RMSE
AUD	2.4267	0.024	2.2924	0.0231	**1.9468**	**0.02**
GBP	2.7593	0.044	2.5272	0.0405	**2.2668**	**0.0381**
CAD	1.9765	0.0322	1.923	0.0312	**1.7579**	**0.0289**
INR	1.337	0.9968	1.0398	0.801	**0.8403**	**0.6973**
JPY	3.0083	3.8442	2.1574	2.8907	**1.7606**	**2.3321**

TABLE 13.8

30 Days Ahead Prediction of 1 USD to Five Different Currencies Using Three Different Models

Currency	BPNN		FLANN		LSTM	
	MAPE	RMSE	MAPE	RMSE	MAPE	RMSE
AUD	2.8238	0.0278	2.7948	0.0276	**2.5193**	**0.0251**
GBP	3.3181	0.0521	3.1564	0.0495	**2.8222**	**0.0466**
CAD	2.4616	0.0384	**2.3773**	**0.0374**	2.3915	0.0375
INR	1.5428	1.1802	**1.2608**	**0.9678**	1.2961	1.002
JPY	3.6031	4.5334	2.5326	3.4303	**2.1865**	**2.947**

daily exchange rate dataset of five different currencies in various short- and long-term time horizon. The performance results of these models depend on the characteristics of given data samples. Sudden high and low frequency of exchange rate forecasting data requires more time to understand patterns and update weights and adjust the model accordingly. Forecasting models (such as BPNN and FLANN), which does not have the memory block, so cannot store the previous values which makes it a struggle to learn these fluctuating data. So, the LSTM model can handle this dataset without any complexity and execute in less number of iterations.

The forecasting performance for different days ahead prediction is tabulated below. As the number of days ahead prediction increases, the value of MAPE and RMSE increases. But in some cases, the error is increasing drastic, and in others, it increases slowly, due to the extracted pattern while forecasting for various days ahead estimation.

The resultant tables reveal that in most of the cases LSTMs have less MAPE and RMSE values in comparison to others, however, in very few cases FLANN have less MAPE and RMSE values. But in overall performance measure, LSTM performed better, and FLANN performed better than BPNN based on the performance measures (MAPE, RMSE) for both short- and long-term days ahead. Figure 13.2 depicts the one day ahead prediction of forex value during training as well as in testing phase of

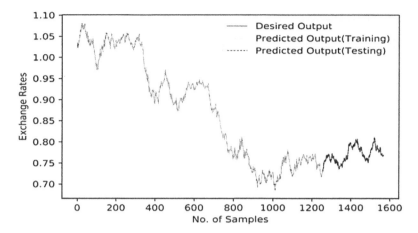

FIGURE 13.2   (i). deep learning-based model (LSTM) predicting nearly the actual trends for Australian Dollar (AUD) data set.

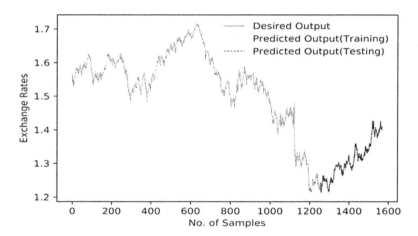

FIGURE 13.3   (ii). deep learning-based model (LSTM) predicting nearly the actual trends for British Pound (GBP) data set.

LSTM deep neural network model for five different currencies exchange datasets. It can also be observed clearly from Figure 13.2 that deep learning based model (LSTM) predicting nearly the actual trends for all five forex data sets.

Deep learning-based model (LSTM) predicting nearly the actual trends for Australian Dollar (AUD) data set is shown below in Figure 13.2 (i).

deep learning-based model (LSTM) predicting nearly the actual trends for British Pound (GBP) data set is shown below in Figure 13.3 (ii).

deep learning-based model (LSTM) predicting nearly the actual trends for Canadian Dollar (CAD) data set is shown below in Figure 13.4 (iii).

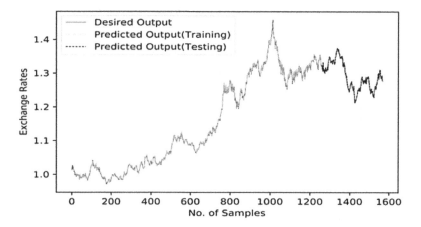

FIGURE 13.4   (iii) Deep learning-based model (LSTM) predicting nearly the actual trends for Canadian Dollar (CAD) data set.

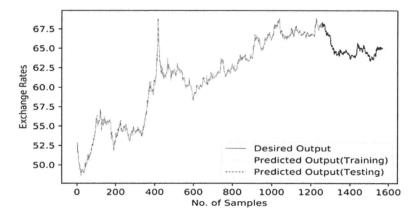

FIGURE 13.5   (iv). deep learning-based model (LSTM) predicting nearly the actual trends for Indian Rupee (INR) data set.

Deep learning-based model (LSTM) predicting nearly the actual trends for Indian Rupee (INR) data set is shown below in Figures 13.5 (iv) and 13.6 (v).

Figure 13.2 Training and testing observations of LSTM model for 1 day ahead prediction for five different currencies: i) Australian Dollar (AUD) ii) British Pound (GBP) iii) Canadian Dollar (CAD) iv) Indian Rupee (INR) and v) Japanese Yen (JPY)

The MSE convergence plot of one day ahead prediction using all the three models BPNN, FLANN and LSTM for the Australian Dollar (AUD) forex data set is shown below in Figure 13.7 (i).

The MSE convergence plot of one day ahead prediction using all the three models BPNN, FLANN and LSTM for the British Pound (GBP) forex data set is shown below in Figure 13.8 (ii).

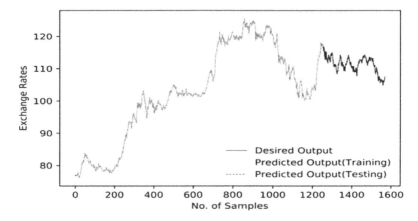

FIGURE 13.6   (v). deep learning-based model (LSTM) predicting nearly the actual trends for Japanese Yen (JPY) data set.

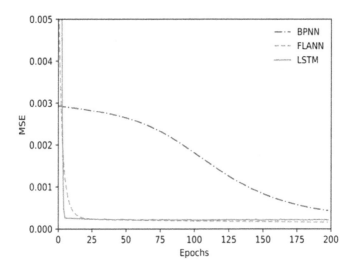

FIGURE 13.7   (i) The MSE convergence plot of one day ahead prediction using all the three models BPNN, FLANN and LSTM for the Australian Dollar (AUD) forex data set.

The MSE convergence plot of one day ahead prediction using all the three models BPNN, FLANN and LSTM for the Canadian Dollar (CAD)forex data set is shown below in Figure 13.9 (iii).

The MSE convergence plot of one day ahead prediction using all the three models BPNN, FLANN and LSTM for the Indian Rupee (INR) forex data set is shown below in Figure 13.10 (iv).

The MSE convergence plot of one day ahead prediction using all the three models BPNN, FLANN and LSTM for the Japanese Yen (JPY) forex data set is shown below in Figure 13.11 (v).

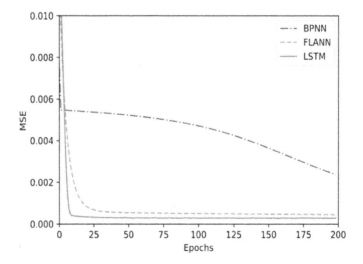

FIGURE 13.8 (ii). The MSE convergence plot of one day ahead prediction using all the three models BPNN, FLANN and LSTM for the British Pound (GBP) forex data set.

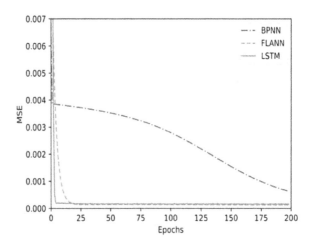

FIGURE 13.9 (iii). The MSE convergence plot of one day ahead prediction using all the three models BPNN, FLANN and LSTM for the Canadian Dollar (CAD) forex data set.

Figure 13.3 MSE convergence plots obtained using three forecasting models (BPNN, FLANN and LSTM) of 1 day ahead prediction for five different currencies: i) Australian Dollar (AUD) ii) British Pound (GBP) iii) Canadian Dollar (CAD) iv) Indian Rupee (INR) and v) Japanese Yen (JPY).

During training phase simulation of the proposed model, Figure 13.3 was obtained. These figures are the MSE convergence plot of one day ahead prediction using all the three models BPNN, FLANN and LSTM for the same five different forex data sets and it reveals that deep learning neural network converges faster with minimum errors than the other two neural network models used in this study.

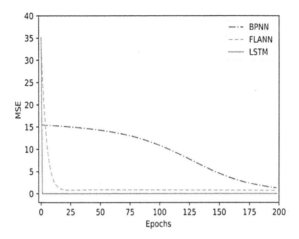

FIGURE 13.10 (iv). The MSE convergence plot of one day ahead prediction using all the three models BPNN, FLANN and LSTM for the Indian Rupee (INR) forex data set.

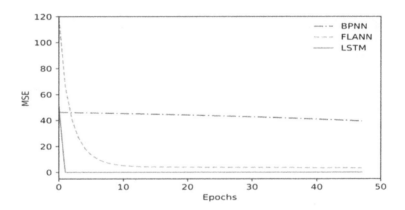

FIGURE 13.11 (v). The MSE convergence plot of one day ahead prediction using all the three models BPNN, FLANN and LSTM for the same five different forex data set Japanese Yen (JPY).

13.6 CONCLUSION

This paper describes the implementation of an especial type of RNN, Long Short-Term Memory network for the exchange rate forecasting in details. Due to its distinct features, gated input and output and memory block LSTM model is performing well in time series prediction. Gates are responsible for the selection of the data, removable of the data and the modification of the data of the block. These gates work as a memory cell by storing previous values and compare them with upcoming variable to update the model by observing the inherited features out of the input patterns. Due to this unique working principle of the LSTM model and from the simulation study made in Section 4, it is clearly observed that the proposed deep learning neural network-based LSTM model giving better accuracy in different time horizons from 1 day ahead to 30 days head in all five forex data sets. As well as it is also converging faster than the other two widely accepted neural network models (i.e., BPNN and FLANN). From the results we also discovered that the error is increasing as the prediction is made for long term time horizon. So, to improve the accuracy of the models in long term, we need to introduce the influencing factors, more statistical features and technical indicators. The prediction accuracy may also be enhanced by exploring other variants of deep neural network-based models.

REFERENCES

1. Taylor, S. J. (1987). Forecasting the volatility of currency exchange rates. *International Journal of Forecasting*, *3*(1), 159–170.
2. Kamruzzaman, J., Sarker, R. A., & Ahmad, I. (2003, November). *SVM based models for predicting foreign currency exchange rates*. In *Third IEEE International Conference on Data Mining* (pp. 557–560). IEEE.
3. Nagarajan, V., Wu, Y., Liu, M., & Wang, Q. G. (2005, June). *Forecast studies for financial markets using technical analysis*. In *2005 International Conference on Control and Automation* (Vol. 1, pp. 259–264). IEEE.
4. Galeshchuk, S. (2016). Neural networks performance in exchange rate prediction. *Neurocomputing*, *172*, 446–452.
5. Huang, W., Yu, L., Wang, S., Bao, Y., & Wang, L. (2006, May). Comparisons of the different frequencies of input data for neural networks in foreign exchange rates forecasting. In *International Conference on Computational Science* (pp. 517–524). Springer, Berlin, Heidelberg.
6. Bui, L. T., & Dinh, T. T. H. (2018). A novel evolutionary multi-objective ensemble learning approach for forecasting currency exchange rates. *Data & Knowledge Engineering*, *114*, 40–66.
7. He, K., Ji, L., Tso, G. K., Zhu, B., & Zou, Y. (2018). Forecasting Exchange Rate Value at Risk using Deep Belief Network Ensemble based Approach. *Procedia computer science*, *139*, 25–32.
8. Ni, H., & Yin, H. (2009). Exchange rate prediction using hybrid neural networks and trading indicators. *Neurocomputing*, *72*(13–15), 2815–2823.
9. Andreou, A. S., Georgopoulos, E. F., & Likothanassis, S. D. (2002). Exchange-rates forecasting: A hybrid algorithm based on genetically optimized adaptive neural networks. *Computational Economics*, *20*(3), 191–210.
10. Jena, P. R., Majhi, R., & Majhi, B. (2015). Development and performance evaluation of a novel knowledge guided artificial neural network (KGANN) model for exchange rate prediction. *Journal of King Saud University-Computer and Information Sciences*, *27*(4), 450–457.
11. Rehman, M., Khan, G. M., & Mahmud, S. A. (2014). Foreign currency exchange rates prediction using cgp and recurrent neural network. *IERI Procedia*, *10*, 239–244.
12. Chao, J., Shen, F., & Zhao, J. (2011, July). *Forecasting exchange rate with deep belief networks*. In *The 2011 International Joint Conference on Neural Networks* (pp. 1259–1266). IEEE.
13. Shen, F., Chao, J., & Zhao, J. (2015). Forecasting exchange rate using deep belief networks and conjugate gradient method. *Neurocomputing*, *167*, 243–253.

14. Yu, L., Wang, S., & Lai, K. K. (2005, May). *Adaptive smoothing neural networks in foreign exchange rate forecasting*. In *International Conference on Computational Science* (pp. 523–530). Springer, Berlin, Heidelberg.
15. Hussain, A. J., Al-Jumeily, D., Al-Askar, H., & Radi, N. (2016). Regularized dynamic self-organized neural network inspired by the immune algorithm for financial time series prediction. *Neurocomputing, 188*, 23–30.
16. Usmani, M., Ebrahim, M., Adil, S. H., & Raza, K. (2018, December). *Predicting Market Performance with Hybrid Model*. In *2018 3rd International Conference on Emerging Trends in Engineering, Sciences and Technology (ICEEST)* (pp. 1–4). IEEE.
17. Kamruzzaman, J., & Sarker, R. A. (2003, December). *Forecasting of currency exchange rates using ANN: A case study*. In *International Conference on Neural Networks and Signal Processing, 2003. Proceedings of the 2003* (Vol. 1, pp. 793–797). IEEE.
18. Majhi, R., Panda, G., & Sahoo, G. (2006, June). *Efficient prediction of foreign exchange rate using nonlinear single layer artificial neural model*. In *2006 IEEE Conference on Cybernetics and Intelligent Systems* (pp. 1–5). IEEE.
19. He, H., & Shen, X. (2007, August). *Bootstrap methods for foreign currency exchange rates prediction*. In *2007 International Joint Conference on Neural Networks* (pp. 1272–1277). IEEE.
20. Ince, H., & Trafalis, T. B. (2006). A hybrid model for exchange rate prediction. *Decision Support Systems, 42*(2), 1054–1062.
21. Graves, A., Mohamed, A. R., & Hinton, G. (2013, May). *Speech recognition with deep recurrent neural networks*. In *Acoustics, Speech and Signal Processing (ICASSP), 2013 IEEE International Conference* (pp. 6645–6649). IEEE.
22. Yu, P., & Yan, X. (2019). Stock price prediction based on deep neural networks. *Neural Computing and Applications*, 1–20.
23. Li, Y., & Cao, H. (2018). Prediction for tourism flow based on LSTM neural network. *Procedia Computer Science, 129*, 277–283.
24. Wang, J., Peng, B., & Zhang, X. (2018). Using a stacked residual LSTM model for sentiment intensity prediction. *Neurocomputing, 322*, 93–101.
25. Hochreiter, S., & Schmidhuber, J. (1997). Long short-term memory. *Neural Computation, 9*(8), 1735–1780.

14 Ethical Issues Surrounding AI Applications

Vidushi Pandey
Department of Information Systems
Indian Institute of Management Kozhikode

CONTENTS

14.1 INTRODUCTION

Advent of Artificial Intelligence (AI) and Machine Learning (ML) technology has ushered us into an era that was once considered a part of science fantasy novels. Today, these applications address problems in sectors like medicine, defence, education, transport, manufacturing, retail, and many more. AI technologies are

DOI: 10.1201/9781003125129-14

playing crucial roles with solutions like computer vision, speech recognition, text analysis and pattern recognition. These have drastically improved our capability to process large amount of data generated in today's sensor-enabled world. Insights from this data have the potential to transform human lives for good. However, like any another technology, AI to is bound to go through a learning curve where unintended outcomes might negatively affect the recipients. The AI community today is not just limited to scientists, developers and engineers, but also involves all the stakeholders that are in one way or another impacted by these solutions. These include citizens, industries, governments, policy makers, lawmakers and most other members society. In order to promote trustworthy, holistic and responsible development of this technology for greater good of society, it is important that all stakeholders are sensitized towards various ethical aspects of this technology. This chapter aims to highlight such ethical issues and approaches that are currently being undertaken to address these issues.

14.2   ETHICAL ISSUES WITH AI APPLICATIONS

Ethical Issues with AI applications are shown below in Figure 14.1.

Despite being an immensely powerful and potentially game-changing technology, AI applications are raising serious ethical concerns about their use. The level of current AI application is not as advanced as to give rise to a robot uprising and put human existence in danger. Such concerns may form an interesting plot of sci-fi movies but are not the immediate pressing issues for society. The immediate serious concerns are related to issues like power imbalance and societal divide that AI can create, labour issues that will be raised, privacy of users and serious threats to democracy due to disinformation capabilities powered by AI tools. These concerns, as summarized in Figure 14.1, are discussed in detail in the following sections.

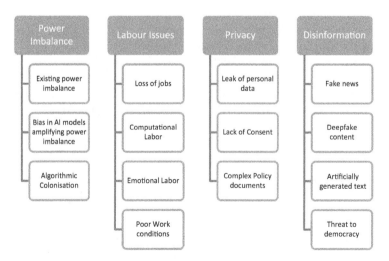

FIGURE 14.1   Ethical Issues with AI applications.

14.2.1 POWER IMBALANCE

Use of AI solutions has often been proposed as a solution to many of world's problems under labels like 'AI for good'. However, access to sophisticated AI applications and their impact on society is seriously plagued by differential power distribution in the society. Unthoughtful use and deployment of AI/ML applications can lead to further widening of this gap between less powerful and more powerful. This issue can be seen from two perspectives:

14.2.1.1 Existing Power Imbalance in Funding Agencies and Organizations Developing AI Solutions

The entire process of conceptualization, design, training and deployment of sophisticated AI solutions is often very costly. Organizations require highly skilled data scientists, software engineers, researchers and UX designers to design AI solutions that would be capable of addressing a practical need satisfactorily. This human power is often accessible to large, heavily funded organizations and corporations which attract these human resources from across the world. Access to human resource in developing AI solutions is often difficult for smaller companies, non-profit organizations and developing/underdeveloped countries. Even academia is facing this issue as quality researchers are often recruited by private firms creating a gap in resource constrained academic research efforts. Such concentration of key human resource under the hands of few powerful agencies can influence the kind of AI solutions that get attention. The agenda of research and development in AI can get impacted by these powerful funding agencies. Areas that make more business sense and can generate more profit are likely to get more research funding compared to applications that may have a greater impact on society but have less earning capacity. The recent incident of Google's ethics researcher Timnit Gebru's termination from the company on grounds of differences in research focus is one example of such scenario.

The latest AI applications employ deep learning algorithms with multiple neural network layers process a large amount of data in parallel. To handle such heavy computing requirements, specialized chips called GPUs or Graphical Processing Units may be required. These GPUs are not only costly to build and procure, but they also consume are large amount of power to handle the intense AI algorithms.

Furthermore, the amount of data required to train such algorithms is also very high. Data collection, pre-processing and cleaning of such data is another layer of cost that organizations have to bear. Investment of such large scale is often affordable to large corporate organizations, while smaller, privately owned or not-for-profit organizations may not be able to afford these costs. All such costs can make AI technology accessible to only a few powerful stakeholders, add to their productivity and profits and in turn further widen the economic and digital divide in the society.

For example, in the case of AI interventions in agriculture, farmers backed up by large corporations have sufficient funds and backup to experiment with such solutions. Even when these solutions may not be immediately successful, these farmers are able to contain the sunk cost, as they have adequate financial support from the industry. Once the AI deployments start paying off, these farmers are likely to gain multiplied output from their farms. On the other hand, small family-owned farms with limited resources would most likely not have the financial flexibility to experiment with these technologies.

This lack or resources will be further amplified once the larger farmers start reaping benefits of increased productivity [1].

This problem of differential access and widening of gap between haves and have-nots isn't new. It has been extant in various domains of society from pharmaceutical research to education, industrialization, internet access and many more. However, identifying that access to AI too falls under this phenomenon and it is important to create mechanisms for addressing such problems.

14.2.1.2 Biased AI Solutions Amplifying Existing Power Imbalance in Society

Poorly designed AI systems can further shift the power balance of the society by unintentionally or intentionally discriminating against certain members of the society. The way an AI system has been conceptualized, trained and tested defines its performance and impact on end users. If these systems are not adequately trained on data representative of all sections of society and if these systems are not appropriately tested with all categories of end users, the system may codify societal biases in their performances. For example, a prediction algorithm designed for selecting candidates in a healthcare program in US was found to be biased against the African American members of the community. In another example, Goldman Sachs and Apple faced backlash when their Apple payment card solution assigned higher credit limits to men in comparison to women with same or even better credit ratings [2].

Even if these biases are identified once the application is rolled out, it is difficult to hold someone accountable, as the company employing the system may not necessarily understand the code behind the application. In Apple's case, the company, developers and Goldman Sachs denied the allegation that algorithm was biased, but could not provide explanation of why the algorithm was making those decisions. Most of the deep learning AI applications are 'Black Box' models, where even the developers do not understand the rules used by algorithms to make decisions. The developers often measure algorithmic success on parameters like accuracy which the code does indeed deliver despite the biases present. Clustering algorithms, for example, are often used to make sense of large chunks of data by dividing it into homogenous chunks of data points. However, unless specifically take care of, the algorithm may not follow 'individual or group fairness' principles, and might result in highly skewed clusters that may amplify existing biases in the society.

Speech recognition systems are widely used across geographies today. But these systems are generally trained on data from native English speakers mostly from western countries. This lack of diversity in training has resulted in non-native English speakers struggling with these systems. In fact, instead of Machine Learning systems adapting to user's needs, often users of these systems are nudged to change their speech to accommodate these devices. This issue can be even more serious for users with serious speech impairments. Such users may be completely unable to use the systems. The problem here is not with the algorithm itself, but due to a lack of diversity in training data, and lack of representation of the wide variety of end users in the input data. Similar issues occur with other forms of AI systems like face recognition not identifying people of certain races or facial differences, computer vision systems not recognizing physically disabled people as human beings due to change in body shape, posture or use of mobility support. Content analysis systems may not consider spellings of dyslexic people.

Algorithmic Coloniality or Data Coloniality are the terms used by scholars in reference to the idea that "the modern-day power imbalances between races, countries, rich and poor and other groups are extensions of the power imbalances between colonizer and colonized". It can manifest in multiple ways in the current AI driven world. Inbuilt racism and other biases in training data and algorithm performance is one aspect that has already been discussed above. Other ways in which this form of 'colonialism' becomes evident are not including developing countries in discussion of AI policies and data agreements, using low cost labour from these countries to get the ghost work of data preparation done, using certain vulnerable populations for beta testing the application before rolling it out in western markets and taking a 'paternalist' approach in 'AI for good' initiatives without allowing developing nations to actually build capabilities of designing AI solutions for their needs [3].

14.2.2 Labour Issues

One of the major perceived threats of AI/ML applications is that these will completely replace humans and lead to massive unemployment in society. There are indeed many examples of AI systems which claim to automate a labour-intensive operation and remove the need of humans as intermediaries. Call centres, customer service kiosks, check out personnel at retail shops, drivers and many more such roles are under the threat of becoming redundant due to AI interventions. There are multiple aspects of this threat that need attention. Two key aspects are:

14.2.2.1 What Kinds of Jobs Are Most Likely to Be Impacted by the Threat of AI?

The key capability of AI/ML as a technology is to be able to predict events efficiently. AI applications for job application filtering try to predict which candidate is mostly likely to perform well on the job, AI applications for medical diagnostic may try to predict if a tumour is likely to be cancerous or benign, autonomous driving vehicle try to predict the next move of vehicles/pedestrian on the road and accordingly make decisions. These and many other examples of AI systems basically rely on the algorithm's efficiency to predict an outcome. The effect these systems will have on the workforce will depend on the importance of this prediction capability in the jobs. For jobs that are completely dependent on the prediction ability like forecasting, legal summary, email response by executive assistants, the threat of replacement would be strong. However, for jobs that are a mix of prediction and some other kind of skills like in medicine, diagnostics or education where the decision-making skill, human touch of the practitioner is also important AI application may complement the existing jobs but not completely replace it [4].

14.2.2.2 Can AI Actually Remove All Need for Human Intervention?

Even for AI applications that claim to be efficient at replacing needs of humans completely, the actual truth may not be the same. AI applications still rely a lot on human workers for smoothening out their edges. Many new kinds of jobs are created to support the performances of AI applications. Human workers are often required for collection of extensive data needed for training the applications. "Computational Labour", refers to this workforce hired on contract by the companies, to help in accomplishing their AI related tasks [5].

These people, often underpaid and from developing countries, spend hours collecting, categorizing and cleaning data for AI applications. In some cases, the results of the applications need to be smoothed out, which requires human support. For example, in content moderation tasks on platforms like Facebook, despite the use of sophisticated AI algorithms, human intervention is still required in many cases. Thus, these AI application despite being positioned to reduce manual labour are also creating need for new forms of manual labour jobs. The problem here is that these jobs are often invisible to end users, leading to issues like mistreatment of workers, lack of fair wages and limited guidelines. The case of workers of the content moderation wing of Indian IT firms suffering severe mental stress is an extreme example of such scenarios. Other forms of jobs that may arise out of AI implementation are the ones that compliment AI usage at customer's end. "Emotional Labour" refers to workers who are hired to help customers/clients accommodate with new AI-based systems and handhold them in the transition process. Catering to the prevalent stereotype of women being more suitable for care and support jobs, the jobs under emotional labour often prefer female workers.

14.2.3 Privacy

Privacy of users as well as non-users who are somehow impacted by AI applications is another important concern that the AI community needs to address. Imagine you have uploaded your holiday pictures on your public Instagram profile. A few days later you see it being used in an advertisement. You approach the advertising company for using your picture without your consent and ask them to remove it. The company tells you that if you didn't want your picture to be used, you should not have made your profile public on social media. Is the company's logic justified? Will you be okay with such use of your picture? Most likely you would not be. However, so many of our pictures, posts and other forms of data that we publicly post is being used by various AI applications for training the models. In most cases, users have no idea that their public data is being used for this purpose and they have not given consent for it. However, many AI companies evade responsibility by putting the blame on people saying if they did not want their data to be used, they should not have made it public. This is not an acceptable way to address this issue. Most of us have no idea that our data can be used for such purposes and hence we never try to prevent or control it. People should have control over their data, and they should have the right to withdraw their data from being used from such models anytime. Now, suppose the advertising company agrees to your claim and you ask them to take down the advertisement. The company does so at their end, but by the time that advertise has spread through various different media channels. Even if the original ad is removed, its multiple copies have been created and shared already. No matter how much you try, you might never be able to get rid of that advertisement. Similarly, what if your data is already being used for training purposes and you decide that you don't want your data to be used in that manner? You ask the company to remove your data point from their training dataset. The company does that. But by this time, multiple training sessions that the algorithm has gone through with your data, your data has already left some mark which cannot be simply removed by removing your data point from the training set. People should have the right to effectively withdraw their data from any AI training process whenever they wish.

The other aspect of privacy is when AI applications like computer vision, voice assistant and other monitoring devices/applications sneakily collect your data without you knowing. In one example, researcher have done experiments and found that Amazon echo often starts recording even in absence of official wake words [6]. These devices may collect your data, store it and use it in improving performance without any intimation to you. Companies may say that these things were mentioned in the 'Terms & Conditions' which users accept; however, we all know that no one ever reads these agreements. Tech companies have done such excellent job of loading these agreements with complex jargons, that it is almost impossible for a regular user to interpret it. Rather than putting all the liability on users for maintaining their privacy, companies need to come up with solutions that can address this problem.

14.2.4   MISINFORMATION, DISINFORMATION AND FAKE NEWS

After the 2016 US presidential elections, investigations in U.S. found presence of co-ordination social media campaigns by a Russian "troll farm", the Internet Research Agency [7] (IRA). The focus of these campaigns was to create an atmosphere of anger and division in the country. IRA had hired round the clock staff who stole identities of real Americans to create fake profiles, interacted with thousands of Americans to understand their behaviour, created fake information posts and rumours, posted content that appropriately blends in with American population without raising a doubt and were said to have serious impact on the harmony and stability of atmosphere in the US around the elections [9].

For achieving these outcomes, the troll farm had invested millions of dollars and hours of human resources. Today, to achieve similar or even more potent results the amount of human involvement and money a troll farm would have to invest can be way lesser, thanks to advancements in AI technology. High powered language generators can generate thousands of texts resembling authentic posts by humans in no time. AI application can now allow you to create realistic pictures and videos of people who never existed. Deepfake technology allows anyone to create highly believable fake videos of people. All these incidents have raised serious issues of misinformation, disinformation and fake issues on social media. Misinformation occurs when the inaccuracy in the information is unintentional, while disinformation refers to intentionally misleading information. These can be in form of text (posts resembling those by real people), photographs, video and audio data. The trending topic and recommendation algorithms of social media platforms often fuel the spread of such false information.

Social media platforms are trying to come up with solutions to filter these posts, but the sophistication of such rumour campaigns is continuously on rise to dodge these policing attempts. Agencies like fact-checkers and scientists who try to debunk these rumours are often under added pressure to provide precise evidence for debunking such false posts. On the contrary, rumour mills spreading such information are rarely under pressure to provide evidence. Not just in political domains, other domains have also started using these malpractices for their vested interests. Facebook this year identified several fake posts on its platform that were created by South Asian telecom companies to discredit their rivals. Facebook removed several pages that created false 'news' and 'memes' against rival companies to discredit their services in front of consumers. Many of the groups and communities where this fake information is shared are closed groups. This makes access of this data to filtering & fact-checking tools even more difficult. Hence, it isn't currently possible to completely curate all the content in circulation on different media platforms.

The effort required to generate a viral disinformation campaign has gone down while the sophistication of these efforts have considerably increased. Most of these applications are based on open-source AI technology like Deep Neural networks (DNN), generative adversarial networks (GANs – artificial image generators) and Generative Pre-trained Transformer (GPT language generators). Access to this technology is freely available to anyone and it can be used to build any kind of application (good or bad). This is raising concerns about open-source publishing of such potent AI technologies. While indeed these technologies will lead to creation of many socially productive applications, the fact that these can very easily be used for many malicious purposes is becoming a growing concern. The latest version of GPT-3 was in fact not made completely public due to such concerns. This is again an ethical dilemma in front of AI community that needs to be addressed.

14.3   APPROACHES TO ADDRESS ETHICAL ISSUES IN AI

The various concerns related to AI applications in society, highlighted in previous section need a holistic problem-solving approach by all stakeholders involved in the AI eco-system. From large corporates to government, academic researchers, whistle blowers, international policy makers, engineers, data scientist and end users, every stakeholder needs to be aware of these potential issues and work in direction of addressing them. Figure 14.2 highlights the key approaches currently in practice to address these ethical concerns. These are discussed in detail in the next sections.

Approaches to address ethical issues in AI is shown in Figure 14.2.

14.3.1   ALGORITHMIC APPROACHES FOR PRIVACY PROTECTION

Often times Machine Learning algorithms require a large amount of detailed user data for training and testing purposes. Companies may have to publish or share summaries of such sensitive data for various purposes. Adversaries with ill intent of misusing this information may try to reverse engineer such summary statistics and get access

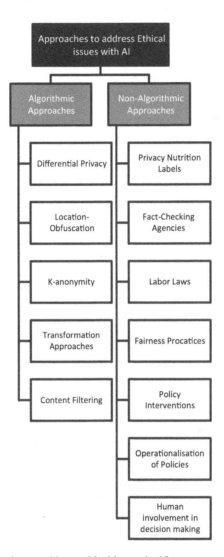

FIGURE 14.2 Approaches to address ethical issues in AI.

to detailed user level data. Anonymizing the data may not be sufficient to prevent such privacy attacks. If the attackers have auxiliary information available from other sources, they may still be able to retrieve original user level data. To prevent such attacks AI experts have proposed various algorithmic techniques to protect the privacy of user data. Some of them are:

Differential Privacy: Differential privacy refers to algorithmic techniques used to split/modify/hide a part of sensitive data in order to make it unusable for adversaries trying to misuse it. One of the approaches is to introduce noise in the data. Thus, instead of providing the actual value x the attacker may receive a value x + N where N is the noise introduce by the system. While the system internally would know how to filter out noise from original data, attackers may not. This will drastically reduce usability of data for attackers. However, if the attackers can query the dataset multiple times, they may be able to find patterns in the noise and be able to filter it out.

Location obfuscation: To protect location and tracking data of users, algorithms may introduce a distance error in order in the original data. This would provide an inaccurate location to the adversary and prevent them from identifying an individual's location.

K-anonymity: This technique hides the actual identity of a user by mixing it with a set of other users' data.

Transformation based approaches: Makes use of cryptography techniques to hide sensitive data.

14.3.2 Non-Algorithmic Approaches to Safeguard User Privacy

Apart from algorithmic interventions, many non-algorithmic interventions are also being made at policy levels to improve privacy of user data. One line of work in these domain focuses on addressing the complexity of 'Terms and conditions' that users often agree to without understanding. A majorant deterrent to users is the heavily complex and technical language used in these agreements. One solution to this problem is use of 'Privacy Nutrition Labels'. The CyLab Usable Privacy & Security Laboratory (CUPS) at Carnegie Mellon University developed the concept of privacy nutrition label to make privacy policies easy to understand and comparable by the end users [10]. Just like nutrition label on a food packet, privacy label is meant to clearly list out key aspects of any application in a clear and easy language. Apple has recently adopted this feature for its iOS14 platform and has mandated developers to provide these privacy nutrition labels for all the applications on its app store [11]. More such interventions are needed to give the users more control over their data and privacy.

14.3.3 Approaches to Handle the Spread of Disinformation

Handling the massive threat of disinformation at various levels requires interventions at both algorithmic level, policy level and at general awareness level. Algorithms built to identify patterns in bot generated data try to find distinct patterns in aspects like sentence construction, repetitiveness, visual distortion, location, frequency of posts etc. Also, there are applications which try to 'poison' the training data, often utilized for training Deepfake models by adding watermarks or utilizing blockchain technology to track data footprints [12].

However, given the rate at which these preventive algorithms are improving, the malicious algorithms too are getting better at same and in some cases higher rate.

A serious issue with only algorithmic filtering is that it may lead to mis-identifying and blocking of genuine content as well. Platforms then have to make this trade-off while tuning their filtering mechanism in deciding whether to be less accurate and prevent any genuine posts from being flagged or should they focus on higher accuracy to remove all malicious content even if it inhibits genuine free speech in some case. Moreover, social media platforms often don't have an incentive in blocking all suspicious content as these kinds of content drive major clicks and may make more business for the platform.

Hence, intervention at policy and awareness level also is also needed to curb disinformation. Stronger rules are required for social media use and misuse. Involvement of fact-checking agencies, sufficient funding and support to such agencies, identifying and tagging reliable and no reliable sources of information are all required to control the menace of fake information on media platforms. Media literacy among the end users is another necessary step to educate them that not all information they come across may be reliable and to sensitize them in identifying and flagging suspicious content. Despite all such efforts, this is an ongoing battle, and new solutions are required to manage this issue.

14.3.4 ADDRESSING BIAS IN AI APPLICATIONS

In order to address the issues of bias that get inbuilt in AI systems and end up discriminating certain sections of society, utmost care has to be taken in the design and training phase of the application development. Ideally, system designers should be aware of possible biases that exist in a given status to avoid them. However, this may not always be known to the system users themselves. Therefore, efforts need to be made in selecting training data that is representative of all categories of end users. Algorithmic techniques are employed at pre- and post-processing levels to reduce bias. Techniques like balancing sensitive data, removing sensitive attributes, transforming model's prediction to satisfy fairness constraints, imposing fairness constraints on the optimization process and innovative data training techniques are used to prevent biases of offline system from creeping in AI systems [13].

Efforts to increase explainability of deep learning models are made to identify which factors are considered by algorithms leading to those bias. A participatory design approach needs to be followed that makes sure target users are involved in all phases of application design.

However, the key challenge is in defining 'fairness'. There are multiple definitions for fairness at both individual and group levels. None of the definitions are exhaustive and cover all aspects of fairness. Thus, selecting what parameters an AI system should adhere to is a fairly complex task. Expecting data scientists and engineers to get involved at level of definitional complexity in addition to their already challenging technical roles is not practical. Organizations need to invest in ethics specialists who can work with AI teams and guide them in such matters.

14.3.5 ADDRESSING RISK AND SECURITY ISSUES IN AI APPLICATIONS

A key aspect related to risk and security of AI applications is assigning accountability. If an autonomous car makes a wrong decision and harms a pedestrian who is accountable for it? The car? The code? The engineers behind the code? The car company? Or the rider who was in the car at that time? This dilemma calls for a deeper look at who should be in control of final decision-making? Depending on the situation, contexts and risks associated with them, the autonomy to make final decisions should be kept with humans. This will enable them to override potentially harmful decisions that AI could make. In applications like enrolment to education institutes, autonomous driving, employment and promotion in offices, disbursing social support, judicial service and all such domains where a wrong outcome may impact a human life in some form, it might make more sense to use AI for recommendation and let human agency make the final decision. However, the humans involved may not necessarily be better at such decision-making. To ensure that humans involved in the process possess sufficient level of expertise, they too need to be trained extensively in real-world scenarios rather than just working with AI systems. The case of Air France flight crash in 2009 is an example of how too much reliance on automated systems and lack of sufficient real-world training may reduce human agency's decision-making capability as well. The Air France AF447 flight crashed in the ocean in 2009 leading to the loss of the 228 lives on board. The accident was a result of 'loss of control' in the aircraft. Loss of control situations often arise when the aircraft (which most of the time runs on auto-pilot systems) withdraws the auto-pilot mode due to inconsistencies in input data and transfers control to manual pilots. In the case of the doomed Air France flight, the autopilot system surrendered control, and the pilots were in shock when they suddenly had to manually fly the aircraft at tricky high-altitude conditions. The pilots could not interpret the system readings correctly, leading to a freefall of the aircraft into the ocean. This accident can partly be attributed to lack of pilot experience in such real-world scenarios due to over reliance on automated systems [14]. With autonomous driving systems being rolled out for commercial use, similar situation is likely to arise even for vehicle drivers. Even if the overriding capability is given to a human, it wouldn't be very useful unless the human in control is properly trained to make such decisions.

14.3.6 POLICY AND ETHICAL FRAMEWORKS

With increasing awareness about the ethical issues related to AI/ML solutions, independent research organisations, governments, non-profits and corporates have all come with multiple policy documents, frameworks and guidelines to address these concerns. The Organisation for Economic Co-operation and Development (OECD) proposed 'Principal for AI' to *promote innovative and trustworthy AI that respects human rights and government values'*. These principles were adopted by the 37 OECD member countries in 2019. Apart from them many other countries as well as G20 countries have adopted AI principles based on OECD's proposal. The principles were designed by an expert group of more than 50 members that included representatives from governments, business, academic community, civil society, labour and scientific communities.

THE OECD AI PRINCIPLES

- AI should benefit people and the planet by driving inclusive growth, sustainable development and wellbeing.
- AI systems should be designed in a way that respects the rule of law, human rights, democratic values and diversity, and they should include appropriate safeguards – for example, enabling human intervention where necessary – to ensure a fair and just society.
- There should be transparency and responsible disclosure around AI systems to ensure that people understand AI-based outcomes and can challenge them.
- AI systems must function in a robust, secure and safe way throughout their lifecycles and potential risks should be continually assessed and managed.
- Organisations and individuals developing, deploying or operating AI systems should be held accountable for their proper functioning in line with the above principles.

Source: https://www.oecd.org/going-digital/ai/principles/

Other such policy-level efforts include UK Data Ethics frameworks, A Proposed Model Artificial Intelligence Governance Framework by Singapore Personal Data Protection Commission, The IEEE Global Initiative on Autonomous Systems, Guidelines on Artificial Intelligence and Data Protection by EU council of Europe and many more. Even private companies like Google and SAP designed and released ethical guidelines for AI implementation. The increasing attention to the ethical concerns regarding AI application is a much needed and appreciable move. However, many of these efforts are also criticised as attempts of 'ethics washing' and not taking any concrete action. The problem lies in effective operationalisation and implementation of these policy guidelines. It is easy to say that we as a company follow the ethical principle, but are there any means to practically implement these and measure their impact? Every organisation is free to interpret the meaning of terms like fairness, transparency, responsible AI in their own way. Hence, not just policies and guidelines but actual operationalisation and implementation of these are the need of the hour. The AI field can take lessons from other domain where similar ethical concerns play a key role. Fields like medicine, law and education that have dealt with such ethical concerns for a long time can provide references for effective operationalisation of ethical values.

Also, companies need to give decision-making powers to ethical committees rather than having them just tick a checkbox of ethical guidelines. There needs to be overall sensitization of developers and engineers about philosophical approaches and ethical values. These sensitization efforts should include not just Western view of ethics, but also perspectives from other cultures like Buddhism, Shinto and Ubuntu.

Expert committees should be available to guide employees throughout the process. Another important role is played by strong AI journalism. In order for end users, developers, companies and governments to understand the technical and ethical aspects of AI, responsible journalism will play a crucial role. Rather than fearmongering and sensationalization, journalism in this field needs to be informative and wide enough to present different perspectives of the stakeholders.

The discussions of all the ethical issues pertaining to AI may seem to be painting a very gloomy picture of the technology for society. However, it has to be understood that every new technological advancement has faced similar concerns. From introduction of automobiles, to industrial machines, computers and IT software, such concerns have always existed and have been handled with deeper understanding of relationship between human and technology. AI technologies, too, will go through this learning curve where all the stakeholders will come up with better solutions through continuous collaborations and knowledge sharing.

REFERENCES

1. https://datasociety.net/wp-content/uploads/2019/01/DataandSociety_AIinContext.pdf
2. https://www.washingtonpost.com/business/2019/11/11/apple-card-algorithm-sparks-gender-bias-allegations-against-goldman-sachs/
3. https://www.technologyreview.com/2020/07/31/1005824/decolonial-ai-for-everyone/
4. Agrawal, Ajay K., Gans, Joshua S. and Goldfarb, Avi. Artificial Intelligence: The Ambiguous Labor Market Impact of Automating Prediction (February 25, 2019). Available at SSRN: https://ssrn.com/abstract=3341456 or http://dx.doi.org/10.2139/ssrn.3341456
5. Shestakofsky, Benjamin. "Working algorithms: Software automation and the future of work." *Work and Occupations* 44.4 (2017): 376–423.
6. https://www.washingtonpost.com/technology/2019/05/06/alexa-has-been-eavesdropping-you-this-whole-time/
7. https://www.ft.com/content/55a39e92-8357-11ea-b872-8db45d5f6714
8. https://www.bbc.com/news/technology-43093390
9. https://cups.cs.cmu.edu/privacyLabel/
10. https://developer.apple.com/app-store/app-privacy-details/
11. https://spectrum.ieee.org/tech-talk/computing/software/what-are-deepfakes-how-are-they-created
12. https://www.mckinsey.com/featured-insights/artificial-intelligence/tackling-bias-in-artificial-intelligence-and-in-humans#
13. https://hbr.org/2017/09/the-tragic-crash-of-flight-af447-shows-the-unlikely-but-catastrophic-consequences-of-automation

15 Semantic Data Extraction Using Video Analysis

An AI Analytical Perspective

Subasish Mohapatra, Aditi Bansal, and
Subhadarshini Mohanty
Department of Computer Science and Engineering,
College of Engineering and Technology, Bhubaneswar

CONTENTS

DOI: 10.1201/9781003125129-15

15.1 INTRODUCTION

The current era of technology offers ample opportunity to users to face up to the mighty stream of data with every click, swipe, share, search and stream. As a result, the digital universe is expanding like never before. An huge volume of data is generated every moment worldwide. The scale is now not limited to kilobytes, megabytes, gigabytes or even terabytes. One of the major contributors to this escalating data is video data. Healthcare, education, media and communications, tours and travels, food and culture, geographical exploration, safety and security, social media and interactive platforms, satellite-generated data, etc. are the key sources generating tremendous amounts of video data on a daily basis. The surveillance data captured from security cameras that are recorded every day add a significant share to the stockpiled video data.

Surveillance videos are a crucial contributor to the unstructured big data [1]. The role of video streams from security cameras is no less than any other visual data sources like social platform data, agriculture data, medical data, sensor data, geospatial data and data evolved from space research. CCTV cameras are installed in almost every corner of the world, where safety is paramount. And this escalating demand for safety and security is driving the need for intelligent surveillance systems [2].

In crowded public places, surveillance cameras act as a third eye covering all types of unusual events, demanding full involvement of human operators. Monitoring, storage, retrieval and processing of such gigantic data have lots of requirements in terms of storage space, time and human efforts. Therefore, in this chapter, we will deal with performing semantic video analysis on the most common source of video data: videos captured by CCTV cameras. We look forward to using this video data, perform analysis and extract the useful portion from it, thereby automating the surveillance process to some extent.

15.2 VIDEO ANALYTICS

Video analytics (VA) is the ability to automatically process and analyze a video segment to derive the required information. It is a more advanced means of video monitoring. VA helps to cut off irrelevant portions of video, making surveillance systems more intelligent and efficient and also reducing the workload on management. It is a subset of computer vision and therefore of AI too. It provides a wide variety of functionalities, including object detection, shapes and faces recognition, video tracking, motion detection, crowd analysis and a lot more. In addition to these functionalities, it also supports an innumerable number of applications in several fields.

15.3 NEED FOR VIDEO ANALYTICS

With the rapid increase in the number of security cameras, video data creation rate is on an exponential rise. To capture behaviours in public places, a large number of surveillance cameras are creatively exploited. Considering the massive amount of data available over time, the next thing to focus on is the facility for data warehousing and data analysis. Imagine the amount of video data we need to deal with, given a single high-definition video camera can produce around 10 GB of data per day.

The space needed for storing large amounts of surveillance videos for a long period is challenging. Instead of storing the whole video data, it will be beneficial to store the analytical output. It will lead to reduction in storage space, solving the storage constraints. Also, deep learning techniques involve two main components: training and testing. Both can be achieved with the highest accuracy through a huge amount of data.

The main benefits of training with vast data are listed below. The complete data can be equally divided into training and testing sets. It is also viable to acclimate variety in data representation by employing this bulk data available. In video analysis, the actual analysis is performed on the frameset extracted from the video. So, the dataset can consist of videos as well as image data. The extracted frameset and the image data are filtered allowing only the useful ones to the model learning stage. Also, a broad training and testing dataset imply a well-learned model, thereby increasing the chances of more accurate results.

15.4   THE WORKFLOW

Semantic data extraction using video analysis aims at making use of enormous video data available to extract useful information. For obtaining the vehicle number, it uses the concept of image processing and computer vision to collect the valuable portion of the video or image data and then implements the concept of optical character recognition [3] to extract further information from it. In other words, it takes video or images as input and produces some text as an output.

Data extraction from surveillance video data can be used for several purposes like crowd analysis, theft detection, violence detection, etc. The workflow of the process may differ with the purpose for which the analysis is performed. This flow of the process for VA can be best understood by considering the fundamental example of identifying the vehicle number of vehicles from the video data and depicted in Figure 15.1. To become familiar with the concepts of VA, the necessary steps involved and where to use it, let us start with the simplest example. The whole process of obtaining the vehicle number from a CCTV captured video is first broken into smaller steps. The methodology for the same is shown in Figure 15.1.

The methodology involves four major stages:

1. **Frame Extraction**: This the first and probably the most straightforward stage. Here, the provided video is converted into a set of frames. The input of this stage is a video, and output is an image sequence obtained from the video.
2. **Licence Plate Detection**: In this stage, the position of the licence plate of the vehicle on the image is detected and segmented using the segmentation model. The segmentation model takes the image as an input and returns the segmented licence plate as output [4–10].
3. **Character Segmentation**: In this stage, the licence plate is further segmented to obtain individual images for each character on the plate [11,12].

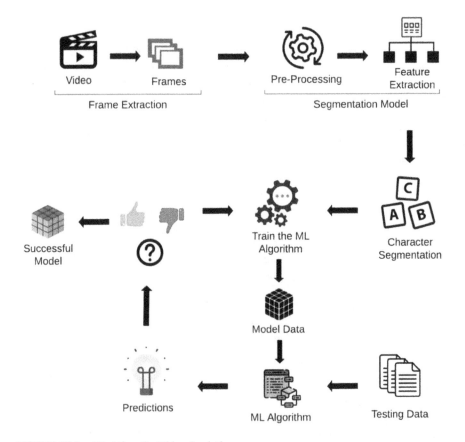

FIGURE 15.1   Workflow for Video Analytics.

4. **Character Recognition**: It is the last phase which will generate the final output. The characters segmented in the previous step are identified using Machine
   Learning [10,13].

15.4.1 FRAME EXTRACTION

Image Analytics is a pervasive field which deals with the extraction of relevant information from digital images or videos by means of some processing techniques.
OpenCV library is an open-source Machine Learning and computer vision library used
to perform operations and analysis on videos and pictures. Here, it is used to extract
continuous image sequences from the video is shown in Figure 15.2. The installed
cameras are used to capture standardized and continuous video feed 24/7. Therefore,
the camera must be positioned such that it captures the required object correctly. Also,
the video should be clear and must have a proper resolution. Sometimes, the captured
video may be present in raw format and, therefore, may require conversion to usable
video format like.avi. Web conversion tools like media converters are used to perform
such conversions. The video is now ready for the first step (frame extraction).

FIGURE 15.2 Obtaining image sequence from the video.

Next, a programmatic way has to be developed to convert the video to static images. This conversion can be easily achieved using the OpenCV libraries and packages. OpenCV library is cross-platform and free for use to aid various computer vision tasks. A simple algorithm using OpenCV can read the video and break it into frames as required [21]. The most important parameter here is specifying the number of frames to extract per second. If the value of this parameter is small, then several duplicate frames are obtained. Moreover, if the value of the parameter is large, some of the frames can be missed. Hence, it is essential to ensure proper value for the number of frames extracted per second is chosen.

Obtaining image sequence from the video is given in Figure 15.2.

Also, in some instances, the objects in the video may remain constant, and the video may not capture any motion. It will generate duplicate frames and processing them is of no use. Thus, an algorithm to remove duplicate frames has to be added. One method of doing it is to calculate the hash value for images and check for duplicates. Once the copies are found, the algorithm keeps only one picture of its kind, and the rest of the duplicates are deleted. A final set of images to be processed further is obtained.

15.4.2 SEGMENTATION MODEL

In the context of computer vision, image segmentation can be thought of as breaking down a digital image into multiple fragments based on pixel characteristics. The objective of image segmentation [14] is to represent an image as something more relatable, meaningful and easier to analyze. Image segmentation is used to separate foreground from background, extract required objects with periphery (known as the range of interest) or cluster pixel regions with similar characteristics in images. More precisely, image segmentation can be described as the process of generating a label for every pixel in an image such that pixels with similar characteristics such as intensity, colour or texture are assigned the same label. The purpose of segmentation here is to detect and extract the licence plate of a car from the image. The extracted frameset from the above procedure is passed through the segmentation model, where we have three main things to do:

- Preprocessing
- Feature extraction
- Localization

15.4.3   Preprocessing

The segmentation step is of prime importance as the rest of the steps are based on it. If the segmentation fails, recognition will also fail to produce the desired output. So, to ensure accuracy, performing preprocessing on data before further processing is necessary. Preprocessing is the primary transformation made on initial input data or the output data from the previous process to make it ready for further processing. It may include some geometrical transformation, colour transformation, standardizing image, image blurring, etc.

Image blurring/smoothening is one of the most used preprocessing steps. It is achieved by convolving the image with a low-pass filter kernel. It is useful for noise removal. When this filter is applied, it removes high-frequency content (e.g., noise, edges) from the image resulting in unwanted boundaries being blurred.

OpenCV mainly provides four types of blurring techniques.

- Avemraging:
  Averaging is a method of smoothing images by reducing the amount of intensity difference between pixels. It is done by combining an image with a normalized box filter. It calculates the average of all pixels under the kernel area and then replaces the central element by the average pixel value. This is done with the help of the function cv.blur() or cv.boxFilter().
- Gaussian filtering:
  The Gaussian filter is linear. Here blurring is achieved by a Gaussian function. It uses a Gaussian kernel rather than a box filter like averaging. It is done using the function cv.GaussianBlur(). Gaussian blurring is highly effective in removing any Gaussian noise from an image.
- Median filtering:
  A median filter is a nonlinear filtering technique that is used to remove noise from an image. It is a preprocessing step to improve the results. Here, the median of all the pixels under the kernel area and the central element is replaced with the median value calculated by the cv.medianBlur() function. It is mostly used where salt-and-pepper noise resides. In the median blurring, the central element is always replaced by some pixel value in the image, whereas in the above filters, the central cost is newly calculated.
- Bilateral filtering:
  A bilateral filter is a noise-reducing smoothing filter. It is highly effective in noise removal and, at the same time, keeps the edges sharp. The function used to do this is cv.bilateralFilter(). We already saw that a Gaussian filter takes neighbourhood pixels while filtering. It does not consider whether the pixels have the same intensity, or it is an edge pixel. It blurs the edges which we do not want. The bilateral filter uses a Gaussian filter, which is a function of pixel difference with a Gaussian filter in space. Both filters make sure that the edges are not blurred.

The colour transformation is also one of the essential steps used while extracting information from images. The colour transformation includes adjusting the brightness, hue, saturation or chromaticity, colour segmentation, colour smoothening and sharpening, etc. Mostly colour transitions like converting RGB to grey or binary proves to be extremely helpful while performing computer vision tasks on digital images as we can easily separate the foreground and background. Moreover, it becomes easier to apply algorithms on binary images. In applications like object detection and colour based extraction, a great deal of extra information can be found that simplifies the image analysis process.

The geometric transformation includes image transformation such as translation, scaling, rotation, distortion of images, etc. to produce a modified view of the image. Such alterations are mostly used as preprocessing steps in various applications where the scanned images are not aligned properly. Geometrical transformations are commonly used in computer graphics and image analysis to obtain a different view of the image or to eliminate the geographic distortion of images.

In the preprocessing step of the segmentation model, the images obtained from the frame extraction step are converted into grayscale images. In a grayscale image, pixels can pick any value from the 256 values lying between 0 to 255. Then these grayscale images are converted into binary images of either black or white pixels. For doing so, a threshold value is chosen, all the pixel values below the threshold value are assigned a pixel value of 0, and those with pixel value above the threshold value are assigned pixel value of 255. Smoothening is done on these images to remove irrelevant lines and edges from the object.

15.4.4 FEATURE EXTRACTION

Feature extraction is the first and the most critical component in object detection and recognition systems. An object is represented by a group of features that may include its colour, texture, shape, etc. These features form the feature vector that is used to recognize and classify the object. The proper extraction of these features is especially important to detect the object correctly. There are various feature extraction techniques available such as HOG, SURF, PCA, etc. Once features have been extracted, Machine Learning models can be built using them, to serve the purpose of accurate object recognition or detection.

In data science, one of the main concerns is the time complexity, which depends mostly on the number of features. In the starting years, the number of features was, however, not a concern. But today, the amount of data and the features contributing information have increased exponentially. Hence it becomes necessary to find out convenient measures to reduce the number of features by identifying and eliminating the least important ones. Things that can be visualized can be comfortably taken as a decision. Feature Mapping [15] is one such process of representing features along with the relevancy of these features on a graph. It makes sure that the features are visualized, and their corresponding information is visually available. In this manner, the irrelevant features are removed, and only the relevant ones are included.

The working of feature extraction depends on the combination of computer vision and our understanding of how a licence plate looks like. In feature mapping, in order to find the licence plate in the image, we pass the characteristics of a licence plate as the feature vector. It includes rectangular shape, and the height is less than the width, ratio of the height of the licence plate to the height of the car, the proportion of the width of the number plate to the width of the car, etc. Once the features are finalized and all portions of the image satisfying the characteristics of the licence plate are found, we need to mark those regions using object localization [16].

15.4.5 Object Localization

Object localization [17] is one of the prevailing computer vision tasks. Computer vision is concerned with the automatic extraction, processing, analyzing, and understanding digital images to procure numerical or symbolic information from a single image or sequence of images. Computer vision tasks include image classification, object localization, object detection, semantic segmentation, instance segmentation, etc. The difference between these tasks can be confusing and difficult to understand and the computer vision task is demonstrated in Figure 15.3.

Image classification is the task of assigning a label to a digital image according to its visual content. The input to image classification model is a digital image, and output is a label describing the category to which it belongs out of a fixed set of classes. Segmentation tasks in computer vision are broadly categorized into two types: semantic segmentation and instance segmentation. Semantic segmentation, unlike classification, assigns a label to every pixel in the image. Here, all the objects belonging to the same category are considered a single entity, whereas in instance segmentation, each object is considered as a distinct entity.

Object detection is the computer vision technique of finding instances of real-world objects in images or videos. It finds its applications in security surveillance, image retrieval, optical character recognition [3], face detection, automated vehicle parking systems, etc. Object localization can be thought of as an intermediate task between image classification and object detection. Object localization works with the

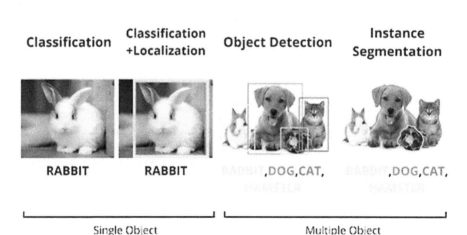

FIGURE 15.3 Computer vision tasks.

FIGURE 15.4   Before and after localization

FIGURE 15.5   Segmented Licence plate.

goal of predicting the exact position of an object in the image with its periphery (i.e., where precisely in the picture, the object is present). The distinction between object localization and object detection is profound. Whilst object localization searches for the primary or the most visible object in a picture, object detection aims to locate all the objects with their boundaries.

In the licence plate detection, after mapping all the features and using object localization to mark them, the image looks as shown in Figure 15.4.

Multiple regions in the image may exhibit the provided characteristics and get marked. From these marked regions, the licence plate is differentiated by performing vertical projection on all these regions. In vertical projection, all the pixel values of all pixels aligned in a vertical line are added. The concept here is, since the licence plate has characters printed on it, there will be variations in the projected pixel values which the rest of the regions will lack. This will ensure that only the licence plate is highlighted. After performing preprocessing, feature extraction, localization and vertical projection of pixels on our image, we segment the required portion of the image, and the result is shown in Figure 15.5.

Segmented Licence plate is given in Figure 15.5.

15.4.6   CHARACTER SEGMENTATION

Now that we have the required image segment, i.e., licence plate, the next thing to do is to segment individual characters from the image. There are many techniques available for character segmentation.[12,18] It includes blob extraction, connected component analysis, Image scissoring algorithm, projection-based method, morphological and partition-based method, template matching and projection-based, smearing, filtering and morphological algorithm, etc. Here are the two most commonly used and easy to implement ways to do it:

1. Boundary extraction using horizontal and vertical projection.
2. Connected Component Analysis (CCA).

15.4.7 Boundary Extraction Using Horizontal and Vertical Projection

Depending on the capture condition, the quality of plate images may not always be suitable. In such cases, before moving to the boundary extraction step, removal of noise, illumination adjustment, etc. are made to improve the quality of images. Next, some image enhancement techniques are adopted in order to enhance the character pixels and weaken the background and noise. Once this is done, a projection-based method is used to extract the characters' boundaries and segment them. Projection-based methods are one of the traditional methods still used in the majority of systems.

Horizontal and vertical projections are done to perform horizontal and vertical segmentation based on information obtained. Horizontal projections are used to find the top and bottom position of characters and remove the unwanted portion present above and below the characters in the licence plate image. In horizontal projection, the sum of pixel values of all the pixels along a particular line in the horizontal line is calculated. Once all values along all horizontal lines are obtained, the mean value is calculated and used as a threshold to get the upper and lower boundary for the characters. The area outside these boundaries is discarded, and the area between is taken up for further segmentation using vertical projection.

Vertical segmentation is used to detect gaps between the characters in the licence plate. Here, the sum of pixel values of all the white pixels lying in each vertical line is calculated. When the values for every vertical line are obtained, based on the result of vertical projection, each character is segmented. The portion of the plate with character will show zero as projection value since it has characters.

In some cases, one-character region is segmented into two, also at times, two characters are grouped as single due to connections for other reasons. Therefore, a refining segmentation process is used to adjust the linking and separation of segmented characters. Finally, an individual segmented image for every character in the licence plate image is obtained and shown in Figure 15.6.

15.4.8 Connected Component Analysis (CCA)

Connected component analysis (CCA) is a two-pass algorithm based on graph theory, where subsets of connected components are uniquely labelled based on a given heuristic. It is an algorithmic application of graph theory, based on traversal methods. One of the fast, simple, easy to understand and implementable algorithms, it is used to find all the connected regions in an image. In order to detect connected areas of

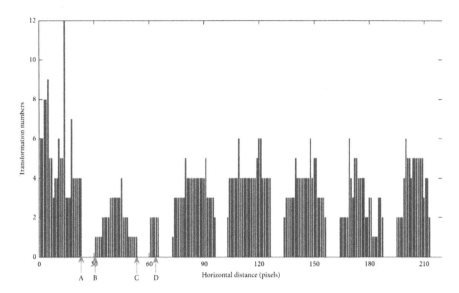

FIGURE 15.6   Vertical histogram projection on the licence plate image.

binary digital images, the algorithm makes two passes over the image, iterating through 2-dimensional binary image data. Starting from the first pixel in the image, we assign binary values to elements in the image, 1 to the foreground (white) pixel, and 0 to the background (black) pixel. In the first pass, the algorithm iterates through every element of data by column and then by row. If the element is in the foreground, it assigns temporary labels to each pixel in the foreground (i.e., white pixels). In the second pass, it performs connectivity checks with the neighbouring pixels (i.e., if the neighbouring pixel also has the same value as the current pixel or say is a foreground pixel).

Suppose the current pixel and the neighbouring pixel in its eight connectivity (pixel lying in immediate north, northeast, east, southeast, south, southwest, west, and northwest of the current pixel), and both are in the foreground. In that case, it assigns the same label (smallest temporary label among both) to them and moves to the next pixel. It continues until all the elements in the image data are scanned. At the end of both passes, it is ensured that each connected region in the image has a unique label assigned to it, and all the pixels in the same region bear the same label.

The algorithm to find connected regions is:
On the first pass:

1. Iterate each pixel in the image one row at a time from top to bottom.
2. If the pixel is background, continue.
3. If the pixel is foreground:
    i. Check the neighbouring foreground pixel of the current pixel.
    ii. If there are no neighbouring pixels in the foreground, assign a unique label the current pixel and continue.

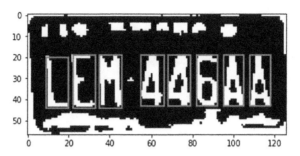

FIGURE 15.7   Character segmentation.

iii. Else, assign the smallest label value from the neighbouring pixel labels to the current pixel.

iv. Save the equivalence relationship between neighbouring labels.

On the second pass:

1. Iterate each pixel in the image one row at a time from top to bottom.
2. If the element is foreground:
   i. Relabel the pixel with the smallest equivalent label.

As in CCA, we consider the white pixels as foreground and black pixels as background, we first invert the binary image of the segmented licence plate and then apply CCA to it. Once all connected regions are found, localization is used to mark the connected parts in the image i.e., characters. The result is shown in Figure 15.7.

15.4.9   CHARACTER RECOGNITION

After character segmentation, the next thing to be done is to recognize the characters correctly. Before that, each character segmented from the previous stage is resized to 20px by 20px. This was done as a preprocessing step for character recognition.

There are a number of ways to perform character recognition, such as template matching, feature extraction based on edge distances, Machine Learning, etc. Our approach is based on Machine Learning as the system accuracy can be improved by improving the training process. Using Machine Learning, an extracted character image is mapped to its actual character.

Machine Learning is the subset of AI that deals with the process of teaching systems to accept data, self-learn from it, improve by experience and then use this learning to produce more useful results. It can be simply defined as a branch of AI that deals with data, processes them, discovers patterns and uses it for future prediction. Machine Learning is categorized as supervised, unsupervised and reinforcement learning. In supervised learning, the machine maps input to output based on its learning over provided input-output pairs. Here, supervised learning is used, as we have an idea of how different characters look like, and different input-output pairs of the character image and its label can be provided as training data.

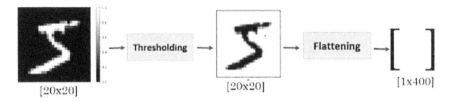

FIGURE 15.8   Preprocessing the training data.

Again, supervised learning is categorized as classification and regression. Character recognition comes under the category of classification. Hence, a Machine Learning classifier is used. To use Machine Learning for character recognition, use the following steps:

1. Collect training dataset.
2. Choose a Machine Learning classifier.
3. Create a training and testing model.
4. Use the model for predictions.

15.4.10 COLLECTING TRAINING DATASET

1. Training images for each character (A–Z and 0–9) are collected.
2. 20×20 grayscale image data and corresponding labels are used as a training set.
3. Some preprocessing like flattening, thresholding, etc. is done to make the data ready for the next step. The processing of the training data is shown in Figure 15.8.

15.4.11 MACHINE LEARNING CLASSIFIER

The ML classifier used here is the support vector classifier. It takes mixed data as input and outputs classes to which data belongs to. The objective of the support vector machine algorithm [19] is to find a hyperplane in N-dimensional space (N = the number of features) that distinctly classify the data points as shown in Figure 15.9. To separate the two classes of data points, many possible hyperplanes could be chosen. Our aim is to find a plane that has the maximum margin, i.e., the maximum distance between data points of both classes. Maximizing the margin distance offers some reinforcement so that future data points can be categorized with more confidence.

Support vector classifier is given in Figure 15.9.

Hyperplanes are decision boundaries that help categorize the data points. Data points lying on either side of the hyperplane can be attributed to distinct classes. Also, the dimension of the hyperplane depends upon the number of features. If the number of input features is 2, then the hyperplane is just a line. Support vectors are data points that are closer to the hyperplane and determines the position and orientation of the hyperplane. Using these support vectors, we maximize the margin of the classifier.

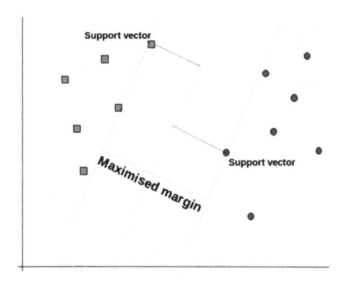

FIGURE 15.9   Support vector classifier.

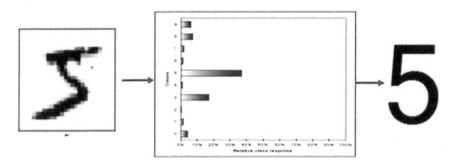

FIGURE 15.10   Classification of characters.

For evaluating the ML model, 4-fold cross-validation was used. Cross-validation is a procedure for evaluating ML models by training several ML models on subsets of the accessible input data and evaluating them on the complementary subset of the data. Use cross-validation to detect overfitting, i.e., failing to generalize a pattern. In k-fold cross-validation, you split the input data into k subsets of data (also known as folds). You train an ML model on all but one (k-1) of the subsets and then evaluate the model on the subset that was not used for training. This process is repeated k times, with a distinct subset reserved for evaluation (and excluded from training) each time.

Figures 15.10 and 15.11 show an example of the training subsets and complimentary evaluation subsets generated for each of the four models that are created and trained during 4-fold cross-validation. Model one uses the first 25% of data for evaluation, and

FIGURE 15.11 4-fold cross-validation.

the remaining 75% for training. Model two uses the second subset of 25% (25% to 50%) for evaluation, and the remaining three subsets of the data for training, and so on.

Each model is trained and evaluated using complementary data sources – the data in the evaluation data source includes and is limited to all of the data that is not in the training data source. Performing 4-fold cross-validation generates four models, four data sources to train the models, four data sources to evaluate the models, and four evaluations, one for each model.

After the SVM classifies all the characters, they may or may not be in proper order and require rearrangement. To keep track of the order of these characters, we store the starting index (x-axis) of each character in an array. The characters are then arranged according to the array to obtain the final output.

15.5 FUTURE ENHANCEMENT

Traffic analysis can be used to adjust traffic light control systems dynamically and to watch traffic jams. It can also be useful in detecting dangerous situations in real-time, such as a vehicle stopped in an unauthorized space on the highway, someone driving in the wrong direction, a vehicle moving erratically or cars that have been in an accident. In the case of an accident, these systems are helpful in collecting evidence in case of litigation.

Vehicle counting, or differentiating between trucks, taxis, buses, cars and so on, generates high-value statistics used to obtain insights about traffic. Installing speed cameras allows for precise control of the driver's illegal activities. Automatic licence plate recognition [20] identifies cars that commit an infraction or, thanks to real-time searching, spots a vehicle that has been stolen or used in a crime.

Smart parking systems based on video analytics help drivers find a vacant spot by analyzing images from security cameras. These are just some instances of the contributions that video analysis technology can offer to build safer cities that are more amiable to live in.

It has also found its application in Industries and plants, where it can be used to track the positions of huge raw materials carrying wagons like a ladle. We can track the ladle number and its position, thus, helping in optimizing the use of ladles.

Also, it can be used to check the correct placement of HSM plates in Steelmaking plants, etc.

15.6 APPLICATIONS

Some applications within the sector of video analytics are widely known to the public. One such example is video surveillance, a task that has existed for about 50 years. In theory, the concept is simple: install cameras strategically to permit human operators to manage what happens in a room, area or public space.

In practice, however, it is a task that is far away from simple. A single operator is mostly responsible for surveillance of more than one camera, and, as several studies have shown, upping the camera counts to be monitored adversely affects the operator's performance. In other words, whether or not an oversized amount of hardware is available out there and generating signals, a bottleneck is made when it's time to process those signals thanks to human limitations.

15.7 HEALTHCARE

Historically, healthcare institutions have invested a large sum of money in video surveillance solutions in making sure the security of their patients, staff and visitors, at levels that are often regulated by strict legislation. Theft, infant abduction and drug diversion are amongst the foremost common problems addressed by surveillance systems.

In addition to facilitating surveillance tasks, video analytics allows us to travel further, by exploiting the data collected so on to realize business goals. For instance, a video analytics solution could detect when a patient has not been checked on according to the needs and alert the staff. Analysis of patient and visitor traffic is extremely valuable in determining ways to shorten wait times while ensuring clear access to the emergency area.

At-home monitoring of older adults or people with health issues is another example of an application that gives excellent value. For example, falls are a significant reason for injury and death in older persons. Although personal medical devices can detect falls, they need to be worn and are frequently disregarded by the patron. A video analytics solution can analyze the signals of home cameras to identify in real-time if a person has fallen. With proper setup, such a system could also determine if an individual took a given medication once they were speculated to, for example.

Mental healthcare is another area during which video analytics can make significant contributions. Systems that analyze facial expressions, body posture and gaze are developed to help clinicians within the evaluation of patients. Such a system is in a position to detect emotions from visual communications and micro-expressions, offering clinicians objective information that may confirm their hypotheses or give them new clues.

15.7.1 SMART CITIES/TRANSPORTATION

Video analytics has proven to be a fantastic help within the realm of transport, aiding within the event of smart cities. A rise in traffic, especially in urban areas, may end up in an increase in accidents and traffic jams if adequate traffic management measures do not seem to be taken. Intelligent video analysis solutions can play a vital role during this scenario.

Traffic analysts often want to adjust traffic light control systems dynamically and to look at traffic jams. It may also be useful in detecting dangerous situations in real-time as a vehicle stopped in an unauthorized space on the highway, someone driving in the wrong direction, a vehicle moving erratically or cars that are in an accident. In the case of an accident, these systems are helpful in collecting evidence just in case of litigation.

Vehicle counting, or differentiating between cars, trucks, buses, taxis and so on, generate high-value statistics used to obtain insights about traffic. Installing speed cameras allows for precise control of drivers altogether. Automatic vehicle plate recognition identifies cars that commit an infraction or, because of real-time searching, spots a vehicle that has been stolen or employed in a criminal offence.

Instead of using sensors in each parking zone, a wise parking system supported video analytics helps drivers find a vacant spot by analyzing images from security cameras. These are some examples of the contributions that video analysis technology can make to create safer cities that are more pleasant to live in.

15.7.2 SECURITY

Video surveillance is an old task of the safety domain. However, from the time that systems were monitored exclusively by humans to current solutions supporting video analytics, much water has passed under the bridge. Facial and licence plate recognition (LPR) techniques can be applied to recognize people and vehicles in real-time and make appropriate decisions. For instance, it is possible to search for a suspect both in real-time and in stored video footage or to recognize authorized personnel and grant access to a secured facility. Crowd management is another crucial function of the security system. Cutting edge video analysis tools can make a huge difference in places such as shopping malls, hospitals, stadiums and airports. These tools can provide an approximated crowd count in real-time and can trigger alerts when a threshold is reached or surpassed. They can also analyze crowd flow to detect movement in prohibited or unwanted directions. This is one of the prominent advantages of those approaches: video content analysis systems are often trained to detect specific events, sometimes with a high degree of refinement. One such example is to detect fires as soon as possible. Or, in the case of airports, to raise an alert when someone walks against the direction intended for passengers or enters a forbidden area. Another great use case is the real-time detection of unattended baggage in a public place. As for traditional tasks like intruder detection, they will be performed robustly, because of algorithms which will filter motion caused by wind, rain, snow or animals. The functionality offered by intelligent video analysis is growing day by day within the security domain, and this is often a trend that will continue within the future.

15.8 CONCLUSION

Video analytics solutions are helpful in our daily tasks. There is a wide range of sectors that can benefit from this technology, especially as the complication of potential applications has been flourishing in recent years. From smart cities to security controls in hospitals and airports to people tracking for retail and shopping centres, the field of video analytics enables processes that are synchronously more effective and less tedious for humans, and less expensive for companies.

Apart from the above applications, it can be used for several applications in different fields depending on the scenario to minimize losses and translate to big profits. The contributions of video analysis technology can help to build safer cities that are more amiable to live in. The functionality offered by intelligent video analysis is growing day by day in the security domain, and this is a trend that will continue in the future.

REFERENCES

1. Subudhi, Badri Narayan, Deepak Kumar Rout, and Ashish Ghosh. "Big data analytics for video surveillance." *Multimedia Tools and Applications* 78(18) 2019: 26129–26162.
2. Singh, Krishna Kant, and Akansha Singh. "A study of image segmentation algorithms for different types of images." *International Journal of Computer Science Issues (IJCSI)* 7(5), 2010: 414.
3. Qadri, Muhammad Tahir, and Muhammad Asif. "*Automatic number plate recognition system for vehicle identification using optical character recognition.*" In *2009 International Conference on Education Technology and Computer*, pp. 335–338. IEEE, 2009.
4. Kim, Sunghoon, Daechul Kim, Younbok Ryu, and Gyeonghwan Kim. "*A robust license-plate extraction method under complex image conditions.*" In *Object recognition supported by user interaction for service robots*, vol. 3, pp. 216–219. IEEE, 2002.
5. Sarfraz, Muhammad, Mohammed Jameel Ahmed, and Syed A. Ghazi. "*Saudi Arabian license plate recognition system.*" In *2003 International Conference on Geometric Modelling and Graphics, 2003. Proceedings*, pp. 36–41. IEEE, 2003.
6. Ozbay, Serkan, and Ergun Ercelebi. "Automatic vehicle identification by plate recognition." *World Academy of Science, Engineering and Technology* 9(41) (2005): 222–225.
7. Shapiro, Vladimir, Dimo Dimov, Stefan Bonchev, Veselin Velichkov, and Georgi Gluhchev. "*Adaptive license plate image extraction.*" In *International Conference on Computer Systems and Technologies*, pp. 2–7, 2003.
8. Dubey, Premnath. "*Heuristic approach for license plate detection.*" In *IEEE Conference on Advanced Video and Signal Based Surveillance*, pp. 366–370. IEEE, 2005.
9. Wu, Cheokman, Lei Chan On, Chan Hon Weng, Tong Sio Kuan, and Kengchung Ng. "*A Macao license plate recognition system.*" In *2005 International Conference on Machine Learning and Cybernetics*, vol. 7, pp. 4506–4510. IEEE, 2005.
10. Hsu, Gee-Sern, Jiun-Chang Chen, and Yu-Zu Chung. "Application-oriented license plate recognition." *IEEE Transactions on Vehicular Technology* 62(2) (2012): 552–561.
11. He, Xiangjian, Lihong Zheng, Qiang Wu, Wenjing Jia, Bijan Samali, and Marimuthu Palaniswami. *Segmentation of characters on car license plates.* In *2008 IEEE 10th Workshop on Multimedia Signal Processing*, pp. 399–402. IEEE, 2008.
12. Zhang, Yungang, and Changshui Zhang. "*A new algorithm for character segmentation of license plate.*" In *IEEE IV2003 Intelligent Vehicles Symposium. Proceedings (Cat. No. 03TH8683)*, pp. 106–109. IEEE, 2003.
13. Saleem, Nauman, Hassam Muazzam, H. M. Tahir, and Umar Farooq. "*Automatic license plate recognition using extracted features.*" In *2016 4th International Symposium on Computational and Business Intelligence (ISCBI)*, pp. 221–225. IEEE, 2016.

14. Chaabane, S. Ben, Mounir Sayadi, Farhat Fnaiech, and Eric Brassart. "Dempster-Shafer evidence theory for image segmentation: application in cells images." *International Journal of Signal Processing* 5(1), 2009.
15. https://www.geeksforgeeks.org/feature-mapping/
16. Bulugu, Isack. *"Algorithm for license plate localization and recognition for tanzania car plate numbers."* (2013).
17. Tang, Sheng, Yu Li, Lixi Deng, and Yongdong Zhang. "Object localization based on proposal fusion." *IEEE Transactions on Multimedia* 19(9), (2017): 2105–2116.
18. Pan, Mei-Sen, Jun-Biao Yan, and Zheng-Hong Xiao. "Vehicle license plate character segmentation." *International Journal of Automation and Computing* 5(4), 2008: pp. 425–432.
19. Gandhi, Rohith. "Support vector machine—Introduction to machine learning algorithms." *Towards Data Science* (2018).
20. Tiwari, Bhawna, Archana Sharma, Malti Gautam Singh, and Bhawana Rathi. "Automatic Vehicle Number Plate Recognition System using Matlab." *IOSR Journal of Electronics and Communication Engineering (IOSR-JECE)* e-ISSN (2016): 2278–2834.
21. Kaur, H., and S. Manviand Balwinder. "Vehicle License Plate Detection from Video Using Edge Detection and Morphological Operators." *Singh International Journal of Engineering Research & Technology ISSN* (2012): 2278–0181.

Index